Psychology and Crime

What does a criminological psychologist actually do? Most people picture a modern-day Sherlock Holmes, helping the police to solve crimes, but the reality is far more interesting and complex. *Psychology and Crime* offers a fascinating introduction to criminological psychology, providing the reader with a comprehensive grounding in everything from cognitive forensics to police interviewing.

Concise, informative and accessible, the book explores a range of theories to understand criminal behaviour, from the physiological to the social. It covers a range of contexts within the criminal justice system where psychology offers unique insights, including police investigation, the perspective of witnesses and victims, and courtroom proceedings. Thoroughly updated throughout to reflect developments in the field, and featuring new chapters covering cybercrime, terrorism and insights from neuroscience, this edition also includes a student-friendly 'Apply your learning' feature and case studies to bring the research to life.

Accessibly written for all levels and with concise coverage of both classic and contemporary psychological theory, this is the ideal book for anyone studying criminal or forensic psychology.

Aidan Sammons has been teaching, writing about, and training teachers of introductory psychology for over 20 years.

David Putwain has taught psychology from GCSE through to doctoral level for over 25 years. His research interests focus on how psychology can be used in applied contexts.

Psychology and Crime

2nd Edition

Aidan Sammons and
David Putwain

Routledge
Taylor & Francis Group

LONDON AND NEW YORK

First published 2019
by Routledge
2 Park Square, Milton Park, Abingdon, Oxon OX14 4RN

and by Routledge
711 Third Avenue, New York, NY 10017

Routledge is an imprint of the Taylor & Francis Group, an informa business

British Library Cataloguing-in-Publication Data
A catalogue record for this book is available from the British Library

Library of Congress Cataloging-in-Publication Data
A catalog record for this book has been requested

ISBN: 978-0-8153-6928-8 (hbk)
ISBN: 978-0-8153-6952-3 (pbk)
ISBN: 978-1-351-25214-0 (ebk)

Typeset in Palatino
by Apex CoVantage, LLC

Contents

Tables

1

Introduction

Imagine asking a member of the public the following question:

- What is a criminological psychologist?
- What does a criminological psychologist do?
- What types of people do criminological psychologists work with?

The answers to these questions are likely to be informed by TV programmes, films and, possibly, high-profile media cases. In the public imagination, the criminological psychologist is a Sherlock Holmes-like figure, solving crimes and mysteries with a combination of arcane scientific knowledge and penetrating insight into the workings of the criminal mind. This makes good television but it does not represent the reality of criminological psychology. Criminological psychologists do sometimes contribute directly to police investigations but this is a relatively minor aspect of a very diverse field. Psychologists are involved in researching the causes of crime, rehabilitating offenders, preventing crime, providing expert advice to law enforcement and the courts and a great deal more. Criminological psychology is just one of a number of academic disciplines that contribute to policing and criminal justice. Others include criminology, sociology, psychiatry and law. Each has its own purpose, assumptions and methods and, consequently, each has something different to contribute to understanding and tackling crime.

Psychology is, broadly, the use of scientific methods to understand the behaviour of individuals. The contribution psychology can make to criminological issues reflects the strengths and limitations of the discipline as a whole. Psychologists undergo rigorous training in research methods, which makes them well placed to conduct investigations and to comment on and evaluate the research and practices of others. However, psychology tends to over-emphasise individual factors at the expense of social ones. In explaining crime, psychologists focus on things like brain function, personality and thinking processes. Sociology and criminology, by contrast, are much more likely to focus on social structural factors like inequality and social class. Although they frequently disagree on where the emphasis should go, each of these disciplines complements the others. In isolation, each tells only part of the story of crime and victimisation but, together, they give a more comprehensive picture. Consequently, this book draws on sociological and criminological research as well as psychological.

The origins of criminological psychology

Criminological psychology emerged as a distinct field in the 1960s but its origins are much earlier. A key influence was the work of Cesare Lombroso in the late 19th century. Lombroso was the first to advance the view that criminality is a heritable, constitutional characteristic. He suggested that criminals were a biologically distinct class of people who exhibited 'atavistic' or primitive features. They committed crimes because they were dominated by their primitive aggressive, sexual and acquisitive urges. Lombroso claimed that their atavistic nature led not only to criminal behaviour but also to distinct physical forms. Consequently, he believed that criminals could be identified from their features, such as heavy brows and strong jawbones. Different types of criminal were said to have different features, so murderers had bloodshot eyes and curly hair whereas sex offenders had thick lips and projecting ears. Lombroso supported his claims with measurements taken from the skulls of known criminals. However, he did not compare these data with measurements of non-criminals and, consequently, did not establish that the features he identified as 'criminal' *only* occurred in the criminal population. He also did not distinguish clearly between criminals and those suffering from various psychological disorders. It is also the case that Lombroso's views reflected many of the prejudices of his time and he was overtly racist in linking criminality with minority ethnicity (Holmes, 2015; see Chapter 12). For these and many other reasons, Lombroso's work is rejected nowadays. However, his important contribution was to insist on empirical evidence and (a version of) the scientific method in presenting his work. This helped to move discussion of criminality away from moral and philosophical discourse and into the realm of scientific research.

Another key early influence on criminological psychology was the psychological laboratory founded by Wilhelm Wundt in Leipzig in 1879 (Gudjonsson & Haward, 1998). Wundt was instrumental in establishing psychology as a scientific discipline where the measurement and experimental manipulation of sensory and behavioural phenomena were foregrounded. Wundt's students studied a range of psychological processes with applications to everyday life. This included topics like witness memory, which is still central to criminological psychology (see Chapter 7). One of Wundt's students, Hugo Munsterberg, settled in the United States, where he advocated for the introduction of applied psychology to the courtroom (with limited success) and carried out extensive research into the effect of leading questions on testimony, the discrepancies between witnesses to an event, the impact of attentional focus and the misleading nature of witness confidence, all of which remain current topics of interest (Memon et al., 2008). However, while psychologists researched and commented on crime and related topics throughout the 20th century, it was not until the 1960s that criminological psychology emerged as a distinct branch of psychology.

Applying psychological principles to crime

Criminological psychology is an example of 'applied' rather than 'pure' psychology. Pure psychology refers to the type of research usually carried out by academics in universities pursuing answers to questions about the basic processes of thinking and behaviour. Although academic psychologists may also be interested in questions about 'real-world' processes, they tend to carry out their investigations in the laboratory. This has the advantage of controlling for the influence of nuisance and confounding variables encountered in real-life situations. The researcher can create her own 'micro-world' where every variable of interest can be isolated and its effect examined free of other influences. Pure researchers usually belong to a theoretical tradition that influences the types of question that interest them and the way they go about answering them. For example, cognitive psychologists typically use laboratory experiments to investigate phenomena like attention, memory and problem solving. This is all done without necessarily considering how such processes might operate in real-life settings.

In criminological psychology, theories and research findings from pure psychology are applied to the questions raised by real-life legal and criminal problems. The pure theoretical approaches can be applied to crime and criminal justice in a number of ways (see Table 1.1).

TABLE 1.1 Examples of pure psychology applied to criminological questions

Pure psychological areas	Criminological psychology topics
Cognitive psychology studies mental processes including perception, attention, memory and problem solving	The distorting effect of perceptual, attentional and memory processes on witness testimony (e.g. the effect of leading questions); techniques to improve witness accuracy (e.g. cognitive interviewing); criminal decision making (e.g. rational choice theory)
Social psychology studies social interaction and the effect of situational and group influences on behaviour	Social influences on criminal behaviour (e.g. gang membership and learning from the peer group); group decision making by juries
Developmental psychology studies changes in psychological attributes over the lifespan, for example, the development of moral reasoning and personality and the influence of parenting and other environmental factors on development	The role of parental attachment and early adverse experiences in criminal behaviour; the effect of victimisation on child development; developmental crime prevention
Learning theory studies how the environment shapes behaviour	The role of learning from the family or peer group in offending; the use of techniques to modify the behaviour of offenders
Biopsychology studies the influence of physiological processes on behaviour, including the workings of the nervous system and the influence of genetics on behaviour	The role of genetics, brain structure and functioning and neurochemistry in offending

Forensic psychology

The terms criminological, forensic, criminal and legal psychology are often used interchangeably, which can be confusing. Criminological, criminal and legal psychology all refer in a general way to the application of psychology to crime and the law. Forensic psychology, however, has a restricted meaning. Forensic psychology denotes expert professional knowledge of psychology as it applies to the courts and legal processes. The majority of forensic psychologists work within the court and prison system, giving expert evidence, advising courts and parole boards, designing and implementing offender rehabilitation programmes and doing research into offending and rehabilitation. In the UK, 'forensic psychologist' is a legally protected title: a person may only use it if he has completed an approved course of study and accreditation and has been granted a licence to practise by the Health and Care Professions Council (HCPC). Anyone who calls himself a forensic psychologist but is not registered with the HCPC is breaking the law and may be prosecuted.

Forensic psychologists may find themselves doing a great range of activities. In their clinical role, they may be asked to psychologically assess individuals who come into contact with the authorities and advise those authorities accordingly. For example, Brown (1997) describes a case in which an adolescent complained to the police that she was receiving frequent, indecent phone calls. Despite continuous monitoring of the phone line, nothing was intercepted. She then alleged that her property was being smeared with paint and some items were shown to the police, damaged as described. She became rather belligerent at the police station and considerable time was spent in enquiries. A forensic psychologist was asked to provide an assessment as to whether the complainant was manufacturing the evidence in order to satisfy some psychological need. The result of the assessment confirmed the police's suspicion that she had fabricated the incidents.

In their experimental role, a forensic psychologist might be asked to investigate questions relating to evidence presented in a criminal case. Brown (1997) gives the example of a case in which three motorcyclists were charged with causing the death by dangerous driving of two other riders. The case hinged on a claim by a police officer that he had seen the motorcyclists speeding and had taken their number plates. But was it really possible to recall four muddy number plates, two and a half inches high, at a distance of 90 yards? Psychologists set up a laboratory experiment in which 100 participants were asked to identify four sets of number plates. These were presented in a degraded form to mimic the real conditions. They found that a few participants could recall one number plate but none could recall all four. Although this cast doubt on the eyewitness evidence given by the police officer, the jury was not convinced and all three of the motorcyclists were convicted.

Aims, organisation and content of this book

The aim of this book is to introduce the reader to a range of psychological research into crime. It is aimed at those who are studying introductory courses in criminal psychology, those who require a basic overview of the field for professional purposes and those who are simply interested in the area. A book of this nature cannot hope to cover such a diverse and complex field exhaustively, so the topics have been selected to reflect what is encountered in most introductory courses and to illustrate the range of topics that criminological psychology covers. Chapter 2 addresses basic questions about how crime is defined and measured and outlines some research on victimisation. Chapters 3, 4 and 5 present a range of explanations of offending including biological, psychological and social causes. Chapter 6 considers how psychological issues come to bear on police investigations through an examination of how evidence is processed, how police interview witnesses and suspects, and the controversial area of offender profiling. Chapter 7 examines how psychological processes affect witness memory and Chapter 8 outlines the psychological processes that affect what happens in a courtroom, with particular emphasis on how juries reach their verdicts. Chapter 9 discusses what happens to convicted offenders through an examination of prison and the alternatives, and Chapter 10 extends this into offender rehabilitation and the contributions of psychology to crime prevention. The field of criminological psychology continually evolves and so Chapter 11 outlines two areas that are of particular current interest, terrorism and cybercrime. Finally, Chapter 12 presents a range of critical perspectives on criminological psychology that offer alternative views to the mainstream one that dominates both the field and this book. In each chapter, a section called 'Apply your learning' invites you to develop your understanding of what you read by applying it to real-world questions and, at the end of each chapter, some further reading is suggested for those who wish to pursue a deeper understanding of any of the topics presented.

2

Defining and measuring crime

The study of offenders and offending requires some agreement between practitioners about which people and acts should be studied. This chapter discusses different definitions of 'criminal', the relationship of offending with age, gender and socio-economic status and different ways of measuring the extent of crime within society. Trends in crime and victimisation are described. Finally, there is a discussion of the psychological effects of victimisation and fear of crime in the general public.

What is a crime? What is a criminal?

The most straightforward answer to the question, 'what is a crime?' is: 'any act that breaks the criminal law'. Under this view, criminal law sets down, in an objective way, those things that society considers harmful. This apparent simplicity hides a great deal of complexity, as it does not address the question of why some acts are criminal and others are not, or why the acts prohibited by law vary between different places and change over time. For example, purchase of alcohol by people over the age of 18 is legal in the United Kingdom but not in Saudi Arabia. An 18 year old purchasing alcohol in the UK has occasioned no crime but the very same person in many parts of the US has. And between 1920 and 1933, under the 'prohibition' laws, most purchase and possession of alcohol in the US was a crime, regardless of age. So the same act – the purchase of alcohol – either is or is not a crime depending on where and when it took place. Even the act of deliberately killing another human being may or may not be a crime depending on whether the killer did so in order to inherit the victim's money, to defend herself against a deadly threat, as a soldier under orders on a battlefield or an official carrying out a judicial execution. No behaviour is *inherently* criminal. Rather, societies define certain acts, under certain circumstances, as criminal for a wide range of reasons. As societies change, so does people's understanding of and response to the act considered criminal. In other words, crime is a social construct.

This raises difficulties for criminological psychologists. If their aim is to study crime and criminals it is important for them to distinguish between those people who are objects of study and those who are not. However, the socially constructed nature of crime makes this a matter of debate. To shed light on this problem it is useful to consider two possible approaches to defining 'criminal', referred to here as the 'legalistic' and 'deviance' approaches.

The legalistic approach

The simplest definition of a criminal is a person who transgresses the laws of her society. The problem with this definition is that it defines as 'criminal' many people who would not normally be considered as such. There are few people who have never broken a single law. Even someone who uses the work telephone for a personal call, takes home some office stationery for personal use or who picks up and pockets a banknote he finds in the street may technically be breaking the law. If we define all such people as criminals then virtually everyone is a criminal. This is clearly unsatisfactory. An alternative is to define criminals as those who have been convicted of a crime by the state. It would follow from this that we should study only those people who have a criminal record. This is also unsatisfactory. In many cases, those responsible for a crime escape detection. If apprehended, they may not be prosecuted and, if prosecuted, they may not be convicted. Thus, many people who have committed criminal acts would not be considered appropriate for study by criminological psychology. There are other problems with the legalistic approach. First, the population of convicted offenders inevitably contains people who have been wrongly convicted. Second, those who have been criminally convicted are, in a sense, 'unsuccessful' criminals. If we were to restrict ourselves to the study of such individuals it is likely we would be using samples biased towards those attributes (e.g. carelessness) that made it more likely they would be caught.

The deviance approach

Some writers (e.g. Sellin, 1938) suggest that the appropriate object of study for criminological psychology is 'deviance', or 'antisocial behaviour', of which legally defined crime is just a part. Under this definition, criminological psychologists should study those people who behave in antisocial ways. Given the problems with the legalistic view, this might seem more satisfactory. Unfortunately, the classification of behaviour as deviant or antisocial is notoriously subjective and an act might be considered as pro- or antisocial depending on one's point of view. For example, defacing a building to draw attention to the oppression of a particular group of people might be regarded as antisocial by the building's owner but prosocial by those sympathetic to the cause being represented. This being the case, it is difficult to see how consensus could be achieved among researchers about the acts they ought to be studying.

Different researchers resolve this issue in different ways but many follow the suggestions of Blackburn (1993) who makes several useful recommendations. First, 'criminal behaviour' should be defined in terms of the conscious breaking of rules. That is, the people of interest to criminological psychology are those who know what the rules are, but do something different. This inevitably means that some behaviour that is legally permissible is nonetheless of interest to psychologists and criminologists whereas other behaviour that is technically criminal is not. So those who park their cars in the spaces reserved for parents with children are not committing a crime but might still be of interest because there is an underlying similarity between this act and other acts that are illegal. This approach allows us to recognise the continuity between, for example, conduct problems in childhood and later delinquency and criminality in adolescence and adulthood. Second, Blackburn recommends that criminological psychology should focus, in the main, on crime as legally defined. The problems this raises notwithstanding, it at least offers researchers a clear framework on which they can agree.

The majority of 'mainstream' criminological psychologists accept this but not all. Those who adopt one of the more critical perspectives on criminological psychology take issue with this apparent willingness to admit, on the one hand, that 'crime' and 'criminal' are social constructs but, on the other hand, treat them as if they were natural or objective facts. Critical perspectives raise questions about how the social construction of crime relates to issues of power, gender and race in society (see Chapter 12).

Variables associated with criminality

Surveys in which people are asked about their own criminal activities suggest that the prevalence of criminality (i.e. the number of people in the population committing crimes) is higher than many people assume. It could even be suggested that petty crime, rather than being an aberration, is actually a normative activity among certain groups. The fact that most people will break the law at some point in their lives notwithstanding, a minority of people commit the majority of criminal offences and certain types of people are over-represented in the offender population. Some of the variables associated with criminality are age, gender, socio-economic status and ethnicity.

Age

Surveys of young people indicate that criminal acts are relatively common among this group. The prevalence and incidence of offending (i.e. the number of offences committed) starts to rise in adolescence and peaks around the age of 18, falling sharply thereafter. This relationship is called the age–crime curve. The majority of offenders are in their teenage years but by the age of 28, 85% of them have stopped committing crimes (Farrington, 1986). However, there are marked differences if different types of crime are accounted for. Property crimes like theft or vandalism follow this pattern closely but fraud and embezzlement are more likely to be committed by older adults (Steffensmeier et al., 1989), principally because opportunities are more plentiful to them.

Moffitt (1993) suggests that the age–crime curve conceals two distinct categories of offender. Adolescence-limited (AL) offenders follow the pattern described above and account for the majority of offenders overall. Life-course-persistent (LCP) offenders are a smaller group but are criminally active throughout their lives. They start to offend at an earlier age following a history of conduct problems in childhood and continue offending into mature adulthood. Moffitt suggests that the two types of offender represent distinct developmental processes. AL offending stems from a 'maturity gap' between a person's biological and social maturity. Although adolescents have reached adulthood biologically, socially they are restricted from many adult behaviours. Delinquency is a reaction against these restrictions and is learned from the peer group through social learning processes (see Chapter 5). As they enter social adulthood, their social maturity 'catches up' with their biological maturity and consequently their motivation to offend disappears. LCP offending, by contrast, is linked to neuropsychological deficits with a range of causes (e.g. genetics, environmental toxins) which, when combined with an adverse developmental environment (e.g. abuse, neglect) result to produce an antisocial personality type with a high propensity to offend at all ages (see Chapter 3).

Gender

Criminal statistics consistently find that men commit more crime than women. Data from the Dunedin Multidisciplinary Health and Development Study, a longitudinal study of around 1,000 people born in the early 1970s, suggest that this is true for most types of offence but there are some exceptions. Rates of drug use and domestic violence are similar between males and females and there are few gender differences in the types of low-level delinquency that prevail in adolescence (Moffitt et al., 2001). The gender–crime gap has been explained in a number of ways. One possibility is that offending patterns reflect constitutional differences between women and men. Males have a higher risk of many types of neurodevelopmental problem that could manifest in an increased tendency to commit crimes. It is also believed that human males have developed a tendency towards aggression through evolutionary processes, which might explain the preponderance of males among violent criminals. However, gender differences in offending might also reflect differences in the socialisation of women and men. Box (1983) found that criminality in women correlated with the degree of female subordination and powerlessness in society. Possibly, societies that stress a more 'traditional' feminine role restrict the opportunities available to women to become involved in criminal activity.

Crime statistics from recent years have suggested that the gender disparity in offending is reducing (Lauritsen et al., 2009). It has been suggested that the narrowing of the gender–crime gap represents the 'dark side' of gender equality as women act on the opportunities for offending previously denied them. However, crime has been falling since the mid-1990s. The gender gap has narrowed principally because rates of offending have fallen faster in men than they have in women (Lauritsen et al., 2009). Where offending by women has apparently increased, this may be because attitudes towards arresting and charging female offenders have changed over time: the actual rate of offending by women has been stable but an increased willingness to process women through the criminal justice system results in a rise in arrests and convictions (Estrada et al., 2016). Feminist views on gender and offending are explored in Chapter 12.

Socio-economic status

It is widely believed that there is an inverse relationship between socio-economic status (SES) and offending. That is, people from lower SES backgrounds are over-represented among the population of offenders. Early studies of the SES–crime link found that the relationship between crime and social class was much stronger for official figures than for self-report measures of offending, possibly reflecting bias in the way that people from different social backgrounds are processed by the criminal justice system. Lower SES individuals might be more likely to be arrested, charged and convicted even if their true rate of offending were the same as those with higher SES. Self-reports of offending correlate relatively weakly with SES. Dunaway et al. (2000) collected data from 555 adults about a variety of demographic variables including personal and family income, use of welfare services, education and employment. They also asked their respondents about offences they had committed in the previous year. Dunaway et al. could only find a weak correlation between SES and general offending. There was variation within this, so SES was a better predictor of violent than non-violent offending and the relationship between SES and offending was stronger among non-white respondents. Dunaway et al. did find, however, that poverty was significantly related to offending. The effect of poverty and neighbourhood conditions is discussed in Chapter 5.

Race and ethnicity

People from minority ethnic groups are over-represented in the crime and victimisation statistics. UK data show that black people are eight times more likely to be stopped and searched by the police than white, 3.5 times more likely to be arrested and four times more likely to be prosecuted. Although non-white defendants are slightly less likely to be convicted than white, there are proportionately more black people in prison than white (16 for every 10,000 white people and 58 for every 10,000 black people; ONS, 2017a). The picture is similar in the US, where black and Hispanic males have a higher lifetime risk of arrest and imprisonment than white and a higher risk of involvement in serious violence (Piquero & Brame, 2008). There are two competing explanations for the ethnic disparity in recorded crime. The differential involvement hypothesis suggests that black and ethnic minority (BEM) individuals commit more crime than white and persist in involvement in crime to a later age than do white individuals typically. Alternatively, the differential selection hypothesis suggests that the real rate of offending is similar across ethnic groups but that BEM individuals are more likely to end up in the crime statistics because they are subject to more police attention through racial profiling and consequently are more likely to be arrested, charged and convicted, especially if, as is sometimes claimed, the courts are biased in their treatment of different ethnicities (see Chapter 8). An associated claim is that the excess of crime among black males is accounted for by the types of 'victimless' crime (e.g. possession of drugs) where the authorities have more discretion about who to arrest, investigate and charge. Critical perspectives on race, ethnicity and crime are explored in Chapter 12.

Measuring crime

Just as it may seem simple at the outset to define what a criminal is, it might also seem relatively straightforward to measure how much crime there is. Surely it is just a matter of counting how many crimes occur? Again, matters are not so simple. The crime rate of a given country or area is calculated by counting how many offences occur and dividing by the number of people who live there. The problem is that there are several ways of counting crimes and they tend not to agree with one another. The three main sources of information about the extent of crime are official statistics, victimisation surveys and offender surveys. Each of these sources of information has its strengths and limitations but all of them distort the 'true' figure of crime to some extent.

Apply your learning

Two candidates are standing for election as local police commissioner. The current commissioner is campaigning on the basis that her policies have resulted in a low level of crime. The challenger is campaigning on the basis that crime is 'out of control' in the locality. How might each justify their campaign position? How might each criticise their opponent's stance?

Official crime statistics

In England and Wales, official crime figures are published by the Office for National Statistics (ONS) on the basis of two sets of data, the crimes recorded by the police and a victimisation survey now known as the Crime Survey for England and Wales (CSEW). Similar arrangements are in place in Scotland and Northern Ireland. Self-report victimisation surveys were adopted as part of the official figures because the police recorded crime rate heavily underestimates the true extent of crime. For a crime to end up in the police statistics, someone first has to notice that it has occurred. Then, they must report it. People may not do this because they believe the crime is too trivial or that the police can do nothing about it. Crimes involving a 'willing victim' (e.g. drug dealing) are unlikely to be reported. Consequently, a large number of crimes never come to the attention of the authorities. While many of these offences are relatively minor, a proportion of unreported crime would be classified as serious.

The police have substantial discretion about the recording of crime. Even if an incident is reported there are several reasons why it may not be recorded as a crime in the official count. The victim may withdraw her complaint. The police may decide that the report is a mistake, a malicious accusation or that there is insufficient evidence that a crime has actually occurred. The decision to 'no-crime' a complaint may reflect an objective, professional decision on an officer's part but 'no-criming' may also be a response to pressure from government to meet law enforcement targets or may reflect a police culture of disbelieving victims. An investigation by Her Majesty's Inspectorate of Constabularies (2014) estimated that around 800,000 crimes a year went unrecorded in England and Wales. This included serious offences. The under-recording rate for violence against the person was 33% and for sexual offences it was 26%. This included 200 reports of rape.

Changes to the way the police record crime can give rise to apparent fluctuations in the crime rate that do not actually reflect the amount of offending. For example, police figures for England and Wales in 2017 show a 27% increase in violence against the person compared with 2016. While this might represent a genuine increase in the level of violent offending, it is likely that at least some of the increase reflects improvements in police recording in response to the HMIC (2014) investigation. In addition, victims' perception of the police can affect their willingness to report some crimes. For example, victims of intimate partner violence may not report offences for fear that their complaint will be dismissed or minimised (Wolf et al., 2003). If the police adopt policies to persuade victims to come forward this can result in an apparent rise in offending when the actual level of crime has not really changed.

Victimisation surveys

In a victimisation survey, a large sample of the population are asked about their experience of crime. In the US, the National Crime Victimization Survey (NCVS) surveys the experience of crime of around 160,000 people in about 90,000 households and has been running continually since the early 1970s. The UK followed in the 1980s, starting with the British Crime Survey (BCS; Hough & Mayhew, 1983). Currently, the CSEW surveys 50,000 households in England and Wales, the Scottish Crime and Justice Survey 6,000 adults each year and the Northern Ireland Crime Survey around 4,000. All use similar methodologies. In the CSEW, the sample is selected at random from the Post Office's list of addresses and approached to take part. Around 75% of those approached participate. Data collection is by structured interview, with one person from the household answering questions about whether they have been a victim of crime, the details of the crime (if any) and their attitudes towards crime and policing. The responses are recorded on a computer. The methodology of the CSEW undergoes revision periodically. For example, in 2009 a parallel survey for children aged 10 to 15 years was introduced so that offences against children could be estimated and, in 2015, fraud and cybercrime were introduced as categories. However, the use of a fairly stable methodology over time has allowed the CSEW to track changes in the incidence of different offences over time.

Respondents are asked about violence, robbery and theft, vehicle crime and damage to property. Data about sexual offences are collected but are not published as part of the main survey results because the low numbers of offences recorded make extrapolation to the wider population difficult.

The CSEW has consistently revealed a far higher number of crimes than do the police statistics. For the subset of crimes covered by the CSEW, the data suggest that somewhere between only a third and a quarter of offences that occur get recorded by the police (Maguire & McVie, 2017). Much of the dark figure consists of relatively minor offences resulting in little or no personal loss or injury. Victimisation surveys and police statistics for more serious offences differ less than for less serious ones. In general, where victimisation surveys employ large samples and robust methodology they are regarded as more accurate and trustworthy than police recorded crime rates. The CSEW has used the same 'core' set of questions since it started, unlike police statistics, which are significantly affected by changes in recording practices. This makes the CSEW much better as assessing trends in offending and victimisation.

This does not mean that victimisation surveys are free of problems. The CSEW relies on respondents' recall of what has happened in the past year, which may not be accurate. Victimisation surveys also tend to put an upper limit on the number of crimes that any single respondent can report. In the CSEW the maximum is five. This is done because otherwise a small number of respondents could inflate the estimated risk of crime in the population. However, a small number of people are disproportionately the victims of repeated offences (Farrell & Pease, 2014) so only recording the first five crimes that a victim reports risks under-representing the level of offending.

The CSEW does not gather data on all offences. Murder, obviously, is omitted, as are crimes against businesses and anyone who does not live in an ordinary residential street address. This includes people living in institutions, student halls of residence and homeless people. Large-scale victimisation surveys tend to underestimate violent crime because people are unwilling to disclose offences committed by a family member or intimate partner to a researcher who is a stranger. Jones et al. (1986) developed methodologies with the aim of gaining respondents' trust and found that reported rates of sexual assault and intimate partner violence were much higher than those reported by the British Crime Survey. They also found that some people's risk of victimisation was much higher than others so, for example, young black women were 29 times more likely to be assaulted than older white women.

Offender surveys

Police and victimisation statistics allow us to estimate only how many offences have occurred, not how many people are committing them. An alternative way of estimating the extent of crime is to focus on the perpetrators rather than the victims. Offender surveys help to shed light on whether changes in the crime rate are due to changes in the number of people committing offences (the prevalence of offending) or changes in the number of offences committed by each offender (the incidence of offending). In the 1990s, offending among young people was measured by the British government as part of its *Youth Lifestyles* survey. The 1998 survey indicated that 26% of young men and 11% of young women had committed an offence in the previous year. Of these, only 12% reported having been cautioned or prosecuted (Campbell & Harrington, 1999). Although at least some of the remainder is likely to have come to the attention of the police, these data support the conclusion that a substantial dark figure exists.

Between 2003 and 2006 the Home Office carried out a national, longitudinal self-report survey of offending called the Offending, Crime and Justice Survey (OCJS). The OCJS initially recruited a representative sample of people from England and Wales aged between 10 and 65, to estimate the prevalence of offending in the general population. The follow-up longitudinal study focused only on those aged 10 to 25, in order to obtain data about how offending behaviour changed over time. Of the former set of individuals, 41% of 65 year olds reported committing at least one offence in their lifetime, with men (52%) more likely to offend than women (30%). The most commonly reported offences were minor thefts and assaults. Around 20% of offenders had done so only once, with 35–40% reporting four or more offences in their lifetime. Across the whole sample, about 10% had committed an offence in the previous year (Budd et al., 2005). As with other research on age and gender, prevalence of offending was highest in the late teens and there were gender differences in both the amount and type of offending. Males were more likely to offend than females and engaged in a wider variety of crimes with the majority of offences by women being minor thefts and assaults. The longitudinal component of the OCJS tracked respondents over a four-year period. It found that over the four years covered by the survey 49% of the sample reported at least one offence. Consistent with the age–crime curve, the prevalence of offending peaked in the mid-teens (14–16 years) and declined subsequently. While the OCJS confirmed that some degree of criminal behaviour is common in the general population, it also showed that a relatively small number of prolific offenders accounted for a disproportionate number of crimes. A group of just 4% of the sample was responsible for 32% of the offences reported (Hales et al., 2009).

Self-report measures seem to agree quite well with other measures of offending such as peer reports and police records (Hindelang et al., 1981). However, they are subject to some criticism. First, they rely on the assumption that the respondents are accurate in their memories and willing to admit to their offences. Given that forgetting increases with time and since respondents are probably less likely to admit their more serious offences, estimates of offending may be in the low side. Second, there is a danger of sampling bias since the most prolific offenders are least likely to be sampled for the survey. For example, if the respondents are surveyed at school, persistent truants are unlikely to be present. Since they are also the most likely to offend, estimates of both incidence and prevalence of offending are likely to be low.

In conclusion, it is impossible to know exactly how much crime is committed. All of the available methods for gathering this information tend to underestimate how much offending there is. At the same time, we should recognise, first, that each source of information compensates somewhat for the weaknesses in the others, so by considering them together it is possible to make reasonable estimates of the extent of crime and, second, that the majority of the dark figure consists of relatively minor and 'victimless' offences.

Trends in crime

Despite their limitations, crime statistics allow us to identify some general trends in offending in the UK. The CSEW/BCS and police statistics show that crime increased steadily from the early 1980s onwards and peaked around the mid-1990s. Since then, CSEW crime rates have fallen almost every year up to 2017 (ONS, 2017b). Police statistics follow largely the same trend, although there are fluctuations caused by changes in how crimes were recorded.

The long-term drop in crime since the 1990s is paralleled by similar falls in many other countries. Data from the US, the UK and Western European countries show that all types of crime rose steadily from the 1960s onward, peaked in the 1990s and have been falling ever since (Tonry, 2014). The international crime drop is interesting because it follows a very similar pattern in countries that have pursued very different criminal justice policies. For example, in the 1980s the US adopted zero tolerance policing and mass incarceration, with unprecedented use of prison sentences for offending (see Chapter 10). Canada did neither but the crime drop has been virtually identical. A great number of explanations for the crime drop have been put forward, including economic factors (a stronger economy leads to greater wealth and less appetite for stolen goods), demographic factors (increased immigration and an ageing population leads to lower offending), changes in laws (tougher firearms laws, looser abortion laws), policing (more police, better targeting of crime) and tougher penalties for crime (greater use of prison and the death penalty). The problem is that these explanations only apply in certain places whereas the drop is very widespread. In addition, explanations linked to the functioning of the economy have struggled to explain why the crime drop has continued even after the global economic crash of 2008.

One hypothesis that might still explain the crime drop is that the rise and subsequent fall in offending is related to the effects of lead pollution on the brain (see Chapter 3). A second is that offending has fallen as a consequence of the adoption of better security methods in Western countries. For example, higher standards of vehicle security have removed opportunities for car theft and, consequently, car crime has fallen. Similarly, security measures have improved in homes and businesses, making them less attractive targets (Farrell, 2013). This fits the evidence on acquisitive crime (e.g. car thefts, burglaries) but it is not obvious how it can explain the reduction in violent offences, including murder. A third possibility is that criminal activity has actually been falling steadily since the Middle Ages as a consequences of long-term cultural changes that have gradually increased people's capacity for individual self-control (Eisner, 2003). In this light, the question is not 'why did crime rates suddenly fall from the 1990s?' but 'why did they rise in the 1960s?' Tonry (2014) suggests that rising crime in the 1960s was a consequence of disruption to the social order in the post-war period related to decolonisation, globalisation, economic restructuring and the breakdown of political consensus. By the 1990s, Western societies had largely absorbed this disruption, allowing the longer term decline in crime to resume. Tonry's argument is compelling but it is not obvious how it could be tested directly, leaving it somewhat speculative. Nonetheless, examination of trends in offending, particularly when different countries are compared, represents an important way of testing theories about the factors that affect offending.

Victimisation

Some people are more likely to become victims of crime than others. The CSEW is useful because, alongside gathering demographic data showing whether particular age or socio-economic groups are more or less likely to be victimised, it also gathers data on people's attitudes, including their fear of crime. This allows a comparison to be made between a person's fear of crime and their chance of victimisation. In general, these data show that most people's fear of crime is exaggerated compared with their chance of becoming a victim of crime.

Property crime

The 2015–2016 CSEW (ONS, 2016) found that the most prevalent types of property crime were vehicle-related thefts and criminal damage, both affecting 4% of households. Thefts from the person and robbery were much rarer, affecting 0.7% and 0.3% of households respectively. One of the factors influencing property crime victimisation is geographical location. People living in urban areas were more likely to be victimised than those in rural areas. The highest rates of property crime were in areas with the highest level of unemployment and, for most types of property crime, people in rented accommodation had a higher risk than owner-occupiers. Younger people were more likely to become victims than older people and people with the lowest household income (£10,000 per year or less) were more likely to be the victims of all types of property crime except for criminal damage, which was more common in higher income groups.

Violent crime

Throughout the 1990s the risk in the general population of becoming a victim of violent crime was around 5%. The 2016 CSEW (ONS, 2017c) found that the risk in 2015–2016 was 1.8%, a substantial reduction. The majority of violent crimes (55%) were classed as 'violence without injury'. Assault with minor injury accounted for 24%, and 21% of crimes were classed as 'wounding', the more serious category.

In the majority of violent crimes, the perpetrator was known to the victim, 43% were carried out by an acquaintance and 20% of crimes were classed as 'domestic violence' where the perpetrator was a partner, ex-partner or family member (although domestic violence tends to be under-reported; see above). Women were more likely to be the victims of domestic violence (7.7% of women; 4.4% of men). In 37% of cases, the perpetrator was a stranger. As with property crime, some people are more likely to be victimised than others. The victims of violence are more likely to be males (2.2% of adult males compared with 1.4% of females). Younger people (16–24 years) ran a higher risk of victimisation, as did those living in more deprived areas.

Intimate violence and sexual crime

The 2016 CSEW (ONS, 2017d) found that women were more likely to be the victims of intimate violence than men. The commonest form of intimate violence for both women and men was non-sexual partner abuse, affecting 5.4% of women and 2.8% of men. There were marked differences in sexual assault victimisation: 3.2% of women had been sexually assaulted compared with 0.7% of men. The majority of sexual assaults were unwanted touching and indecent exposure; 0.7% of women had been the victim of rape or attempted rape compared with fewer than 0.1% of men. As with property and other violent crimes, sexual offences affect some groups more than others. Younger people experienced domestic violence more frequently than older. Young women aged 16–19 were significantly more likely than other groups to be the victims of sexual assaults, with 11% of this group being affected. Those with a lower SES ran a higher risk of victimisation. For example, 17% of women in the lower income bracket had been the victim of domestic violence compared with 4.3% in the highest income bracket. A similar trend was apparent for men but it was less marked.

Repeat victimisation

Surveys show that victimisation is not evenly distributed. Many types of crime disproportionately affect younger, poorer people. However, what is not readily apparent from headline figures is how often the same people are victimised repeatedly. One of the strongest predictors of whether a person will become a victim of crime is whether they have been victimised in the past. Pease (1998) estimates that 1% of people are the victims of 59% of all personal crime. Repeat victimisation often involves the same offenders, who select the same or similar victims because of past success. Farrell and Pease (2014) identify a number of reasons for repeat victimisation:

- Domestic violence gives rise to repeat victimisation because the victim and perpetrator are likely to reside in the same place; the fact that victims are reluctant to report such crimes means that there are few restraints on the perpetrators.
- Some shops are repeatedly targeted because they stock sought-after goods (e.g. electronics and drugs) and are situated in high-traffic areas.

- In hate crimes, the offender(s) may be motivated to victimise an individual in multiple different ways; and because victims of hate crime are often easily identifiable (e.g. having a disability or belonging to a minority ethnic group), they may be victimised by multiple offenders.

- Workers in some professions, including police officers and nurses, are regularly exposed to individuals who are likely to attack them.

- Those who frequently commit offences themselves run a high risk of repeat victimisation, since they interact regularly with other offenders and may also possess things like drugs or cash, which make them an attractive target.

Farrell and Pease distinguish between two explanations of repeat victimisation. The risk-heterogenity explanation involves a target being victimised by multiple offenders (as when a shop is targeted by many shoplifters). The alternative is an event-dependent explanation where a target is victimised *because* they have been victimised previously. Either process can give rise to supertargets that account for a disproportionate amount of victimisation.

Effects of victimisation

It is almost inevitable that a person will experiences some degree of distress as a result of being victimised. Shapland and Hall (2007) identify a range of effects:

1 shock, and a loss of faith in society
2 guilt associated with the idea that they could have avoided victimisation
3 physical injury
4 financial loss, either through loss of property or effects on employment
5 psychological symptoms including anxiety and depression and post-traumatic stress disorder (PTSD)
6 social effects such as avoiding certain places or activities
7 increased fear of victimisation, and increased actual risk of victimisation (see above).

It is difficult to predict exactly what consequences an individual will suffer since this depends not only on the offence but also the victim's personal circumstances, other life events, previous experiences of victimisation and their personality.

The main determinant of the victim's reaction is the seriousness of the crime. Victims of less serious offences typically suffer relatively little distress and victimisation has little or no impact on their subsequent behaviour (Averdijk, 2011). However, serious, violent victimisation generally has a highly disruptive effect. Immediately following a serious crime, victims are likely to experience confusion and disbelief. Assuming that they define the event as a crime they make a decision about what to do next. This could include doing nothing, telling someone else (e.g. a friend or family member) or informing the authorities. As discussed above, much crime goes unreported to the police. Reporting the crime to the authorities may have a positive effect on the victim if the perpetrator is caught as they may feel that justice has been served or they may be recompensed for their losses (Ruback & Thompson, 2001). By way of contrast, reporting the crime may have negative consequences if the victim is disbelieved, if police and other officials are unsympathetic and, if the case goes to trial, if the defence lawyers treat the victim in an aggressive or humiliating way when they give evidence (Symonds, 1980).

In some cases, the trauma of victimisation can give rise to PTSD, an anxiety disorder characterised by (1) re-experiencing the event (e.g. in flashbacks, night-mares or intrusive mental images); (2) avoidance of stimuli associated with the trauma and emotional numbing; and (3) hyperarousal, irritability, anger, insomnia and problems concentrating. People with PTSD run a higher than average risk of developing further psychological problems such as depression, drug and alco-hol problems. Gale and Coupe (2005) collected data from 149 victims of robbery who were interviewed three weeks after the crime and again around nine months later. The victims' immediate response was increased fear of crime, particularly at night. Nine months later, fear of crime had diminished but was still elevated. Three weeks after the crime around half the victims had sufficient symptoms to warrant a diagnosis of PTSD. Nine months later, this had fallen but still a third of victims met the criteria for PTSD. There was individual variation, so while the mental health of two-thirds of the victims improved over time, the mental health of 25% actually deteriorated. A similar, albeit more serious, pattern is identifiable among victims of sexual assaults. Resick (1987) found that rape survivors experi-enced significant effects on anxiety, mood, fear of revictimisation and self-esteem. Levels of distress fell for the first three to six months following victimisation and then stabilised, so that four years later adverse psychological effects were still present.

Not all victims of violent and sexual crime go on to develop PTSD. Research on trauma suggests that a range of demographic variables have an influence. Women are at a higher risk than men, as are members of minority ethnic groups, those with a lower socio-economic status and those with a history of psychological problems (Kelly et al., 2010). The risk of PTSD following victimisation depends on several variables including the seriousness of the crime and the level of social support to which the victim has access. Resick (1987) found that adjustment following victi-misation was related to the degree of distress they felt immediately following the crime. Those with the highest distress had the highest risk of chronic psychological symptoms. More recently, Kunst et al. (2011) asked 172 victims of violent crime about their emotional reactions during victimisation, their subsequent anger at hav-ing been victimised and their level of PTSD symptoms. Around 46% of victims met the criteria for PTSD. Those who reported the greatest levels of anger had a signifi-cantly higher risk of PTSD. Kelly et al. (2010) suggest that the risk of PTSD among victims of serious crime can be reduced by:

■ Engaging with victims as soon as possible, ideally while they are still receiving acute medical care.

- Providing support in victims' communities.
- Integrating support services so that the social, financial and mental health needs of victims are all met.

Fear of crime

Victimisation surveys have generally found that people have a fear of crime that is disproportionate to their actual chances of being victimised. CSEW data for 2015–2016 (ONS, 2017e) show that the overall risk of victimisation was 15.2% but respondents estimated their risk at 19.1%. Different groups judge their risk of victimisation in different ways, so those most at risk (people aged 16–24 years) tended to underestimate their risk whereas those aged 35 years and upwards significantly overestimated their chances of victimisation. Only people in the 25–34 age group were largely accurate. Despite the continual fall in crime since 1995, 60% of adults believed that crime was rising but this has dropped in recent years: in 2009 over 80% of respondents believed that crime was rising.

The main reason for the public's misperception of their risk of being victimised seems to be that they gather information about crime from media sources such as newspapers and television programmes that do not accurately reflect the reality of crime. News media tend to focus on unusual and horrific events. Murders receive extensive coverage, although murder, in the UK, remains an extremely rare crime. In order to attract audience share, news media will tend to focus on sensational events even if these are the exception rather than the norm. Even where actual crime statistics are reported, news reports tend to focus on aspects of the data that portray a rise in victimisation and pay little attention to reported falls in the crime rate (Ainsworth, 2000). The result is that the public are constantly exposed to accounts of murder, rape and abduction, and may come to believe that the frequency with which these are reported reflects the actual chance of being so victimised. The same is true of fictionalised crime in films and television programmes that regularly features statistically rare crimes such as violent attacks on strangers. In light of this, it is not surprising that people tend to have an inaccurate perception of the likelihood that they will be affected by crime. However, people are more accurate in their perception of crime in their locality, presumably because this is based on first-hand experience whereas perception of crime nationally is more likely to be based on the media (ONS, 2017e).

Chapter summary

There is debate over which people and acts should be studied by criminological psychologists but most researchers agree that research should focus principally on crime as legally defined. Although around half the population commits a crime at some point in their life, criminal behaviour is most frequent among young men.

Official statistics, victimisation surveys and self-reports are all ways of measuring crime. They have a tendency to underestimate the extent of crime (particularly police recorded crime) and there is a 'dark figure' of unrecorded criminal activity. However, data from multiple sources suggest that, in recent years, crime has been falling although there is dispute about why. Victimisation is not evenly distributed in the population. Young people and those from low SES groups are most heavily victimised. The psychological effects of victimisation include anger, depression and anxiety, with victims of more serious crimes at significant risk of developing PTSD. Generally, people have an exaggerated fear of being victimised and believe that the incidence of crime is greater than it actually is. The main reason for this is that they obtain information about crime from media sources that exaggerate its incidence.

Further reading

The Crime Survey for England and Wales website presents data and analysis from the CSEW including short reports on different aspects of the criminal statistics. It is regularly updated. www.crimesurvey.co.uk.

Biologically oriented explanations of offending

Apply your learning

Kai has been convicted of a violent assault. He was standing in the queue at a fast food outlet having spent the evening drinking with friends. Kai claims that another customer 'jumped the queue' in order to get served before him and insulted him when challenged. Kai punched and kicked the victim repeatedly, leaving him with significant injuries. Kai has several previous convictions for violent behaviour and has been known to the authorities for a long time. As a child, he was put under child protection because of parental neglect related to drug dependency and his violent father, who himself had several convictions for violence and theft. Kai's guilt is not in doubt, but the judge has asked for reports before passing sentence.

List all the features of Kai's case that you believe may be relevant to understanding his offence from a psychological viewpoint. Outline how each feature could have contributed to what he did. As you read this chapter, add to your analysis of the case any new ideas you encounter.

Biologically oriented explanations of offending rest on the idea that offenders, as a group, are different from non-offenders in their biological structure and/or functioning. This was an influential idea in the early days of criminological psychology (see Chapter 1). However, the idea of the 'born criminal' fell out of favour during the 20th century when criminology shifted to an emphasis on environmental explanations (see Chapter 5). In the 1990s there was a resurgence of interest in biological factors and there is now widespread acknowledgement that theories of offending that do not incorporate them are necessarily incomplete. This chapter starts by reviewing evidence for some of the biological differences that have been found between offenders and non-offenders and outlining their putative role in criminal behaviour. There follows a discussion of where these differences may come from, focused on a selection of possible causes: genetics, environmental pollution, traumatic brain injury and adverse childhood experiences.

Biological differences between offenders and non-offenders

The biological view assumes that an individual's behaviour is organised by his nervous system, particularly his brain, and criminal acts are a consequence of this. Biopsychology does not claim that there are specific brain areas or processes that cause people, for example, to burgle houses, file false tax returns or assault their spouses. Rather, an offender's nervous system interacts with social and other environmental influences to give rise to tendencies to behave in particular ways (e.g. aggression) that become criminal acts when they violate the law. Biopsychological research has tended to focus on aggressive crime as it is relatively straightforward to identify (unlike, say, financial fraud), is a pressing social problem and has clear links to the large and well-researched body of biological knowledge about aggression. This makes it an obvious target for researchers wishing to investigate biological influences on offending.

Low heart rate

One of the most consistent findings in the biopsychology of offenders is that they have a lower heart rate than non-offenders. The association is remarkably robust and is found in children, adolescents and adults and across different cultures (Portnoy & Farrington, 2015). Low heart rate (LHR) can predict aggression and conduct problems in children and violence in adults independently of other variables such as personality and family history (Farrington, 1997). What is not clear is *why* offenders have LHRs. One possibility is that LHR indicates a chronically low level of activity in the nervous system. The individual finds this uncomfortable and offending provides risk and excitement, thereby raising their arousal level to a more comfortable level (the *sensation-seeking* hypothesis). A second possibility is that LHR reflects a diminished capacity to experience fear. Since fear, intuitively at least, plays a part in stopping people from acting on their antisocial impulses then fearless people might be more prone to offending (the *fearlessness* hypothesis). Relatively few studies have addressed this issue directly, but Portnoy and Farrington (2015) suggest that using LHR as a biomarker for antisocial behaviour may lead to practical applications for reducing offending. For example, improving a child's early environment with enhanced diet and education seems both to increase heart rate and reduce later behavioural problems and offending (Raine et al., 2003) and LHR may be useful in predicting those individuals who may benefit most from treatments designed to reduce behavioural problems in children (Cornet et al., 2014). LHR is also relatively easy to measure and therefore to incorporate into studies of how biological and other factors interact to produce criminal behaviour (Raine & Portnoy, 2012).

Brain structure and functioning

Biopsychologists regard aggression as an innate, genetically influenced, set of responses that have evolved because they confer a survival advantage. Aggressive behaviour benefits an animal if it allows it to compete successfully for territory, food, mates and so on. Aggression, violence and crime are not synonymous but it is possible that the same evolved brain systems that regulate aggression in other species might be involved in aggressive crime. Aggression in mammals can be predatory (as in hunting for food), social (as when establishing dominance over others of the same species) or reactive (as when responding to a threat) but it all depends on signaling between several brain structures including the prefrontal cortex, the amygdala, the hypothalamus and the periaqueductal grey. Electrical stimulation of the hypothalamus of cats and rats causes social or predatory aggression, depending on exactly where the stimulation is applied (Fuchs et al., 1985; Kruk, 1991). Damage to the amygdala in monkeys can either inhibit or disinhibit aggressive behaviour, again depending on the site of the lesion (Miczek et al., 1974; Pinel et al., 1977) and damage to parts of the prefrontal cortex can also facilitate aggressive responses (de Bruin et al., 1983). These structures are also present in the human brain, raising the possibility that violent offending may result from some degree of abnormality in one or more of these areas. However, what is true of a rat or cat may not be true of a human. Their brains are similar but not identical and their evolutionary history is different. Investigating the human brain through systematic lesioning or electrical stimulation is impossible for ethical reasons so it is hard to link offending to brain abnormality purely on this basis.

Some relevant evidence comes from clinical case studies where violent crime correlates with brain damage caused by disease or injury. For example, in 1966, Charles J. Whitman murdered his mother and wife before murdering 14 strangers and wounding 31 more. Whitman was killed by a police officer and, in the subsequent post-mortem, a tumour was found that had affected his hypothalamus and amygdala. Whitman's diary contained accounts of unpredictable, inexplicable rage in the months leading up to the shooting and he had sought medical treatment shortly before his shooting spree (Lavergne, 1997). Whether the tumour actually caused Whitman's actions is disputed but Siegel and Victoroff (2009) identify 18 similar cases in which violent and sometimes homicidal human behaviour was associated with a brain tumour affecting brain areas implicated in aggression by animal studies. This includes two where surgical removal of part of the amygdala resulted in a reduction in aggression (Mark & Sweet, 1974; Hood et al., 1983). These examples imply that the same brain systems govern aggression in humans as in other animals. However, such cases are also highly unusual: most violent criminals do not have obvious brain pathologies. Consequently, on their own, they cannot sustain the view that violent offending is the result of biological abnormality.

Biopsychological research advanced significantly with the development of brain imaging technology in the 1970s and 1980s. Computerised axial tomography (CAT) and magnetic resonance imaging (MRI) allowed researchers to create images of brain structure with much greater detail than conventional X-rays, which are poor at imaging soft tissues like the brain. The development of positron emission tomography (PET) and functional MRI (fMRI) allowed researchers to create three-dimensional images that indicate activity in different brain areas. They work by tracking the movement of radioactive glucose (PET) or haemoglobin molecules (fMRI). When a brain area grows more active, it uses more oxygen and glucose and consequently blood flow to that area increases. By measuring changes in blood flow it is possible to infer brain activity. Volkow and Tancredi (1987) were the first to use PET to investigate the brains of violent individuals but early investigations were limited by the relatively poor images produced by the scanners and the prohibitive cost of using them to investigate large samples. However, technological improvements by the mid-1990s had started to address these issues, allowing Raine et al. (1997) to conduct a landmark investigation of brain functioning in violent offenders.

Raine et al. used PET scanning to compare brain functioning in 41 people charged with homicide who were pleading not guilty by reason of insanity (the *murderers*) with 41 non-offenders who were matched to be as similar as possible (the *controls*). All the participants were injected with a glucose-based radiotracer, after which they completed a continuous performance task (CPT) in which they watched a screen that projected random stimuli and pressed a button only when they saw a particular stimulus (the target). A CPT engages a number of brain systems, making it useful for assessing brain functioning. The murderers' and controls' brain activity during the task differed in several ways. The murderers had lower glucose metabolism in the prefrontal cortex, parts of the parietal cortex and the corpus callosum (the 'bridge' between the two hemispheres of the brain). They also showed asymmetries of glucose metabolism that were not present in the controls: activity was lower in the left than the right hemisphere in several structures, including the amygdala. The differences observed by Raine et al. are important because most of them related to brain areas that were already implicated in aggression by prior research. For example, the prefrontal cortex had long been regarded as playing a role in the inhibition of inappropriate impulses; this is consistent with the finding that prefrontal activity was found to be lower in the murderers. Other areas not previously associated with violence (e.g. the cerebellum) showed no differences.

The investigation of Raine et al. (1997) had a significant impact because it was the first to use PET scanning with a large enough sample and sufficient controls to support reasonably firm conclusions about the role of brain abnormalities in violent crime. It established the paradigm for the use of neuroimaging to investigate offending and gave rise to a strand of criminological research whose influence has grown in the intervening years. It is also notable for the caution Raine et al. exercised when interpreting their results and the clarity with which they drew attention to the limitations of their research. In particular, they emphasised the relatively poor resolution of their scanning technology, the potentially confounding influence of mental illness among the murderers, the narrow subset of violent offenders represented by their sample and the fact that no comparison was made with a group of non-violent offenders, making it impossible to know whether the differences they detected were due to their being violent or their being offenders. Raine et al. also stressed that their findings do not mean that violence is caused by biological factors alone and that violent offending depends on the interaction of these with 'social, psychological, cultural and situational factors' (p.505). This last point is often lost when such evidence is presented to the public via the mass media, particularly when it is accompanied by brightly coloured and impressive looking images that purport to identify the 'brain centre' responsible for crime or some other behaviour (O'Connor et al., 2012).

Over the past 20 years, evidence has confirmed a great number of initial suggestions from Raine et al. about the role of specific brain areas in offending. The structures most strongly implicated are the prefrontal cortex and the limbic system, a set of interconnected structures that includes the amygdala. The most consistent finding is that offenders have unusually low activity levels in the prefrontal cortex, often accompanied by a reduction in the volume of grey matter in the same area. Imaging studies have also shown that the activity of the left and right amygdalae is asymmetric in violent offenders and that violence is associated with a reduced amygdala volume (Raine & Yang, 2006).

These differences may contribute to criminal behaviour in a number of ways. The prefrontal cortex is responsible for executive function: planning, decision making and impulse control. Impairments of the prefrontal cortex limit an individual's capacity to use information about emotions to predict the outcomes of their actions. Consequently, their behaviour is strongly influenced by short-term rewards and they tend to act impulsively (Damasio, 1996). In this view, then, violent – and other – crime occurs because the offender is relatively poor at anticipating and learning from punishment, meaning they do not stop themselves from acting on their impulses where an individual with an unimpaired prefrontal cortex would be able to do so. The amygdala is involved in emotional regulation and plays an important role in how mammals respond to threat. In general, as threat increases, an animal will first freeze, then attempt to flee and then, when no other choice exists, attack the source of threat. If the functioning of the amygdala is impaired, an individual might be unusually sensitive to threats and, consequently, violent behaviour might be triggered by relatively innocuous situations (Blair et al., 2005). Alternatively, a relatively unresponsive amygdala might impair an individual's capacity to both experience fear and recognise it in others. This would remove two important inhibitions on offending: the fear of the consequences and the recognition of the effect offending has on the feelings of others (Mitchell and Beech, 2011). This may be the underlying problem in psychopathy (see Chapter 4).

Brain chemistry

The nervous system relies on a vast array of chemicals that transmit signals between its cells. Normal development and functioning requires these neurotransmitters, neurohormones and hormones to be present in the correct proportions. Offenders differ from non-offenders in that they tend to be deficient in the neurotransmitter serotonin. A review of 20 studies found that low levels of a serotonin breakdown product (5-HIAA) were reliably associated with antisocial behaviour towards both people and property (Moore et al., 2002). The relationship between serotonin and offending is stronger in men than women, which implies that the factors that contribute to offending might differ between genders. In addition, serotonin levels tend to increase with age, which may explain why offending generally decreases over the lifespan. Although studies in this area share the limitation that it is breakdown products like 5-HIAA that are measured, not actual serotonin levels, the association is robust enough to support the conclusion that serotonin levels are a contributory factor in offending. Another neurotransmitter implicated is dopamine. Increases in aggressive behaviour correlate with increased dopamine levels and when drugs are used to increase or decrease dopamine activity there is a corresponding effect on feelings of anger and aggressive behaviour (Seo et al., 2008). In many brain areas, serotonin regulates dopamine, so where serotonin levels are low, dopamine levels rise excessively. It may be that low levels of serotonin prevent the prefrontal cortex from successfully regulating negative emotional states arising in the limbic system, thereby increasing the risk of a violent response in situations that are interpreted as a threat or a provocation.

Influences on the nervous system

There is now abundant evidence that some types of offending are attributable to differences between the brains of offenders and non-offenders. However, this leaves unanswered the question of *why* these differences exist. There are many influences on the development, structure and functioning of the nervous system that may be relevant in understanding crime. Four of these are discussed below, selected because they illustrate the range of factors that may be involved.

Genetics

Genes are sequences of deoxyribonucleic acid (DNA) that transmit information from one generation to its offspring. A human being has around 20,000 genes (Ezkurdia et al., 2014), inherited from their parents and organised into 23 pairs of chromosomes. Together, they provide a 'blueprint' for the development of the individual. The majority of genes are shared by all humans but around 1% of them exist in different forms called alleles. These contribute to the differences between people, influencing physical traits such as eye colour and psychological and behavioural traits such as personality. Genes are relevant to crime because some of them influence the development of the nervous system. They may therefore be responsible for the differences in the brain that are associated with offending.

The consensus among biopsychologists is that genes influence criminal behaviour. This view rests on evidence from family history studies, twin studies and adoption studies. A family history study is conducted in order to ascertain whether a specific trait (in this case, offending) runs in families. If it does, this provides evidence that genetic influence plays a role. Osborn and West (1979) report that 40% of the sons of criminal fathers go on to get a criminal record themselves, compared with only 13% of the sons of non-criminal fathers. Other studies report similar results (Cloninger et al., 1978; West, 1982). Although suggestive of a genetic influence on offending, these findings could also indicate an environmental influence: sons might acquire criminal tendencies through social learning or the correlation might be due to the influence of a third variable that affects both father and son such as social class, deprivation or poor education (see Chapter 5).

This problem is avoided by the twin study methodology, because it eliminates the confounding effect of shared environmental influences, at least in principle. A twin study compares monozygotic (MZ; genetically identical) and dizygotic (DZ; non-identical) twin pairs. It rests on the assumption that, in both MZ and DZ twins, criminality is affected by environmental factors to the same extent, because both MZ and DZ twins develop in equivalent environments: they are born into the same family, at the same time, go to the same schools etc. If it is found that the MZ twins are more similar in their criminality than the DZ twins this must be due to their greater genetic similarity. The similarity between twins is expressed as a correlation or concordance. A 25% concordance means that 25% of the time *both* twins show evidence of criminality whereas in the remaining 75% of cases only one does. Early twin studies showed strong evidence of a genetic influence on offending but the samples used were small and the methods used to determine whether the twins were MZ or DZ were unreliable. Large-sample studies using reliable tests of zygosity have been carried out since the 1970s. Christiansen (1977) used 3,586 twin pairs and found concordance rates of 35% (MZ) and 13% (DZ) for males; 21% (MZ) and 8% (DZ) for females. Dalgaard and Kringlen (1976) found concordances of 26% (MZ) and 15% (DZ) for females. These findings indicate a genetic influence on offending. Two points should be stressed, however. First, the MZ concordances, while greater than the DZ, are still fairly low, indicating a substantial environmental contribution. Second, there are questions about the assumption of equal environments in twin studies. The greater similarity of MZ twins may be due to the fact that they share a closer relationship than DZ twins and are treated more similarly, especially since a DZ pair may be different sexes whereas a MZ pair cannot.

Adoption studies compare the rates of criminality between people who were adopted early in life, their biological parents and their adoptive parents. Broadly, the biological parents supply the genes and the adoptive parents the environment so where the adoptees are more similar to their biological parents this suggests a genetic influence on criminality and where they are more similar to their adoptive parents the environment is a more significant influence. Crowe (1972) found that where the biological mother of an adoptee had a criminal record, so did nearly 50% of adoptees. By contrast, where she had no criminal record, this figure was only 5%. Hutchings and Mednick (1975) examined criminality in both biological and adoptive fathers. If both had a criminal record, 36.2% of the sons also became criminals. When only the biological father was criminal 21.4% did so and when only the adoptive father had a criminal record so did 11.5% of the sons. When neither father had a criminal record, 10.5% of the sons did. More recently, Hjalmarsson and Lindquist (2013) analysed data from every person adopted in Sweden between 1943 and 1967, finding that criminality in the biological parents was significantly associated with criminal convictions in the adoptees. As with family history and twin studies, these findings support the view that offending is genetically influenced.

Again, there are several reasons to treat these findings with a degree of caution. First, they also indicate a significant influence of the environment. Second, greater concordance between offspring and biological mothers may be due to prenatal factors like maternal stress or drug taking rather than a genetic influence. Third, adoptees may be placed in environments similar to those from which they were adopted, possibly another branch of the same family. Fourth, children may be adopted years after their birth, leaving room for a significant environmental influence from the biological parents early in life.

These objections notwithstanding, the accumulated evidence supports the view that offending is influenced by genetics. A systematic review of twin and adoption studies by Mason and Frick (1994) estimates the size of this genetic influence at around 50%; this figure is confirmed by recent studies using more sophisticated methodologies (Beaver et al., 2009). The influence is not uniform, however. Aggressive offending seems more influenced by genes than is non-violent offending (Eley et al., 2003), and the genetic influence appears much stronger in life-course-persistent than in adolescence-limited offenders (Moffitt, 1993, 2005; see Chapter 2). In general, the question of *whether* genes influence offending is widely regarded as settled. Research in recent years has shifted to focus on the questions of *which* genes are involved and *how* they exert their influence.

Where it comes to aggressive offending, several genes have been identified as potentially significant (Raine, 2008). One is the MAOA gene, which codes for monoamine oxidase, a chemical that breaks down serotonin. When the MAOA gene is 'knocked out' (made inactive) in mice they become very aggressive (Cases et al., 1995). In humans, MAOA exists in at least two versions (alleles), L-MAOA and H-MAOA. Carriers of the L-MAOA allele produce less monoamine oxidase than H-MAOA carriers. They also have lower volumes in several key brain areas including the prefrontal cortex and the amygdala (Meyer-Lindenberg et al., 2006), structures that are important in offending (see above). Low-activity MAOA alleles are associated with impulsivity and aggression (Buckholtz and Meyer-Lindenberg, 2008) and seem to make carriers unusually responsive to provocation. McDermott et al. (2009) compared L- and H-MAOA carriers on their response to someone who frustrated them. The participants played a financial game in which they were led to believe that another player had deprived them of either a small or a large amount of money. They were subsequently given the opportunity to punish that player by requiring them to consume a quantity of unpleasant hot sauce. When they had experienced only a small loss, the L- and H-MAOA carriers responded similarly. However, when they had experienced a large loss, the L-MAOA carriers were much more likely to punish their opponent. Although somewhat artificial, and not of offenders, this study by McDermott et al. goes some way to illuminating how a specific allele may influence behaviour in ways that may be analogous to offending situations. Other research directly supports an association with offending. Beaver et al. (2010) found that L-MAOA is more frequent among gang members and offenders who use weapons and Stetler et al. (2014) compared violent and non-violent offenders, reporting that L-MAOA was carried by 61% of the violent but only 20% of the non-violent offenders. Carriers of L-MAOA scored higher on measures of impulsiveness than those with the H-MAOA allele.

Two points should be noted. First, it is difficult integrating these findings with what else is known about the relationship between serotonin and aggression. If L-MAOA carriers make *less* monoamine oxidase we would expect them to have *higher* serotonin levels than H-MAOA carriers whereas the evidence suggests an association between low serotonin and aggression. Second, none of these findings indicates that the L-MAOA allele *inevitably* gives rise to aggression or criminality. The expression of the L-MAOA allele in behaviour depends on other developmental influences. Caspi et al. (2002) and Fergusson et al. (2011) report that heightened impulsivity and aggression tends to result when L-MAOA carriers are subjected to early traumatic experiences like violent abuse. Despite this, and rather misleadingly, the association between aggression and L-MAOA has led to it being dubbed the 'warrior gene' (Gibbons, 2004). The L-MAOA allele has been reported to be more common in some ethnic groups than others (Lea and Chambers, 2007). The argument has been advanced that this reflects an evolved warlike and aggressive tendency that, in turn, may explain the inflated rates of crime among some ethnic groups (e.g. the Maori). Those taking a critical perspective on criminological psychology have argued that this represents a form of scientific racism, as the genetic factors 'inherent' in the ethnic group are privileged over the societal reasons that may also explain the inflated crime rates (see Chapter 12).

Genetic influences and evolution

Controversial interpretations aside, the presence of genes that affect impulsivity and aggression is generally thought by biopsychologists to be the result of evolution. Evolutionary accounts of offending are rooted in the assumption that the genes that sometimes manifest as criminal behaviour have arisen and persisted in the human population because, over evolutionary time, they have conferred an advantage on those who carried them by allowing to compete successfully with other individuals. There is evidence that human beings have evolved a general tendency to be aggressive as, compared with other species, human aggression is more often lethal than in other species. Gómez et al. (2016) compared intraspecific violence in 600 human populations and 1,024 mammal species. The death rate from intraspecific violence in non-humans was 0.3% whereas in humans it was 2%. The suggestion that aggressive traits have evolved to allow individuals to compete for resources is supported by evidence of human-on-human violence throughout history. Allen et al. (2016) found that incidence of sharp-force trauma (i.e. from edged weapons) correlates with times when food was scarce because of famine or drought.

The evolutionary view would also draw attention to the fact that men are, in general, more likely to offend than women, especially violent offences. Gottschalk and Ellis (2010) focus on the role of sexual selection in criminality. Following conventional evolutionary theory, they suggest that human females tend to invest more resources in their offspring than males and therefore tend to be choosier about their choice of mate. This promotes competition among males for mating opportunities.

Among the evolutionarily advantageous strategies males could adopt are some that could manifest as antisocial behaviours such as:

- Deception (e.g. promising to be faithful during courtship and then leaving once the female is pregnant).
- Intimidating, injuring and killing rival males.
- Exaggerating their capacity as a provider, e.g. by stealing resources from others.
- Using force when mating is not voluntary.

An evolutionary account of crimes such as assault, murder, rape, theft etc. is necessarily somewhat speculative but does at least provide a set of grounding assumptions against which the operation of genes on the nervous system can be understood. At the same time, it should be acknowledged that there are competing explanations for the same behaviours (see Chapters 4 and 5), and that biopsychologists themselves insist that evolutionary and genetic influence on offending must be understood as just that: influences, rather than causes. Feminists have also advanced a critical view of such claims (see Chapter 12).

Environmental toxins: lead pollution

One of the most significant challenges to genetics as an explanatory factor in offending is that crime rates fluctuate (see Chapter 2). While the prevalence of particular genes/alleles does change with time, over the course of short timescales (i.e. decades) the genetic composition of the population remains steady while the amount of violent offending can change markedly. This implies that factors other than genes have an impact on offending. One potentially important factor is pollution from the environment. A large number of toxins are known to affect brain development, including methylmercury, manganese and lead (Grandjean & Landrigan, 2014). Of these, lead has attracted particular scrutiny because environmental lead levels show a close relationship with levels of violent crime. This was first reported by Nevin (2000), who collected data about environmental lead pollution in the US over the course of the 20th century and compared these with crime data. It emerged that lead levels correlated almost perfectly with the rate of violent crime committed 23 years later. Environmental sources of lead include paint and petrol, both of which formerly contained lead as an additive. Having risen over the course of the 20th century, environmental lead levels in the United States peaked in the mid-1970s, falling thereafter as a result of tougher environmental legislation. Violent crime in the US rose steadily in the US in the post-war period, peaking in the early 1990s and then falling to a historic low in 2014. Nevin's explanation for the relationship is that exposure to lead early in life affects brain development in ways that later increase the risk of offending. Stretesky and Lynch (2004) compared air-lead levels and crime rates in 2,772 counties in the US finding a significant correlation between lead levels and both violent and property crimes. They also found that the relationship was strongest in counties with the highest levels of deprivation. Mielke and Zahran (2012) found the same relationship in an analysis of six US cities. Research has repeatedly confirmed the correlation between lead levels and crime. Nevin (2007) found it in data from Britain, Canada, France, Australia, Finland, Italy, Germany and New Zealand. Significantly, legislation to reduce lead levels in much of Europe was enacted in the 1980s and the fall in crime rates came correspondingly later than in the US, again after a delay of around 20 years.

There is a plausible route from lead exposure to offending. Lead exposure results in lower IQ, poorer educational attainment, generalised cognitive deficits, hyperactivity, conduct disorders and aggression, all of which are linked to criminality in adulthood (Narag et al., 2009). The degree to which brain development is affected depends on the level of exposure and age, so earlier exposure results in greater deficits. Neuroimaging studies using MRI indicate that childhood lead exposure results in a reduction of grey matter in large parts of the prefrontal cortex (Cecil et al., 2008), which is consistent with the findings discussed above.

However, there are some difficulties interpreting the evidence linking lead pollution with crime. First, there are inconsistencies between some findings, particularly those concerning property crime and murder. Reyes (2007) found a strong relationship between lead exposure and violent assault but only a weak link with murder or property crime. Second, there are many other variables that plausibly could influence offending rates, including economic conditions, policing and judicial policies and drug use. Because these can fluctuate alongside environmental lead levels it is difficult to isolate lead as a causal factor in crime. Similarly, higher lead exposure tends to occur in economically disadvantaged areas, so factors such as poverty and social disorganisation may explain the relationship. In the absence of experimental studies, which clearly would be unethical to conduct, conclusions about a causal link between lead exposure and offending are not possible. One promising direction for research is the use of prospective, longitudinal designs. This involves recruiting participants early in life, assessing them for various risk factors including lead exposure and then following them up at regular intervals. One such study already shows an association between lead levels at three years of age and behavioural problems at six years (Liu et al., 2014) but it will be some years before data are available about adult offending. Until then, the role of lead pollution remains a speculative, albeit plausible, hypothesis.

Traumatic brain injury

Another potential source of brain deficits is physical injury. Traumatic brain injury (TBI) refers to injury to the brain incurred through mechanical force to the head and can occur in many ways including sporting injuries, car accidents and physical violence. TBI can be *focal*, where there is clear damage to a specific brain area, but is more often *diffuse*, where there is subtler and more widespread injury. Severity can range from the mild disruption associated with concussion (disorientation but no loss of consciousness) to severe, where there is lengthy loss of consciousness and a significant risk of psychological impairments in the longer term. The effects of TBI are cumulative, so repeated mild TBI can still add up to significant injury over a period of time. Around 8.5% of the population have had a TBI but those most at risk are young men (Yates et al., 2006). Other risk factors are living in a town or city, having lower socio-economic status, and alcohol and drug use (Williams, 2012).

There is substantial evidence of an association between TBI and offending. Williams et al. (2010a) surveyed 453 adult offenders in custody and found that 64.9% had experienced some degree of head injury. In 16% of cases the TBI was moderate to severe and where the TBIs were mild they were often repeated. Schofield et al. (2006) randomly sampled 200 Australian adult prison inmates and found that 82% had experienced TBI, 42% having lost consciousness as a result. Research has focused more on male than female offenders but the prevalence of TBI may be higher among women (Slaughter et al., 2003). Similar findings have been found in juvenile offenders (Allely, 2016). There is also some evidence of a relationship between severity of TBI and severity of offending. Raine et al. (2005) found that, while TBI was common in adolescent offenders, those who went on to become persistent offenders in adulthood had significantly more TBIs with loss of consciousness than those who stopped offending as they entered adulthood. Similarly, Williams et al. (2010b) found that young offenders with more TBIs showed a greater level of violence in their offences.

One interpretation is that TBI leads to diffuse brain injury that produces the deficits in executive functioning, impulse control and emotional regulation that lead to offending (see above). However, the picture is complicated by the fact that mental illness and substance abuse are elevated in the prison population and it is not clear whether TBI operates independently of this or whether, for example, TBI elevates the risk of substance abuse, which then leads to a greater risk of offending (Williams, 2012). There are also questions about the direction of causality between TBI and offending. It is possible that those who commit crime start out with a greater propensity for risk taking or poorer impulse control that increases both their risk of incurring a TBI and their risk of offending. In an attempt to resolve this issue, Schofield et al. (2015) identified 7,694 individuals from Western Australia who had been admitted to hospital for TBI. These were compared with 22,905 matched individuals with no TBIs to see if there was a relationship with criminal convictions. Importantly, people who had been convicted of crimes committed *before* they incurred their TBI were excluded. They concluded that TBI was a causal influence on later offending in both males and females, moderately increasing their risk of criminal convictions. Although it is very difficult to separate out the influence of TBIs from other variables, there is sufficient evidence to support the view that addressing TBI in the criminal justice system would bring significant benefits in the form of reduced offending rates and more successful rehabilitation.

Adverse childhood experiences

A final influence on brain development that may be relevant in understanding offending is exposure to severe and chronic stress. Maltreatment as a child increases the risk of offending in adulthood, possibly by as much as 50% (Caspi et al., 2002). One way of measuring the impact of negative experiences in child-hood is the Adverse Childhood Experiences (ACE) scale originally developed by Felitti et al. (1998). Using ACE involves assessing whether the person experienced any of 10 adverse events in childhood. These include emotional, physical or sex-ual abuse, witnessing household violence and having a household member impris-oned. Higher ACE scores are associated with poorer health, earlier death, greater risk of drug and alcohol abuse and imprisonment (Felitti et al., 1998). It is possible that stressors experienced in childhood affect brain development in ways that lead to offending. Stress affects brain structure and functioning in both animal models and humans (Anda et al., 2010). Bremner and Vermetten (2001) report that chronic and severe stress causes changes in the prefrontal cortex and the limbic system and alters the metabolism of both serotonin and dopamine. Jackowski et al. (2009) found that severe stress is associated with reduced grey matter in the prefrontal cortex and Ahmed-Leitao et al. (2016), reviewing neuroimaging studies, report that childhood maltreatment correlates with reduced amygdala volume. While these studies do not specifically address offending they provide evidence that early adversity pro-duces measurable changes in the brain. These include the areas relating to executive function and emotional regulation that are implicated in criminality (see above).

Research using the ACE scale is at an early stage but there appears to be a rela-tionship with overall risk and severity of offending. Baglivio et al. (2015) found that ACE scores of six or higher were predictive of earlier first arrest and a pattern of chronic offending. Fox et al. (2015) studied 22,575 offenders in the US. ACE scores were significantly higher in chronic, violent offenders than in those who commit-ted a single, non-violent offence. Suggestive as these findings are, it is necessary to be cautious. High ACE scores are associated with a number of different outcomes besides offending including increased risk of victimisation (Ports et al., 2016). It is not yet known how different variables interact to produce criminal and other out-comes, neither is it clear why some individuals appear to be resilient to the effects of childhood adversity although the mediating effect of the L-MAOA and other alleles (see above) may provide part of the answer.

Biopsychology and offending: general considerations

The biological view of crime makes many people uneasy. One criticism is that an emphasis on genetics implies that crime is an inevitable and insoluble problem. In response it could be said that, while genes do seem to be an influence on offending, biopsychology has done much to reveal how genes interact with other influences like neurotoxins and childhood adversity. Even if nothing can be done about an individual's genetic inheritance, biopsychology holds the promise of preventing offending by, for example, acting to reduce exposure to pollutants, supporting the parents of at-risk children or by improving children's diet, education and physical activity in the early years (Raine et al., 2003). The accusation that biopsychology implies that attempts to rehabilitate offenders are futile can be answered similarly.

Far from promoting a fatalistic view, biological psychology may help make rehabilitation more effective if it can be used to match offenders with the most appropriate forms of treatment (Cornet et al., 2014). It also leads to non-obvious but apparently effective interventions with offenders like giving dietary supplements (Zaalberg et al., 2010).

A second criticism is that biological psychology threatens to undermine the notion of criminal responsibility. The prerogative of the judicial system to punish a criminal rests on the understanding that the offender's actions were freely chosen. If they were influenced by their genes or their brain structure, then their crimes were not the result of free choice and, therefore, it would not be legitimate to punish the offender. However, the English judicial system (along with many others), takes the view that a person lacks criminal responsibility only if (1) they did not understand the *nature* of their act; or (2) they did not understand that the act was *wrong*. Glenn and Raine (2014) point out that even in cases where there is strong evidence of a genetic or neurological factor in a person's offence, this does not, in itself, show that the offender lacks rationality, so it remains for the courts to judge criminal responsibility, not the scientists. Glenn and Raine do argue, however, in favour of assessing criminal responsibility on a scale and using neuropsychological testing as part of the assessment, as is the case in the Netherlands.

A third criticism is that the biological approach invites application in predicting future offending and this raises ethical concerns. In the case of convicted offenders, attempts to predict future offending are uncontroversial. Behavioural, psychological and social variables are already widely used in prison systems all over the world to make decisions about whether offenders should be released. The biological understanding of risk factors is not sufficiently advanced at present to increase the accuracy of the methods already in use and the measures required (e.g. brain scans) are impractical to take, so there is currently no justification for using them, although this may change in the future (Glenn & Raine, 2014). Much more problematic is the possibility of predicting risk of offending in people who have not committed any crime. On the one hand, there is a potential benefit to society of identifying those at risk and diverting them from offending through suitable interventions. On the other hand, there is a threat to civil liberties if an individual's rights are curtailed on the grounds that they *might* commit a crime. This risks undermining the principle that people are presumed innocent until proved guilty and it is clear how easily a biopsychological knowledge of offending could be misused if it took the form of, for example, mass genetic screening (Rose, 2000). It is not yet possible to use biological factors in this way but this could change as understanding grows, so the ethical and civil liberties implications of this issue will require continued consideration.

Chapter summary

There is substantial evidence that the nervous systems of offenders are different from those of non-offenders. Their heart rates are lower and, particularly in the case of aggressive offenders, there are structural differences in the limbic system and prefrontal cortex of the brain. These differences are consistent with the view that offenders have unusual emotional responses, find it difficult to inhibit their antisocial impulses and do not learn easily from punishment. There are several factors that could contribute to these abnormalities. Genetics is one and it is widely accepted that genes that affect the metabolism of the neurotransmitters serotonin and dopamine influence the risk of criminality, although this is in combination with adverse childhood experiences. Other influences on criminality include neurological damage caused by lead pollution and traumatic brain injury. It is difficult, given the accumulation of evidence, to reject the idea that offending has a substantial biological basis.

Further reading

Raine, A. (2013). *The Anatomy of Violence: The Biological Roots of Crime*. London: Allen Lane. An explanation of the field by a world-leading researcher.

Psychologically oriented explanations of offending

The previous chapter examined criminality from a biological perspective. This chapter presents a number of individual psychological perspectives on offending including unconscious motivations, personality and cognitive processes. The range discussed here is by no means exhaustive but gives some indication of the diversity of psychological views on criminal behaviour. The distinction between 'biological' and 'psychological' perspectives is somewhat arbitrary and, in the case of personality theory and psychopathy, there is inevitably a crossover. This to be expected since a long-term tendency within psychology as a field is to integrate biological, psychological and social perspectives.

Apply your learning

Alan, a reformed offender, describes how he ended up in prison:

I grew up in the recession of the 1970s. Jobs were scarce. My teachers didn't expect much of me and saw me as a troublemaker. My father was violent towards my mother. I loved my mum and I hated the way he treated her but I came to see that the world was full of victims and perpetrators and I didn't want to be a victim. In my teens I started hanging around with a gang, nothing that serious. We'd go out drinking and there were rivalries with other gangs. One night we were in a bar and this lad knocked my drink over. Next thing I knew we were all over him, kicking and punching him. I stabbed him. I was revolted but at the same time I needed to show everyone that I was a hard man.

How could the psychological theories discussed in this chapter explain Alan's offending? Which do you believe provides the most plausible explanation and why?

Psychodynamic theories

Starting with Sigmund Freud, a number of psychoanalytical thinkers have turned their attention to crime as one possible manifestation of irrational, unconscious, pathological processes. While the psychodynamic approach is no longer a significant force in criminological psychology it gave rise to a number of hypotheses about the causes of offending that remain important, including the notion that criminality is linked to disruption of early childhood attachments.

The psychoanalytical tradition regards the personality as having three components. The foundation of the psyche is the id, which generates self-serving and pleasure-seeking impulses. If manifested, these would result in highly antisocial behaviour. The pleasure-oriented demands of the id are redirected by the ego, whose primary orientation is towards reality. The ego, in turn, is guided by the superego, which embodies the moral rules that a person acquires during socialisation within the family. If the ego acts contrary to the superego's moral rules it is punished with guilt and anxiety. In a well-adjusted person, the ego is able to act in ways that satisfy the id's demands for gratification but that are morally acceptable to the superego. It follows from this that tendencies to behave antisocially are, from a psychodynamic viewpoint, the result of an inadequate or dysfunctional superego, which, in turn, results from an abnormal relationship with the parents during early childhood. Criminal behaviour can be the result of a superego that is weak, deviant or overly harsh (Blackburn, 1993). A person with a weak superego would experience little or no anxiety when contemplating antisocial acts and little or no guilt after committing them. Since it is this anxiety and guilt that keeps people 'on the straight and narrow' they would have few inhibitions against acting on the selfish and aggressive impulses from their id. Alternatively, the person could have a deviant superego. If a young boy has a good relationship with a criminal father he would internalise his father's pro-criminal values in the usual course of development, meaning that he would lack any sense that criminal acts were wrong. Finally, if the superego is excessively harsh and punitive the person may engage in criminal behaviour (e.g. 'compulsive' stealing) in order to be punished for it.

There is a tendency to dismiss psychoanalytically derived theories out of hand on the grounds that they are 'unscientific', which is not entirely fair. Two strengths of the psychodynamic tradition are that it stresses the importance to offending of stable personality traits and how they interact with the immediate situation and recognises that there are many routes to offending, so the same behaviour might have different causes in different individuals (Andrews & Bonta, 2010). It also identifies childhood influences as significant in crime, particularly poor-quality interactions between child and parent (Blackburn, 1993). Consequently, psychodynamic theories have contributed to the field by identifying important variables linked to criminality. However, the grounding assumption, that criminal tendencies are a manifestation of unconscious conflicts and motives, is very difficult to gather direct evidence for. Because the relationships between family variables and offending can be explained in other ways (e.g. genetics and social learning) it is relatively rare now for criminological psychologists to draw directly on psychoanalytical theories.

Attachment, delinquency and offending

One influential development of the psychodynamic approach is the view that criminality is related to problems forming attachments with primary caregivers early in life. According to Bowlby's (1951) 'maternal deprivation hypothesis', an infant requires a close and continuous relationship with its primary caregiver. Because the attachment an infant forms with its caregiver is a prototype for all the other relationships the child will form throughout its life, disruption of the attachment relationship results in an inability to form meaningful relationships with others. In some individuals, this 'affectionless' character leads to delinquent and criminal behaviour. Bowlby's theory was based on a comparison of 44 juvenile thieves (who had been referred to a child guidance clinic) with a matched group of adolescents who had mental health problems but no history of criminal behaviour. Bowlby reported that 39% of the thieves had experienced significant interruption to their maternal attachment whereas in the non-delinquent group this was only 5%. While Bowlby's research has been extensively criticised for its unrepresentative sample, poor control group matching and the way he classified attachments as disrupted, and although later researchers did not find as clear-cut a relationship as Bowlby (Rutter, 1971), attachment remains an important theme in criminological psychology. Bowlby did not distinguish between *disruption* of attachments (an attachment forms but is then discontinued) and *distortion* of attachments (an attachment forms but is affected by adverse circumstances such as parental conflict). A more recent psychodynamic theory by Fonagy (2003) proposes that the attachment relationship provides the context within which an individual learns self-control over their innate aggressive and violent tendencies. Distorted attachments interfere with the process by which they 'unlearn' to be violent early in life, leaving the person prone to aggression and impulsivity in adulthood because they have a diminished capacity to understand the mental states of others. There are interesting parallels between this view and the biological account of offending given in Chapter 3 and research continues to support the view that attachment is an important influence on offending. McElhaney et al. (2006) reviewed 74 studies, finding that insecure and disorganised attachment is significantly associated with antisocial behaviour in adolescence, and Ogilvie et al. (2014) conducted a meta-analysis of 30 studies, concluding that insecure attachment is more common in violent, non-violent and sexual offenders than in non-offenders.

Eysenck's personality theory

Eysenck's (1964) theory shares the psychoanalytical assumptions that offending is linked to stable personality traits and that the root cause of most criminality is the failure to contain immature pleasure seeking and selfish impulses. However, Eysenck was a vociferous critic of psychodynamic psychology and, beyond these assumptions, his approach to crime was very different. Eysenck linked offending to three personality traits that he claimed are present in all people: extraversion (E), neuroticism (N) and psychoticism (P). These should not be thought of as types of people but as dimensions along which people can vary. An individual's unique personality is the result of their individual combination of E, N and P. The dimensions are independent of each other so two people might have very similar E and N levels but different levels of P. Eysenck's central claim is that people who are high in all three traits are particularly prone to offending. E, N and P are largely genetically determined and relate to general properties of the nervous system. People who are high in E have a low level of activity in their nervous system (low cortical and autonomic arousal). They therefore require more stimulation from their environment than people who score lower in E, and, according to Eysenck, they are harder to condition. People who are high in N have unstable nervous systems and react very strongly to aversive stimuli, making them anxious and also less conditionable. People who are high in P have characteristics associated with mental disorders like schizophrenia and tend to be cold, uncaring, solitary and aggressive (Eysenck added the P dimension in later versions of his theory). According to Eysenck, the high E and N makes a person seek out excitement and risk but they are unlikely to learn from the punishment that follows antisocial acts. At the same time, their high P steers them away from social contexts that support prosocial behaviour, resulting in an individual with a high risk of engaging in crime.

Eysenck's theory generates predictions that are relatively easy to test. E, N and P are straightforward to measure using self-report pencil and paper tests. If it is true that high E, N and P lead to criminal behaviour then we would expect to find higher E, N and P scores in offenders than in the general population. Although Eysenck himself claimed impressive support for his theory, others suggest that matters are not so clear. The associations between E, N, P and offending only appear in very narrowly defined samples (e.g. psychopaths; see below) and when 'ordinary' offenders are analysed, the associations tend to reduce or disappear (West, 1988). A review by Farrington et al. (1982) found that 'officially' defined offenders had high N but not high E, whereas in self-reported offenders E was high but N was not. Subsequent research has reported similarly inconsistent results. Although measures of P and N tend to be higher in offenders than non-offenders, some studies find that offenders have higher E, some lower and some about the same (Hollin, 1989).

Part of the problem may be that samples of convicted offenders only include those who were caught and found guilty, so studies comparing them with noncriminal controls may actually only indicate the characteristics of 'unsuccessful' offenders. Another problem is that Eysenck's E actually measures two different traits, impulsivity and sociability and only impulsivity is actually related with criminality. A meta-analysis of 52 studies by Cale (2006) found that impulsivity was quite strongly related to antisocial behaviour while sociability and neuroticism showed only a weak relationship. Apart from the inconsistent findings, others have taken issue with Eysenck's concept of P because it is not clear what it measures. It appears to be related to psychopathic tendencies but not in a consistent way (Blackburn, 1993). It has also been criticised as being circular in that questionnaire items that measure P tend to refer to antisocial behaviour, so reporting antisocial behaviour results in high P scores, which are then used to explain antisocial behaviour.

While Eysenck's attempt to formulate a 'unified theory of offending' is widely regarded as having failed, his contribution to the field is significant. His theory was arguably the first fully worked-out psychological theory of offending and remains impressive for the way it went beyond a merely descriptive analysis of offenders to provide a causal explanation of criminality that included genetic, biological, psychological and social processes. Eysenck founded a tradition of research that has identified important personality influences on offending and many of his ideas have remained influential in the field. For example, the view that aggressive offending results from a combination of impulsiveness and an inability to learn from punishment is central to the biopsychological view of offending discussed in Chapter 3 and has been a significant influence on research into the relationship between psychopathy and offending.

Psychopathy

Psychopathy is a personality disorder with three distinguishing traits: (1) a callous, unemotional character and a lack of guilt; (2) arrogance, deceitfulness and narcissism in relationships with others; and (3) a tendency towards impulsive, irresponsible and antisocial behaviour (Cooke et al., 2006). Psychopathy overlaps with other problems including antisocial personality disorder and conduct disorder but has the distinguishing feature that, while those disorders are associated with *reactive* aggression (reacting violently to threat or provocation), psychopaths are characterised by *instrumental* aggression: they use aggression as a means to achieve other goals (Frick et al., 2003), which makes them particularly dangerous. Neumann and Hare (2008) estimate that about 50% of more serious offences are committed by individuals with psychopathic traits, who are also much more prone to recidivism than other offenders. Psychopathy is usually identified using a checklist of traits and behaviours such as a lack of empathy, impulsiveness and a high need for excitement (e.g. the Psychopathy Checklist; PCL-R; Hare et al., 2000). Diagnosis of psychopathy depends on having a score above a designated cut-off score but it is best understood as a dimension, so the difference between a psychopath and a non-psychopath is more a question of degree than of kind. Psychopathy is not diagnosed in children but psychopathic features, particularly callous and unemotional (CU) traits, are frequently present in children who later develop the full disorder. Such individuals are unusually aggressive in early childhood, have problems following rules (e.g. in school) as children, and gravitate towards delinquent peers in adolescence. In adulthood, they are prolific, non-specialist offenders with an irresponsible and parasitic lifestyle. The predominant feature throughout life is a lack of empathy and a disregard for the wellbeing of others (Viding et al., 2014).

Psychologically, psychopaths have a very specific set of deficits: (1) they are relatively unreactive to pain and distress in others; (2) they have difficulty recognising fear and sorrow (but not anger) in others; (3) they have an impaired ability to learn from punishment and other negative experiences; and (4) they have difficulty understanding moral rules whose purpose is to avoid harming others (White & Blair, 2015). Most people empathise with others and find their distress aversive. Over the course of their early development they learn, from this and from externally imposed punishments, that harming others has negative consequences for themselves and so they learn an aversion to harming others. Psychopaths lack empathic responses to others and their capacity to learn from punishment is impaired, so they do not build up a conscience in the same way as other people (Viding et al., 2014; cf. Eysenck's view of criminality).

Lalumière et al. (2008) suggest that psychopathy represents an evolutionary strategy that allows some individuals to take advantage of the fact that the major-ity of humans have an evolved inclination to cooperate. In such an environment, a tendency to lie, cheat and manipulate others could be advantageous, provided that such individuals are not too common (as otherwise people become more vigilant and opportunities to deceive others disappear). This is speculative, but psychopa-thy is widely regarded as having a biological basis and there is certainly evidence that it is influenced by genetics. Beaver et al. (2011) studied general psychopathic traits in 759 twin pairs, estimating heritability at 44%. In a study of CU traits Viding et al. (2005) found substantially higher concordance in MZ than DZ twins, estimat-ing the influence of genes on this trait at 67%. A review of 24 studies by Dhanani et al. (2017) found good evidence of a genetic influence on psychopathy, this being strongest for the CU traits. However, these heritability estimates still indicate a sig-nificant environmental influence. Auty et al. (2015) investigated this by comparing PCL-R scores from fathers and sons who were participating in a prospective, longi-tudinal study of factors affecting delinquency. A number of other risk factors were also measured. A correlation was found between the psychopathy scores of fathers and sons. Psychopathy in the sons was also associated with the father's employ-ment problems, alcohol abuse, family disruption and poor parental supervision. Although supportive of a genetic contribution, it also seems that the fathers' psy-chopathic traits made them more likely to be unemployed, meaning that they spent more time in the home where they consequently had a negative effect on the sons' developmental environment.

Brain imaging studies have linked psychopathy with structural and functional abnormalities. For example, Ly et al. (2012) found evidence that the cerebral cortex was thinner in psychopaths than controls, particularly in the area of the left insula. Carré et al. (2013) report that those with stronger psychopathic tendencies show lower levels of amygdala activity. While these findings are suggestive, there are problems. Griffiths and Jalava (2017) reviewed imaging studies where psychopathy had been diagnosed using the PCL-R which should, in principle, make patterns across studies easier to find. Results regarding the amygdala were inconsistent, with some finding reduced amygdala volumes and activity, others finding increases and some showing no differences. Evidence of differences in the hippocampus were more consistent but still many of the studies found no differences between the psychopaths and the controls. Part of the problem is that different studies use different cut-off scores to distinguish psychopaths and the dimensional nature of psychopathy is often overlooked, so an individual with a PCL-R score of 25 might be in the psychopath group in one study, but would be in the control group in a different study. In addition, psychopathy is strongly associated with drug and alcohol abuse, so this could be a confounding influence in many studies. There are other problems with the evidence base. Many studies have examined the heritability of antisocial behaviour (see Chapter 3) but relatively few of these have distinguished between psychopathic and non-psychopathic offenders, which makes it difficult to say how much of the apparent heritability of antisocial behaviour is attributable to psychopathy or vice versa. A similar problem exists with research into the role of brain abnormalities (Lalumière et al., 2008).

Some critics have questioned the usefulness of the entire concept of psychopathy on the grounds that it is circular: psychopathy is diagnosed on the basis of the individual's self-reported tendency to commit antisocial acts, which is then used to explain why they commit antisocial acts (the same point has been made about Eysenck's P dimension; see above). Walters (2004) suggests that evidence is lacking that psychopaths represent a discrete, identifiable subgroup of offenders; that the PCL-R has relatively poor predictive power when identifying recidivists; and that it over-emphasises individual psychological factors in offending to the exclusion of all else. Horley (2011) adds that terms like 'psychopath' work against the effective rehabilitation of criminals because offenders incorporate the label into their own self-concept and because, once they have been labelled psychopathic, society responds by, for example, imposing harsher punishments or withholding opportunities for therapeutic rehabilitation (see Chapter 5 on labelling theory and self-fulfilling prophecies). Defenders of the concept respond that, at the very least, psychopathy is useful as a predictor of criminality and recidivism. Harris et al. (1991) found that 80% of psychopathic offenders reoffended within a year of release and that their psychopathy scores were a stronger predictor of reoffending than 16 other variables combined. DeLisi (2009) goes further, arguing that since offenders have an obvious, negative effect on others, that we should not be shy of using negative labels like 'psychopathic' to describe them. Furthermore, since about 5% of 'career' offenders are responsible for the vast preponderance of crime and since 'career offender' overlaps significantly with 'psychopath', psychopathy should actually be regarded as the 'unified theory of crime'. While this may overstate the importance of the concept there is no doubt that it continues to stimulate a great deal of research.

Moral development

The cognitive perspective in psychology is concerned with the processes of thinking. Kohlberg (1976) advanced an influential cognitive theory of how moral reasoning develops. Although it is not a theory of criminality as such, since criminal acts are usually also immoral, it is potentially of relevance to understanding criminal behaviour. Following the work of Jean Piaget, Kohlberg suggested that moral reasoning advances with increasing age, becoming more complex and abstract in line with more general intellectual development. Kohlberg investigated moral reasoning in children and adults by presenting participants with moral dilemmas, short scenarios that pose a moral problem. The best known concerns a man whose wife is dying but who cannot afford the medicine that might save her. The participant is asked whether the man should break into the pharmacy and steal the medicine. Kohlberg was not so much interested in whether the participant answered yes or no, but wished to examine the reasoning behind their decision. From the kinds of justification that people gave Kohlberg distinguished three distinct levels of moral reasoning. Each level contains two stages, giving six stages in all (see Table 4.1).

If Kohlberg is correct, we might expect that criminals will show a lower level of moral reasoning than non-criminals, as lower levels afford more justifications for offending than higher. The majority of studies have focused on adolescents, but there is consistent support for this prediction. Arbuthnot et al. (1987) reviewed 15 studies and found that, in all but three of these, significantly more delinquents were functioning at level 2 than level 3. Thornton (1987) found a correlation between adolescents' moral reasoning and teacher reports of their antisocial behaviour. Nelson et al. (1990) reviewed 15 studies and found the same association between

TABLE 4.1 Levels and stages of moral development in Kohlberg's theory

Level	Stage	Description
1. *Pre-conventional* Rules and social expectations are external to the individual	Obedience and punishment orientation	'Right' and 'wrong' are determined by what is punished and what is not
	Instrumental purpose and exchange	'Right' and 'wrong' are determined by what brings rewards rather than the avoidance of punishment
2. *Conventional* The individual has internalised the rules and expectations of others	Interpersonal accord and conformity	'Right' is defined in terms of what pleases others
	Social accord and system maintenance	'Right' is defined in terms of conformity and respect for authority
3. *Post-conventional* The individual adopts universal moral principles and distinguishes their rules from the rules and expectations of others	Social contract, utility and moral rights	'Right' and 'wrong' are determined by values and opinions. Individual rights can be more important than laws
	Universal ethical principles	'Right' and 'wrong' are based on ethical principles adopted by the person that are essentially separate from the mores of society although the two may coincide

offending and immature moral reasoning. Van Vugt et al. (2011) found a significant inverse correlation between level of moral reasoning and risk of recidivism among offenders. Some evidence suggests that offenders' moral reasoning is only lower in areas related to their offending. For example, Palmer and Hollin (1998) found that non-violent offenders' moral reasoning was lower in areas relating to property and the law but not in other areas (e.g. helping others). The poorer moral reasoning of offenders may be related to parenting. Blackburn (1993) suggests that moral development in children depends on adequate opportunities for role taking, which may be lacking in the families of delinquents and offenders. This view is supported by the observation that parental rejection is associated with poorer moral development (Palmer & Hollin, 1996) and higher levels of moral development are facilitated by a democratic parenting style where children are involved in discussion of moral decisions with parents and peers (Powers, 1988). Palmer (2003) suggests that a lower level of moral reasoning influences offending because it supports an egocentric bias in thinking and hostile attributions about others' behaviour. These limit consideration of the impact of offending and prime the individual to react antisocially to other people's (innocuous) actions.

Although this research supports a link between moral reasoning and offending, several points should be stressed. First, Kohlberg proposed a theory of moral *reasoning*, not a theory of moral *behaviour*. The link between thinking and behaviour is rarely straightforward and it is obvious that anyone can have well-worked-out moral positions that they fail to act on. Second, the link between moral behaviour and offending is stronger for some types of crime than others. Thornton and Reid (1982) found that those convicted of crimes carried out for material gain (e.g. robbery and theft) were more likely to show preconventional moral reasoning than those convicted of impulsive crimes like assault. This is not surprising since the former type of crime typically involves planning and, hence, reasoning, whereas the latter type does not. Third, interventions that have tried to enhance delinquents' moral reasoning have met with limited success: moral reasoning improves but moral behaviour does not (Gibbs et al., 1995). Ultimately, there does appear to be a relationship between moral reasoning and offending but beyond the work of Palmer (2003) relatively little research has been done recently to integrate moral reasoning with other variables in criminality. Since it was not Kohlberg's intention to produce a theory of crime, it is fairest to regard it as complementary to other explanations of offending.

Social cognition

Social cognition is a term that covers a range of thinking processes involved in understanding the self in relation to other people. This includes self-perception, perception of others, interpreting others' behaviour and solving problems involving other people. It would be impossible here to examine all the themes contained in the large and well-developed research literature on social cognition and offending (see Fontaine, 2012), so only two illustrative examples are discussed: the role of cognitive and emotional deficits in aggressive offending; and the use of cognitive strategies to justify offending.

Cognitive and emotional deficits

Criminality may be linked to deficits in social understanding. Aggressive/violent offending may be the outcome of situations in which an individual forms incorrect mental representations of the consequences of their actions (Richardson et al., 1994). For example, misunderstanding of others' motives and goals (e.g. interpreting innocuous or ambivalent behaviour as provocative or threatening) may incline the individual to respond aggressively. This idea underpins anger management training (see Chapter 10). Alternatively, the inability to understand others' pain and distress may remove an important inhibition on hurting others. Deficits of this kind may relate to the capacity to empathise (feel what other people are feeling, an emotional process) or mentalise (work out what other people are thinking, a cognitive process). For example, Jolliffe and Farrington (2004) found a weak negative association between aggression and empathy and a stronger negative association with cognitive perspective taking, although a meta-analysis by Vachon et al. (2014) found only a weak link between empathy and aggression. One problem with the evidence base is that these studies rely almost wholly on self-reports, which are prone to response bias through social desirability. Winter et al. (2017) addressed this criticism by using more objective measures in a comparison of offenders and non-offenders. Responses to videos with emotional and neutral content were recorded, along with performance on a mentalising task and a factual reasoning task. The results suggested that aggressive offending was associated with deficits in empathy (emotional) rather than mentalising (cognition). Similarly, Mariano et al. (2017) found that offenders were lower than controls on a variety of empathy measures and had more difficulty recognising the emotional states of others. Significantly, this is consistent with research indicating deficits in brain areas associated with recognising others' emotional states (see Chapter 3).

Moral disengagement

Another theme in the social cognition of offenders is the use of moral disengagement strategies (Bandura, 1990). Individuals who are contemplating a criminal act may experience an uncomfortable internal conflict (or cognitive dissonance) between, for example, the desire for material gain and the moral knowledge that stealing from others is wrong. Moral disengagement describes a set of strategies used by offenders to reduce this cognitive dissonance. It can take several forms:

- Moral justification. Deciding that the end justifies the means.
- Euphemistic labelling. Using language that sanitises antisocial acts.

- Advantageous comparison. Identifying other types of offending as worse.
- Diffusion of responsibility. Sharing the responsibility with co-offenders and so feeling less individual culpability.
- Displacement of responsibility. Blaming someone else, e.g. a ringleader.
- Distortion of consequences. Mentally minimising the amount of harm that would result.
- Victim blaming. Attributing the responsibility for victimisation to the victim themselves.
- Dehumanising the victim. Regarding the victim as lacking human attributes and therefore being a legitimate target.

The use of moral disengagement is a significant predictor of offending (Shulman et al., 2011) and has been identified in a variety of antisocial and criminal acts including terrorism, executions, juvenile delinquency and white-collar crime (Fontaine, 2012). Alleyne et al. (2014) examined the role of moral disengagement strategies in violence by gang members. Gang membership is a factor in a young offender's escalation from general criminality to violent criminality. The social processes involved in gang membership are crucial to this escalation as by identifying as a gang member the individual becomes sensitive to threats to their collective identity (e.g. through rivalry with other gangs). In order to maintain gang membership, the person feels pressured to adopt the gang's pro-violence norms (see Chapter 5). Alleyne et al. compared gang and non-gang members on their endorsement of moral disengagement strategies and found that gang members were significantly more likely to use all the above strategies except for diffusion of responsibility and distortion of consequences. Dehumanisation emerged as particularly important in the relationship between gang membership and violence, supporting the view that a reduction in empathy is an important factor in aggressive crime.

There is substantial evidence for the role of cognitive distortions in a range of offences. For example, child molesters have a marked tendency to minimise the harm their offences cause. That said, there is relatively little evidence that sex offenders have beliefs that are *qualitatively* different from non-offenders; the differences are more often in how strongly the relevant beliefs are held (Gannon, 2009). Chen and Howitt (2012) examined cognitions of 290 offenders convicted of drug, sexual, property and violent crimes. All four categories of offender held beliefs that legitimised their own offending but maintained a negative view of perpetrators of other offence categories. The tendency to make advantageous comparisons between their own and others' offending may go some way to explaining why criminals often specialise in one particular type of offence.

The association between the social cognitions of offenders and their activities is potentially of use in reducing crime. However, research is a long way from disentangling the relationship between social cognition and offending. It is unclear whether moral disengagement precedes offending or appears subsequent to it, so it is difficult to tell whether such cognitions play a causal role in the onset of offending or are a consequence of dealing with the moral conflicts that offending raises. Rebellon and Manasse (2014) suggest that there is a reciprocal relationship between pro-crime attitudes and offending behaviour but that behaviour influences attitudes more strongly than vice versa. Gannon (2009) also highlights a lack of evidence regarding the exact role played by social cognition. For example, it is not clear whether sex offenders actively interpret victims' behaviour in offence-supporting ways, or whether they do this only retrospectively. A problem here is that the majority of studies use self-reports measures and offenders are liable to report their thinking in self-serving ways. Gannon suggests that understanding of this area will make more progress once researchers more widely adopt implicit measures of social cognition in their research designs.

Rational choice theory

The rational choice theory (RCT) of crime is based on the idea that crime is the outcome of weighing up the costs and benefits of offending and acting accordingly. It originated in economics (e.g. Becker, 1968) but has been developed as a psychological theory within the cognitive tradition by, among others, Cornish and Clarke (1987). RCT starts from the assumption that people seek to benefit in some way from their actions and that criminal behaviour is one of several alternatives available. Accordingly, the individual assesses the potential benefits (e.g. material gain) and the potential costs of offending (e.g. the effort involved; the risks of getting caught and punished) and makes a comparison with the costs and benefits of alternative actions. If the benefits of offending outweigh the costs and the alternatives are less 'profitable' then the individual will choose to offend. Unlike in classical economics, where the person is assumed to be a completely rational actor, Cornish and Clarke recognise that the decision-making process is not purely logical but is constrained by a number of factors including the time available, the offender's cognitive ability and the information they possess. However, the essential proposition is that offenders *choose* specific crimes for specific reasons and in order to understand crime it is necessary to understand that decision-making process.

A number of studies support this general idea. Rettig (1966) gave students a hypothetical scenario describing an opportunity to commit a crime (e.g. likely benefits, risk of detection, likely degree of punishment) and found that the degree of punishment had the biggest influence on the decision to commit the crime. Similarly, Feldman (1977) found that respondents were rational the majority of the time, in that they reported willingness to commit a crime when potential rewards were high and costs low. Of course, results obtained from simulations may not apply to real offenders and crimes. However, there is supportive evidence from Bennett et al. (1984), who interviewed convicted burglars about their decision making during offences. They found that their reasons clustered around three themes: risk (e.g. the chance of being seen or caught), reward (potential material gain) and ease of entry (how difficult it would be to break into the property). Of these, risk was reported to be the most important. One criticism of research like that of Bennett et al. is that the offenders used were unsuccessful ones (i.e. they got caught) and the reasoning processes of 'successful' offenders may be different. Wright and Decker (1994) addressed this by interviewing 105 active burglars in two US neighbourhoods, 75% of whom had never been convicted. While they described a largely rational approach to selecting victims and acting on offending opportunities (e.g. burgling the houses of known drug dealers because the rewards were greater) Wright and Decker also identified important constraints on rationality, such as identifying with a 'street culture' that effectively ruled out legitimate employment as an alternative to offending. Other research has produced mixed results. Piliavin et al. (1986) found that changes to rewards influenced the probability of offending but changes to costs did not and Nagin et al. (2009) found that changes to the severity of judicial punishments (e.g. increases to prison terms) make little difference to crime rates. Apel (2013) found evidence that changes to perception of risk (e.g. increases in police numbers or police concentration on crime 'hot spots') does influence crime rates but only weakly.

One reason for the relatively weak relationship between rewards, costs and offending is that RCT assumes that offending is planned behaviour whereas many crimes, especially violent ones, appear to be impulsive responses to an immediate situation. Cornish and Clarke acknowledge this limitation and suggest it be regarded as a perspective on crime from which specific theories of offending can be developed, rather than a general theory of offending. Another problem is that research into RCT has tended to focus only on financial rewards and judicial punishments and the importance of other types of reward and cost has not been accounted for. Addressing this criticism, Loughran et al. (2016) took a range of measures from a sample of 1,354 adolescent offenders. They used self-reports to measure extent of offending and the perceived risk of a range of crimes including fighting, armed robbery, assault with a weapon and theft. They also asked about the perceived personal rewards of offending (how much of a thrill or 'rush' it would give); perceived social costs and rewards (e.g. approval or disapproval from peers); and financial gains from both legal and illegal activities. They found that the relative value of the rewards and costs combined correlated closely with severity of offending and that changes to the costs/rewards were associated with changes in the probability of offending for all types of crime. This suggests that RCT has potential as a general theory of crime if the psychological rewards and costs are factored in alongside the external contingencies. Akers (1990) suggests that such 'psychological' formulations of RCT add nothing to our understanding that is not already present in more established theories like social learning theory (see Chapter 5). However, given the popularity of economic analyses among policymakers in the form of 'behavioural economics' it is likely that RCT will continue to generate research into crime and crime prevention (see Chapter 10) for the foreseeable future.

Chapter summary

Psychological theories of offending explain crime in terms of mental processes, using theoretical constructs like personality and cognition. The psychodynamic tradition views criminality as a consequence of unconscious mental processes. It has provided useful pointers to later researchers but is no longer widely accepted. The exceptions are theories based on the importance of childhood attachment to later offending, which increasingly converge with other lines of research. Eysenck explained criminality as being due to a particular personality pattern (high E, N and P). This theory failed because research did not find the predicted relationship between personality and offending, and the theory has been accused of circularity. However, Eysenck's ideas have been a significant influence on research in the biological tradition and into psychopathy, a personality disorder with a strong relationship with offending. Psychopaths lack empathy with others and learn poorly from punishment. It is claimed that psychopathic offenders are responsible for a significant proportion of all crime. There is evidence that psychopathy is influenced by genetics and differences in brain structure and functioning. However, opinion is divided between those who see it as a viable general theory of offending and those who fear that it under-emphasises important influences on criminality and may work against attempts to rehabilitate offenders. In the cognitive tradition, offending has been linked to limited moral development, although only for some types of crime, and cognitive psychology has been more influential where theorists have addressed the role of specific cognitive processes. Research into social cognition has shown that crime is linked to deficits in social understanding, particularly empathy, and there is a great deal of evidence that distortions and biases of thinking are associated with offending. However, it has yet to be established that they play a causal role in criminal careers. In recent years there has been interest in the idea of the 'rational criminal', whose decision to offend or not is the outcome of the calculation of the costs and benefits of offending. There is evidence that manipulating the costs and benefits of offending can make criminal acts more or less likely. However, the variety of criminal acts that are possible may mean that no single general psychological explanation of offending is likely to account for all. That said, all of the theories considered here are useful insofar as all point to ways in which offending might be prevented.

Further reading

Andrews, D. A., & Bonta, J. (2016). *The Psychology of Criminal Conduct*, 6th ed. London: Routledge. This is probably the most comprehensive presentation of a specifically psychological view of offending.

5

Socially oriented explanations of offending

This chapter focuses on theories that explain offending in terms of the processes that happen between people. Social learning theory suggests that criminality is a set of learned attitudes and behaviours and there is an exploration of the role mass media might play in offending. Social-psychological and sociological perspectives suggest that crime is a consequence of relationships between individuals and groups and there is a discussion of three influential theories, labelling, self-fulfilling prophecy and social identity theory. Finally, there is a review of research into the role of social variables including poverty and the neighbourhood in crime. As with the previous chapters, the line between psychologically and socially oriented theories is somewhat arbitrary and most of these theories refer to both individual and social processes.

Apply your learning

Saffi has been caught shoplifting. She is 14 years old and has not been in trouble with the authorities before. She was with a group of young people who were chased by a store detective who suspected that they were stealing. Only Saffi was caught and the shop manager called the police, who arrested her and took her to the police station. Saffi admitted stealing some low-value items of jewellery. The arresting officer has a choice: she can arrange for Saffi to be formally cautioned and released with no further action or she can advise that Saffi be prosecuted.

What justifications could be given for each course of action? What are the pros and contras? How could social theories of offending guide the officer's decision?

Social learning theory

Social learning theory (SLT) originated in an earlier explanation of crime called differential association theory, which suggested that some individuals become criminals and others not because of the different people they associate with (Sutherland, 1939). SLT starts from the same assumption: that criminal behaviour is qualitatively no different from any other sort and is learned from other people. It was developed as a general theory of behaviour by Bandura (1977) and as a theory of criminal behaviour by Akers (1973). In simple terms, an individual learns deviant ways of thinking and acting by observing the people around them. Whether they then imitate these ways of thinking and acting depends on the extent to which they are reinforced for doing so. A reinforcement is any consequence that makes a behaviour stronger. Akers specified four key factors in the development of deviance and criminality:

- Differential association (i.e. the people from whom behaviour is learned).
- Imitation (i.e. the process of acquiring attitudes and behaviour from others).
- Definitions (i.e. the attitudes and values that support offending).
- Differential reinforcement (i.e. the perceived consequences of imitation).

Imagine a young person who starts to associate with a peer group that shoplifts. Within the group they are exposed to pro-criminal attitudes such as, 'no-one loses out – the shops don't even notice the stuff has gone.' They are also told about, or may observe directly, members of the group stealing things. They may be told about ways of not getting caught. Whether the person starts to imitate these attitudes and behaviours depends on whether she expects that she will be reinforced. Reinforcements might be approval from other group members or material gains from stealing. If criminal attitudes and behaviours are competing with non-criminal attitudes and behaviours whichever receives stronger or more frequent reinforcement will win out. The family and peer group are clearly important contexts for the learning of criminality but the school, the neighbourhood and the media may also act as important influences.

While Akers's formulation tends to emphasise the contexts in which learning occurs, Bandura (1977) is more focused on the *mechanisms* of learning. Behaviour is learned from other people who act as models. Whether an individual selects another person as a model depends on a number of variables including their status and their perceived similarity to the observer. By attending to the model's behaviour, the observer can form a mental representation of their behaviour and may then imitate it, but only if there is a motivation to do so. Motivation is based on the person's expectancies about the likely result of imitation. If the learner observes that the model is reinforced for her action, she forms the expectancy that she also will obtain reinforcement and consequently become more likely to imitate. Conversely, if the model is observed to be punished, then the probability of imitation will decrease.

Because it was carefully formulated to be so, SLT is open to empirical testing. In a series of classic studies, Bandura et al. (e.g. 1963) demonstrated that four and five year olds could learn aggressive behaviours through observing an adult model. They were shown an adult behaving aggressively (both physically and verbally) towards an inflatable known as a 'bobo doll'. Some of the children observed the model being reinforced for this by being praised by another adult. A second group observed the model being punished (told off). A control group observed the aggressive behaviour being neither reinforced nor punished. When later given the opportunity to play with the bobo doll the children who had observed the model reinforced were seen to imitate many of the verbal and physical behaviours exhibited by the model. Imitation of the model was also observed in the control group. Those children who had seen the model punished were comparatively much less likely to behave aggressively towards the bobo doll. Importantly, all the children had *learned* the model's behaviours: when later offered reinforcement, the 'punishment' group produced just as many aggressive acts as the group who had originally seen the model reinforced.

While such studies have gone a long way to identifying the key variables that influence observational learning they have come under fire for their artificiality and research in the Bandura tradition has been accused of neglecting naturalistic settings. Akers's research, contrariwise, has tested SLT using survey data from large samples. Akers et al. (1979) collected data from 3,065 US adolescents, asking about the extent to which they drank alcohol and used marijuana alongside other questions about who they had seen doing this, whether their peers/parents approved or disapproved and the positive and negative consequences they had experienced or observed. The results showed that, together, the four mechanisms (differential association, imitation, definitions and reinforcement) explained 68% of the variability in marijuana use and 55% of the variability in underage drinking. Unfortunately, many subsequent studies have only addressed differential association (e.g. by using measures of peer delinquency) with the other three mechanisms being relatively under-researched (Ward & Brown, 2015). However, Pratt et al. (2010) carried out a review of 133 studies that investigated the four core ideas of SLT. Strong support was found for the roles of differential association and definitions in crime and delinquency and modest support for the roles of differential reinforcement and imitation, which closely matches the findings originally reported by Akers et al. (1979).

A range of other research supports SLT, at least indirectly. If criminality is learned, we might expect to find it in the families and/or the peer groups of offenders. As was discussed in Chapter 3, crime tends to run in families. In a longitudinal study of 397 families, Farrington et al. (1996) found that 6% of the families accounted for half of the criminal convictions received. Having a mother, father, sister or brother with a conviction predicted strongly whether the son would also get one. This is at least consistent with SLT, although the same pattern could be explained in other ways: genetic influences; the fact that family members are exposed to the same risk factors (e.g. poverty); or that the authorities are biased against the family members of convicted offenders, resulting in labelling and self-fulfilling prophecy (see below). Another consistent finding is that delinquency in the peer group is a predictor of delinquency in the individual (Kiesner et al., 2003). Again, this is consistent with SLT although Blackburn (1993) points out that this pattern applies mainly to minor offences – vandalism, petty theft and so on – and not the more serious types of crime. Furthermore, it is not necessarily clear whether peer delinquency causes people to become criminals or whether those with antisocial tendencies seek out a delinquent peer group, although longitudinal data from the US National Youth Survey suggests that delinquency in the peer group plays a causal role in later offending, through its influence on criminal thinking (Walters, 2016).

SLT has reasonable empirical support for its main claims and it has been very influential, with elements being incorporated into many other theories of offending. It is applicable to a wide range of types of crime, including violence, drug offending and 'white-collar' offending in occupational and professional contexts. Another strength of the theory is that it stresses the uniqueness of the individual and allows that different people may commit the same crimes for different reasons because each individual's motivation and expectations are based on his unique learning history.

Having said this, SLT does have several significant limitations. The research base relies heavily on self-reports to measure the key variables; these are susceptible to bias. Furthermore, much of the research is correlational, making it difficult to draw firm conclusions about cause and effect relationships with offending. At the same time, the experimental research that has been done, Bandura's for example, tends to use rather artificial designs and measures of behaviour that, while *related* to offending, are not the thing itself (for obvious ethical reasons). Another criticism is that SLT gives too little weight to factors besides learning. Bandura (1986) has since presented a social cognitive theory of behaviour that gives cognitive processes, such as beliefs, a central role in determining behaviour. Similarly, Akers (2009) has developed his theory to include the influence of structural variables such as social class, gender, race and ethnicity. However, a drawback remains that social learning theory assumes that all the differences that occur between people are the result of learning, whereas a great deal of evidence now suggests that biological factors influence people's vulnerability to criminogenic environments (see Chapter 3) although Fox (2017) points out that there is nothing in SLT that precludes integration of the biological and social learning approaches to offending.

The influence of TV, films and videogames

Early studies by Bandura and others showed vividly that young children could easily acquire aggressive behaviours from models. This observation has fed anxiety about the possible influence of mass media (e.g. films, television and comics) on antisocial behaviour and criminality. The link with SLT is clear, as films, televisions and comics offer a ready supply of models that viewers and readers are actively invited to identify with. Plots involving aggression, violence and criminality are common. Concerns about the effect this might have, especially on children, led to the establishment of a line of psychological research that has been hotly debated ever since.

The news media tend to focus on 'copycat' crime, where it is thought that specific incidents have been inspired by media content. For example, in 2003 in the US, Devin Moore was arrested for stealing a car. At the police station, he seized a handgun from one of the officers and killed three people. He claimed that, after playing the videogame 'Grand Theft Auto – Vice City' for hours on end, he had lost the capacity to distinguish between the game and real life. This formed part of his legal defence of 'not guilty by reason of insanity'. The jury rejected this plea, finding him guilty and sentencing him to death (Helfgott, 2015). Attention grabbing as they are, incidents like these have attracted relatively little research from criminological psychologists, although Helfgott identifies 53 such examples, including crimes inspired by fictional books, films, television and media coverage of other crime. Surette (2013) concludes that, in most cases, the role of the media is to act as a source of information on *how* to offend for people who were anyway going to commit crimes for some other reason.

Research has instead focused principally on the ways in which media exposure may affect aggression in the general population. Sparks and Sparks (2002) suggest six mechanisms:

- Catharsis. It may allow a 'safe' way of expressing their aggressive impulses (a Freudian idea; see Chapter 4).
- Social learning. It provides examples of aggressive behaviour that people may learn from.
- Priming. It puts people in a state of 'readiness' to be aggressive, making them more likely to react in hostile ways.
- Arousal transfer. It makes people excited and this can then be expressed as aggression in other situations.
- Desensitisation. Repeated exposure to violence may reduce people's empathic response to others' distress, removing an inhibitor of aggression.
- Cultivation of fear. It influences people to construe the world as a threatening and hostile place.

There is support for all of these mechanisms except catharsis (Kanz, 2015). However, there is an ongoing debate about what studies of media and aggression actually show, how relevant it is to offending and whether parents, policymakers and the public should be worried.

Much early work was conducted in the laboratory. Such studies involve showing participants either violent or non-violent films and then giving them the opportunity to aggress against someone else by giving them electric shocks (e.g. Berkowitz, 1969). More recently, researchers have shifted towards blasts of white noise or the administration of unpleasant hot sauce as a measure of aggression. Very often, those shown the violent film give more electric shocks (blasts of white noise, more hot sauce etc.) suggesting a moderate influence of viewing violence on subsequent aggression (Coyne, 2007). However, several problems limit the conclusions that can be drawn. First, the laboratory situation is rather artificial and so may elicit unnatural responses from the participants. Second, the forms of 'aggression' used in such studies do not represent real-world aggression particularly well, so they have little link with real-world crime. Beyond the experimental approach, researchers have looked for correlations between what people watch and how they act. Belson (1978) questioned teenage boys about the programmes they liked and their aggressive behaviour. Those who watched a great deal of violent content were more likely to report using violence in their everyday lives. Again, there are limitations. First, the data were gathered retrospectively and therefore may not accurately reflect actual viewing or behaviour. Second, the data are correlational so it is difficult to say whether what they watched influenced how they acted or whether the more aggressive individuals sought out more violent content. A development of this early research was the adoption of longitudinal designs, where the same individuals provide data regularly over a period of time. Milarsky et al. (1982) measured media consumption and aggression in 3,200 children, finding small associations between early viewing habits and later aggressive behaviour. Compared with other variables (e.g. the family) the influence was relatively minor.

Other researchers have used situations where television was to be introduced for the first time. These can be used as natural experiments: if the media have an effect on antisocial behaviour we might expect an increase in aggression following introduction. Williams (1986) studied a small Canadian community ('Notel') into which television had recently been introduced. Observational, peer and teachers' ratings of aggression were compared with measures taken from other communities where television was already available. In Notel, over a two-year period, there was a steady increase in measured aggression whereas in the other communities there was none, suggesting that television has a real-world impact. Similar research in the US has used actual crime rates as the outcome measure and found that the introduction of television is accompanied by an increase in crime (Hennigan et al., 1982) but results have been inconsistent, with Howitt (1998) finding no such effect in the UK.

Reviews of the large amount of research that now exists suggest that exposure to violent media has a short-term effect on aggressive thinking, emotion and behaviour, particularly in children (Anderson et al., 2010). Evidence of a longer term effect is weaker and there is relatively little evidence of a direct link between media consumption and offending (Browne & Hamilton-Giachritsis, 2005). One reason for the weak association is that some individuals may be more susceptible than others. Browne and Pennell (1998) compared the responses of offenders and non-offenders to violent films. The offenders showed a stronger preference for violent content, got more excited when viewing violence and identified more with violent characters. Browne (1995) suggests that parental abuse or exposure to violence in the home might make some individuals vulnerable to the effect of media violence. Kanz (2015) supports this view with an analysis of longitudinal data from 3,400 young people in Germany. She gathered self-report data on violent media consumption, delinquent and criminal behaviour, pro-violence attitudes and parenting style. Kanz found that exposure to media violence led to an increase in pro-violence attitudes but that this was much greater among children whose parents showed little empathy in child rearing. On balance, then, films and television have a weak but significant effect on offending in vulnerable individuals.

More recently, debate has shifted to the impact of videogames. Concerns have centred on the fact that they have a degree of interactivity that is absent from films and television, and because, in recent years, videogame hardware has developed to the point where it can supply a remarkable degree of realism. As with earlier research into films and television, experimental studies support an effect on aggression. Lin (2013) compared participants who played a violent game, watched recorded game-play or watched a film. Measures of aggressive cognition, emotion and behaviour were highest in the players. McGloin et al. (2013) found that increasing the degree of immersion felt by game players with more realistic graphics and a more 'natural' controller resulted in greater cognitive aggressive following a boxing game. Lin (2013) did not find that the degree of identification between the player and the game character affected aggression but Sauer et al. (2015) reports that where players identify with a heroic character post-game aggression is lower than when they identify with an anti-heroic one. Again, there are inconsistencies in the findings so while it is widely reported that violent gaming leads to emotional desensitisation, a brain imaging study by Szycik et al. (2017) found no differences in the activity of emotion-relevant brain areas of 28 'excessive' players of violent games and a control group when they were exposed to distressing images. A meta-analysis by Anderson et al. (2010) found that violent videogame exposure was associated with increases in aggressive cognition, emotion and behaviour, increased arousal and reductions in empathy and prosocial behaviour. However, Ferguson and Kilburn (2010) are critical of these conclusions. First, they point to the large number of studies using measures of 'aggression' of questionable relevance to real-world violence. Second, they question the evidence selected by Anderson et al., objecting to their use of unpublished data in their review. Third, they accuse Anderson et al. of ignoring inconvenient observations, such as the enormous growth in violent videogaming at a time when violent crime was falling sharply across Europe and the US. As things stand, there are now entrenched ideological positions on both sides of the debate so further progress seems unlikely. The American Psychological Association's Task Force on Violent Media report on the matter (Calvert et al., 2017) concludes that, while the current evidence base firmly supports an effect of violent videogames on aggression, evidence is lacking for a link with criminality.

Labelling and self-fulfilling prophecy

Labelling is a sociological theory associated with the work of Becker (1963). Becker's interest was deviance, of which crime is just one example (mental illness is another). His starting point was that no behaviour is inherently deviant. Rather, deviance is created when a societal group creates rules about what is acceptable and what is not. Certain behaviours then become deviant insofar as they break those rules. For example, a society may agree that there is such a thing as 'private property' and that depriving a person of his own private property is wrong. Such an act would be 'stealing' and those who do it would be labelled by society as 'criminals'.

Once a person has been labelled as a 'criminal', society assumes the right to treat him differently because he poses a threat to the social order. He can be imprisoned, made to pay a fine, ordered to keep away from particular areas or people and so on. The stigmatisation and sanctions visited on the criminal serve to regulate his behaviour and as a warning to others. Becker's theory suggests that, having been defined as a criminal by society, the individual then takes on the label 'criminal' as part of his own identity. He starts to think of himself as a criminal, defines himself in opposition to those who make the rules, associates with other 'outsiders', adopts their criminal ways of thinking and acting and so on. So, in Becker's view, those who become habitual lawbreakers do so as a consequence of the way society labels them. Because labelling theory recognises that criminality is defined by society, and some groups within society are more powerful than others, it raises the possibility that ideas about crime serve the interests of the powerful, rather than the interests of society as a whole. This has been an influential idea among those who take a critical perspective on psychology and crime (see Chapter 12).

Labelling theory claims that the deviant/criminal label applied by the authorities to the individual is incorporated into their self-concept. If so, the self-concepts of delinquents and offenders would be expected to contain more 'deviant' elements than those of non-offenders. There is support for this view. Ageton and Elliott (1974) examined the self-concepts of adolescent boys who had never come into contact with the police. Those who were subsequently arrested tended to adopt delinquent self-descriptions while those who were not labelled by the authorities remained the same. However, several studies have found that a delinquent self-concept tends to be present *before* any contact with the authorities (Gibbs, 1974), which raises questions about the direction of causality: do people who are labelled start to think in criminal ways or are people who think in criminal ways more likely to get labelled? McGrath (2014) interviewed 69 female and 325 male young offenders after sentencing in New Zealand. Respondents were asked questions about the impact of being labelled, such as 'Even though the court case is over, do you still feel that others will not let you forget what you have done?' Their responses were used to assess the level of stigmatisation perceived by each offender. Data were also obtained about subsequent offending. Interestingly, there was a positive relationship between perceived stigmatisation and reoffending in females but not in males, suggesting that labelling may interact with gender in influencing criminal outcomes.

Another prediction of labelling theory is that being 'officially' labelled by the authorities will increase an individual's subsequent risk of offending. It appears so. Petrosino et al. (2013) reviewed 29 studies that compared subsequent offending in delinquents who were 'processed' by the criminal justice system (prosecuted, convicted and punished) with those who were 'diverted' from the system (e.g. by referring them to support services). Compared with 'diverting' offenders, 'processing' was associated with a 5 to 6% increase in subsequent delinquency. Bernburg et al. (2006) examined the role of the peer group using longitudinal data from 1,000 adolescents who were aged 12 and 13 at the start of the study. The researchers collected self-reports of delinquent behaviour, delinquency in the peer group and involvement with the justice system. They found that involvement with the justice system signifi-cantly increased the probability of subsequent offending and was associated with increased delinquency in the peer group, including gang membership. Labelled individuals start to associate with other delinquents because, having internalised the 'criminal' label, they identify with them and because they are blocked from asso-ciating with non-delinquent groups as the stigma of being labelled leads to social rejection. Increased contact with delinquent and criminal peers then leads to greater risk of offending through social learning (see above). Bernburg et al. suggest that official labelling embeds the individual in a network of deviant social relationships, increasing their exposure to criminogenic influences. Some individuals are more susceptible to the effects of labelling than others. Besemer et al. (2017) found that getting a criminal conviction significantly increased men's later self-reported offend-ing, but only in respondents whose parents also had a criminal conviction. It may be that those whose parents have criminal convictions have fewer social resources with which to resist the effects of labelling. Being associated with a 'criminal' family, they are more likely to be singled out for monitoring and harsher treatment by the authorities, giving rise to a self-fulfilling prophecy.

Self-fulfilling prophecy (SFP) is a social-psychological idea that overlaps with labelling theory. In an SFP, a prediction comes true because it has been made. For example, a boy whose father is a convicted criminal might be expected by other people to develop criminal tendencies himself. Although he may be no more anti-social than his peers, his teachers more readily notice his misbehaviour, punish him more harshly and ignore or explain away any positive and prosocial behaviour on his part. He may receive less time and attention than the other pupils. Over time, the boy makes less progress in his learning and develops a negative attitude towards school and authority. Although minor acts of antisocial behaviour are common in adolescents, this boy might be more likely to be caught by the police, because his 'criminal family' reputation means he is more closely monitored. If he is caught then he may be more likely to be charged with an offence rather than let off with a warning. The result is that the boy develops into an adult criminal because the expectations and behaviour of others smooth the path towards offending, while simultaneously blocking off the alternatives. The classic study of self-fulfilling prophecy was by Rosenthal and Jacobson (1968), who randomly selected some primary school children and informed their teachers that these children had been psychologically tested and were 'growth spurters' who could be expected to make substantial intellectual gains in the near future. Subsequent testing showed signifi-cant increases in the IQs of the 'growth spurters' compared with the other children, presumably as a consequence of their teacher's altered expectations. Some have disputed the validity of this finding but there is strong support for the influence of teachers' expectations on student progress (Hattie, 2009).

Although plausible, it does not automatically follow that a similar process applies to offending. It would be unethical deliberately to label a randomly assigned group of children as 'future offenders' to see what might happen and so direct evidence is not available. However, there is some suggestive research in this area. Meichenbaum et al. (1969) repeated Rosenthal and Jacobson's study in a group of female juvenile delinquents and found that teachers' expectations and behaviour did change, leading to better performance than matched controls in a subsequent examination. This does suggest that delinquents are responsive to others' expectations (although in a prosocial direction rather than an antisocial one). Jahoda (1954) reports that among the Ashanti people of Western Africa there is a practice of naming boys after the day of the week on which they were born. The day of birth is believed to determine the boy's temperament, so boys born on a Monday are believed to be placid, those born on a Wednesday are supposed to be aggressive. Police records apparently showed a high number of arrests for men born on a Wednesday and a low number for those born on a Monday. Jahoda concludes that the men's names influenced how they were treated by others throughout their development, resulting in different patterns of behaviour. However, beyond isolated studies like these, self-fulfilling prophecy as a factor in offending has received relatively little attention and the idea has largely been subsumed into the body of research concerning labelling.

Labelling fell out of favour as a theory of crime in the 1980s because, while the evidence indicates some effect, it is not a major influence on offending (Tittle, 1980) and because it oversimplifies the relationship between attitudes, self-concept and behaviour (Blackburn, 1993). A frequent objection to labelling theory is its overly deterministic view, as if an innocuous individual is one day arbitrarily labelled as a criminal and instantly turns into a career deviant. An extreme view of labelling is clearly untenable – there are far too many other processes involved in criminality – but relatively few of those researching labelling in the 1960s and 1970s ever took such an extreme position, so it has perhaps been unfairly caricatured (Paternoster & Iovanni, 1989). Recently, there has been a revival of interest in labelling and the studies discussed above show that it can play a role in understanding the development of criminal careers through its effect on social networks. Such studies, albeit that they rely heavily on self-reports and frequently use samples that are relatively limited, imply that law and order policies involving 'crackdowns' on youth offending may ironically contribute to increased criminality. Although 'get tough' policies often meet with approval in the media, they serve to trap some individuals in a criminal career that they might otherwise have avoided with negative consequences for the offender and their victims, and an economic cost for society.

Social identity theory

Social identity theory (SIT; Tajfel & Turner, 1979) is about the relationship between an individual's sense of self and the social groups to which they belong. It originated in an attempt to explain prejudice, discrimination and intergroup conflict but has been applied to a great range of behaviour, including crime and deviance. It does not present an explanation of crime as such but is useful in understanding certain types of offending. SIT claims that a person's individual sense of identity is based on membership of social groups. Membership gives the person an understanding of what it means to be a group member, what attributes members have and how members differ from those of related outgroups. For example, someone who categorises herself as a teacher will assume a set of ideas about what a teacher does (probably involving activities like planning, teaching and assessing), what a teacher is like (perhaps being interested in people and committed to helping others) and a set of ideas about other occupational groups and how they relate to and compare with teachers (for example, seeing teachers as similar to nurses but quite different from stockbrokers). A person's social identity fluctuates as their situation makes different group memberships salient (Hogg et al., 2004). People classify others according to whether they are members of the salient social group or of a related outgroup. This serves two purposes. First, it simplifies the world and reduces uncertainty. Second, it acts as a source of self-esteem. By making favourable comparisons with outgroups, the person gets to feel good about who she is. Because ingroup membership is potentially an important source of self-esteem, people are motivated to protect their social identities. Consequently, there is a strong motivation to conform with the social norms of the ingroup.

Boduszek and Hyland (2011) suggest that criminality can be understood as a way of achieving a successful social identity. People try to join social groups that will give them a high status as this will enhance their self-esteem. At school an individual may wish to join the group representing social popularity, academic success and so on. Those who fail in their attempts to join the high-status groups (e.g. because of lower intellectual and social capacities) experience lower self-esteem, rejection and discrimination from the high-status group. One way of escaping the negative consequences of failure is joining an alternative social group that provides a more successful identity. They can achieve high status by joining a deviant or criminal group, especially if it has norms that allow them to define their failure to join the mainstream as a form of success. For example, Emler and Reicher (1995) suggest that delinquency in adolescent boys is most common among those who feel they cannot meet adults' high academic expectations. They use delinquent acts to establish a social identity that affords them a favourable reputation among their peers.

One area of criminality in which social identity theory has been applied is in understanding gang membership. In the US, where it has been studied most extensively, it is young people aged 14 or 15 who are most at risk of gang involvement. Membership typically lasts two to three years, with a small number becoming adult members (Goldman et al., 2014). Gang membership is associated with increased risk of both criminal behaviour and victimisation (Taylor et al., 2008) and gang-related activity is economically and socially costly to the community in which it occurs. Goldman et al. (2014) analyse gang membership in terms of social identity, highlighting a number of points:

- Gang membership is more common among people who feel marginalised, where opportunities to join high-status groups are limited.
- Joining a gang offers a way of achieving a distinct identity and a sense of belonging to people with otherwise poor relationships in the family, school and community.

- Members tend to be very loyal to their gang as they need to protect the sense of identity that comes from gang membership and will remain members even though the costs (e.g. risk of violence) are very high.

- Those who join gangs experience a subjectively elevated status, as the social prestige attached to the gang is experienced personally.

- Gang members attach a great deal of importance to respect and feel they must retaliate if *any* member has been disrespected as their identity is heavily invested in group membership.

- Since the norms of the gang include violent criminality, members will conform with these in order to maintain their status as group members.

As noted in Chapter 4, social identity as a gang member is also associated with a range of moral disengagement strategies that serve to disinhibit violent behaviour.

SIT makes an interesting contrast with many other explanations of crime in that offending is regarded as a strategy adopted by the individual to fulfill psychological needs. In this light, offending is an expression of the same desire for identity, status, respect and pleasurable experiences that other individuals achieve in prosocial ways (Goldman et al., 2014). This view draws objections from those who would rather view criminals as qualitatively different from law-abiding people but it coincides with recent innovations in offender rehabilitation that view offending as a deviant attempt to satisfy universal human needs (e.g. the Good Lives Model; Ward & Maruna, 2007). SIT does not attempt to provide a complete explanation of offending. Rather, it is complementary to other explanations. While SLT explains how an individual might learn to aspire to gang membership through exposure to models in the community and the media, SIT explains why the peer group is such a powerful influence on offending. Analyses like those of Goldman et al. show clearly how SIT can be integrated with the evidence base on offending, but the theory has so far stimulated relatively little research designed as a direct test of hypotheses about offending.

Poverty

There is a link between poverty and offending. Official measures of poverty and offending show that crime happens disproportionately in poorer areas and that poorer people are substantially over-represented in prison populations. Harlow (2003) reports that half of US prison inmates have either lived in social housing or had parents who received welfare benefits; further, that 60% did not finish high school, compared with 20% of the general population. It has been argued that official statistics exaggerate the association between poverty and offending, as it may be that poorer people are more likely to be caught and/or sanctioned rather than being more likely to offend per se. Tittle et al. (1978) reviewed 35 studies and found only a weak association between poverty and self-reported offending, lending weight to this view. However, the studies reviewed by Tittle et al. relied on measures of trivial offences or non-offences and used samples that tended to exclude those suffering the severest deprivation. When these problems are addressed, the evidence shows a significant effect of poverty (Hay & Forrest, 2009). Wozniak (2016) reviewed 43 studies of the poverty–offending relationship, reporting a strong association and some indications that poverty is particularly influential on violent offences. Hay and Forrest (2009) analysed five years of data from the US National Longitudinal Survey of Youth, gathered from 12,000 people who were aged 14 to 21 at the start of the study. Self-reports of assault, theft and vandalism were taken, along with data about family income. Forrest found that children who were living in poverty during their ninth year were 45% more likely than the general population to offend in their teenage years. Those who spent their first 10 years of life in poverty had a 79% greater risk of offending. These results confirm that poverty contributes to offending and suggest a dose-response effect whereby greater exposure to early deprivation increases the risk of adult criminality.

There are competing explanations of this relationship. The simplest is absolute deprivation. This view suggests that people commit offences because they are unable to afford the necessities of life. A related but more sophisticated view is relative deprivation. This occurs when an individual makes a comparison between their own situation and members of a reference group (e.g. other people living in their city) and observes that they are less well off. This gives rise to anger and frustration both of which provide the motivation to offend. Although there is an association between measures of both absolute and relative deprivation and offending, neither explanation is widely accepted. Critics object that both approaches are based on a sentimental view of offenders as being 'compelled' to commit crimes and are based on the fallacy that the causes of crime are essentially economic (Ousey & Lee, 2012).

Current analyses focus on the relationship between structural inequality and processes that contribute to offending. Poverty causes a range of factors to concentrate in particular areas, for example, unemployment and inequality. These combine to undermine the capacity of the community to control its members through their effect on family structure, community involvement and the supervision of young people (Wilson, 2012). Support for this view comes from Bellair (1997), who found that, once the effect of community ties was controlled, the association between deprivation and offending disappeared. Low income is associated with poor parental supervision and separation of children from parents, both of which are significant influences on adult offending. Those living in poverty are likely to be juggling several jobs, unable to afford adequate childcare and enduring significant stress, contributing to high levels of conflict within the family (Wozniak, 2016). Cohen (1955) suggests that long-term, persistent poverty undermines commitment to conventional values around crime and offending, giving rise to a criminal subculture. A number of studies implicate poverty in offending via neighbourhood processes (see below). In addition, poverty increases the risk of neurological damage via its effect on nutrition, parental drug use, abuse and neglect (Moffitt, 1993). The difficulty is that poverty covaries with many other criminogenic influences and it can be difficult to disentangle them (such as childhood adversity and environmental pollution; see Chapter 3). It should be stressed that poverty is neither a necessary nor a sufficient explanation for offending. Although they correlate, many people experience extremes of poverty and deprivation but do not offend and plenty of crimes are committed by people who have never experienced poverty. Finally, it should not be overlooked that poverty is also an important factor in victimisation: poorer people, and people living in deprived areas, are more likely than others to become the victims of crime (see Chapter 2).

Neighbourhood influences

Offending is not evenly distributed across locations; there is more crime in some neighbourhoods than others. A neighbourhood is a geographical area with an associated social community in which people have regular social interactions with each other. Opinion varies about how many members a typical neighbourhood has, with Antonaccio et al. (2017) arguing for a figure around 600 people. Poverty tends to be concentrated in particular neighbourhoods, so there is an association between poverty, neighbourhood and offending. A question that emerges from this is this: Does the neighbourhood play a role in causing offending? This is difficult to untangle because the three may be connected in many ways. Poorer people tend to gravitate towards particular neighbourhoods. Those neighbourhoods tend to be exposed to higher levels of pollutants such as lead, which may affect development (see Chapter 3). Some neighbourhoods attract offenders because they offer more opportunities for offending as there is a supply of suitable victims and some criminal activities may generate additional crime in the vicinity (for example, robberies may increase in close proximity to locations of drug dealing).

The correlational/cross-sectional design of most studies of neighbourhood influences makes it difficult to identify causal relationships but a rare exception is the Moving to Opportunity programme sponsored by the United States Department of Housing and Urban Development in the 1990s (Sanbonmatsu et al., 2011). In this programme, 4,600 volunteer families living in deteriorating social housing were randomly assigned to one of three conditions: one group received housing vouchers that could only be used to rent homes in low-poverty areas; a second group received vouchers that could be used in any location and a third group were used as controls. Compared with the other two groups, youths who moved to low-poverty areas showed a significant reduction in arrests for violent offences. Because the groups were randomly assigned, this suggests that the change of neighbourhood had a causal influence on offending.

The neighbourhood may directly affect criminality in at least two ways. The first is social learning, where the presence of a concentration of offenders in a particular neighbourhood may facilitate offending by other individuals. Livingston et al. (2014) analysed 10 years' worth of crime data from Glasgow, in Scotland. The city was divided into 600 neighbourhoods and official records were used to plot the location of all reported crimes, as well as whether each crime was committed by an already active offender or a newly active offender. They found that the presence of already active offenders in a neighbourhood was associated with an increase in newly active offenders. Controlling for other factors, a 1% increase in already active offenders led to a 5 to 6% increase in newly active offenders. Livingston et al. suggest that the existing offenders 'recruit' new offenders via social learning and peer influence processes. Mennis and Harris (2011) identify a similar 'contagion' effect for juvenile delinquency. This implies that the authorities in charge of resettling offenders after release should avoid concentrating offenders in particular neighbourhoods. A second influence is collective efficacy (CE). This is the capacity of a community to enforce desirable social norms. Where CE is high, social cohesion and trust are present and residents act in ways that informally police the community, such as reporting truancy and scolding youngsters who misbehave. This conveys the impression that offending is not tolerated. Where this is lacking, an important inhibition on offending is removed. Sampson et al. (1997) surveyed residents of 343 neighbourhoods, measuring CE by asking residents what they believed their neighbours would do when faced with different situations (e.g. observing someone spraying graffiti on a local building). CE was assumed to be higher where people reported that their neighbours would be likely to intervene. Sampson et al. found a negative correlation: in neighbourhoods where CE was high, crime rates were lower and vice versa. This finding has since been replicated in many other cities including Stockholm, Los Angeles, Tianjin and Brisbane (Hipp & Wo, 2015).

Overall, research indicates that some neighbourhoods have features that directly affect crime rates in the locality. However, research to disentangle the mass of variables involved in neighbourhood effects is at a relatively early stage and there remain controversies about the mechanisms involved. For example, Antonaccio et al. (2017) found that, in Russia and Ukraine, CE did not seem to influence offending but that the moral attitudes of local residents did and Lieven et al. (2015) found that school influences accounted for most of the variation in juvenile offending between neighbourhoods, suggesting that the influence of the neighbourhood on crime is not universal. However, research on neighbourhood influences is valuable as it may guide policymakers to intervene in and support communities in ways that reduce offending.

Chapter summary

Socially oriented theories of offending locate the causes of crime in the interactions between people. The most influential social explanation of offending is social learning theory. It claims that offending is the result of learning of criminal attitudes and behaviours from other people, such as family members and the peer group. There is a great deal of support for SLT, although it has difficulty accommodating individual differences in people's response to social influences and should be considered alongside biological and psychological explanations. An implication of SLT is that exposure to the mass media (TV, films, videogames and music) affects aggressive behaviour. It is widely agreed that the mass media affect aggression but it remains controversial how profound the influence is and whether it really matters on a practical level. Labelling theory suggests that criminality is the result of a process whereby powerful groups in society define some people as deviant and they become trapped in a net of social forces that doom them to adopt a criminal career. Although it is no longer accepted that labelling causes criminality there is evidence that it can amplify criminal tendencies. Social identity theory is concerned with the role that social groups play in a person's identity and behaviour. It is potentially useful in understanding some types of offence, such as those committed by gang members. Finally, a range of social variables has been connected with offending, including poverty and neighbourhood processes. This research has helped to shed light on demographic differences in offending and has much value as a source of ideas to inform crime reduction policies.

Further reading

Akers, R. L. (2009). *Social Structure and Social Learning: A General Theory of Crime and Deviance*. Livingston, NJ: Transaction Publishers. This is the most complete presentation of social learning theory as it relates to crime.

Becker, H. S. (1963). *Outsiders: Studies in the Sociology of Deviance*. New York: Free Press. A classic of the sociology of crime and deviance and a good starting point for understanding critical perspectives on offending.

Psychology and police investigations

In a Western democracy, the police have a number of interrelated roles including preventing crime, preserving public order and detecting criminal offences. The investigation of crimes may be supported by scenes of crime officers (SOCO), who collect evidence at crime scenes, and forensic investigators and scientists who may be employed by the police force or by other organisations. A comprehensive survey of the psychology of policing is beyond the scope of this book. Instead, a selection of topics is presented that illustrate the intersection of police investigations and psychology. There is a discussion of how the collection, processing and interpretation of forensic evidence may be affected by psychological processes. There follows a comparison of 'standard police interviews' with psychologically informed alternatives including ethical interviewing and cognitive interviewing. Finally, there is a discussion of offender profiling. Chapter 7 also covers topics of relevance to policing, including the use of aids to suspect identification.

The processing of forensic evidence

Forensic investigators collect and interpret evidence that may be used to identify suspects, eliminate people from an investigation and support legal arguments in criminal cases. They may appear in criminal trials as expert witnesses for either prosecution or defence and there is an expectation that those working in these roles will be objective in the collection, processing and interpretation of physical evidence. However, there is growing recognition that there are limits on forensic investigators' capacity to do this. Cognitive forensics (Found, 2015) is a branch of psychology concerned with the application of knowledge about processes such as perception, memory, decision making and expertise to forensic science. Until the 1990s, forensic identification evidence such as fingerprints, toolmarks, handwriting and bite marks presented in criminal cases tended to be accepted by the court automatically and cross-examination rarely questioned the basis of the expert witnesses' certainty (Saks & Koehler, 2005). However, the increasing use of DNA evidence since the 1980s led to a re-evaluation of many forms of expert forensic testimony. This was partly driven by the large number of 'DNA exonerations', in which people imprisoned or executed on the basis of expert forensic testimony were shown to be innocent. The result has been an increasing focus on the validity of forensic expert judgements and a growth in psychological studies of how such judgements are made.

A landmark study of forensic judgements was reported by Miller (1984). Student participants were asked to determine whether the handwriting on some allegedly forged cheques matched some other handwriting samples. Half the participants were given a context describing the case, including the information that witnesses had reported seeing the author of the comparison samples signing the cheques. The other half were given no context and simply asked to determine if the cheques matched the comparison samples. Although none of the comparison samples actually matched, the majority of those given the context information judged that they did. All of the 'no-context' group judged correctly that the samples did not match. This suggests that forensic investigators may unconsciously take on irrelevant information when making judgements about evidence. Miller's study was limited by its small sample of non-expert participants but a follow-up study in which a larger sample of students was extensively trained in the analysis of hair samples, produced very similar results (Miller, 1987). Where context information was given, errors were made in 30.4% of comparisons, while only 3.8% of comparisons without context information were erroneous. While Miller met with resistance from the forensic science community, there is now much more widespread acceptance of the risk of bias in forensic evidence analysis (Found, 2015).

In the area of fingerprint analysis, Dror et al. (2006) recruited five expert examiners to check the match between a crime scene fingerprint and a comparison specimen. All were told that the evidence came from a case where another expert had mistakenly judged that there was a match. In fact, each expert was given case evidence and comparisons from one of their own prior cases where they had judged that the case evidence and the comparison sample matched. Three of the five experts reported that there was no match, in effect, reversing their own judgements under the influence of the context information. This study used a very small sample and a very strong biasing context but does suggest that the judgements of forensic experts (as opposed to student volunteers) can be affected by extraneous case information. There has been some controversy about findings in this area. Hall and Player (2008) gave 70 fingerprint experts the task of evaluating the match between a 'latent' fingerprint on a £50 note and a comparison print. They did this in their usual workplace, under normal conditions (e.g. there was no time limit). The context was manipulated by supplying information either that the evidence was from a murder case (high emotion) or from a case of passing forged banknotes (low emotion). Although the participants reported that they had been affected more by the high-emotion case, Hall and Player found no difference between the judgements made by the participants in each condition, suggesting that forensic experts are less affected by context than the student participants often used in such studies. However, Dror (2009) rejects Hall and Player's conclusions, pointing out several problems: some of the experts did not read the context information, so could not have been biased by it; the participants knew it was a study, so they may not have performed as they normally would when analysing evidence; and there are data in the results that suggest that the context did have an effect, as those in the 'high-emotion' condition were less likely to report that there was some agreement between the case evidence and the comparison sample.

Further investigations have explored the conditions that moderate the effects of bias. Stevenage and Bennett (2017) gave a fingerprint-matching task to student participants. They were given context information about a DNA analysis of the evidence, being told (1) that DNA evidence suggested the fingerprints should match; (2) that the DNA suggested they should not match; or (3) that the DNA evidence was unclear. They found that biased decisions were much more likely when the participants were under time pressure and the DNA context was misleading. Dror (2017) investigated the possibility of bias introduced by computer systems used in fingerprint analysis. The Automated Fingerprint Identification System (AFIS) compares case fingerprint evidence against databases of stored prints and produces a candidate list of matches, ordered by similarity, for the forensic examiner to check. Dror has found that experts tend to spend less and less time examining each possible match as they work their way down the list and they tend to make more false positive matches (i.e. concluding that the prints match when actually they do not) with candidates at the top of the list and more false negative matches with candidates further down.

It is now accepted that the judgements of forensic experts are susceptible to bias, although in some areas more than others. Analysis of handwriting, hair and fingerprints appear more affected by context information than that of firearms and shoeprints. In any case, there is a strong argument for forensic examiners to take measures to protect against bias. Dror (2017) recommends that forensic examiners should be exposed only to the evidence they are analysing and measures should be adopted to shield examiners from any other information about the case to reduce the possibility that investigators will be biased by the case context. Found (2015) suggests that peer review of analyses should be routine, with results being checked by colleagues who have no knowledge of either the case context or the results of the first analysis. Unfortunately, these precautions are routine in very few organisations.

Understanding the impact of human factors on forensic evidence is important since both prosecution and defence at a criminal trial may draw on expert forensic testimony when constructing their cases. It is in the interests of justice that the testimony offered be as accurate as possible and that an honest assessment of its limitations is available. This is because forensic evidence can be especially powerful in the eyes of the jurors who decide the case. This is partly attributable to the popularity, over the past 20 years, of television dramas based on the forensic investigation of crimes, notably *CSI: Crime Scene Investigation*. These programmes present a rather inaccurate view of forensic analysis. Consequently, many viewers of such programmes hold unrealistic beliefs about forensic science including that forensic laboratories always have the most up-to-date equipment and forensic investigators almost never make errors (Cooley, 2006). Cooley and Turvey (2014) suggest that the 'CSI effect' leads to expectations on the part of jurors that may impact criminal trials in various ways. Jury decisions are discussed in Chapter 8.

Police interviews

The police interview people in order to obtain information that may help them to solve crimes. Gudjonsson (1996) distinguishes four categories of people who may be interviewed:

- Victims are the people against whom an offence has been committed.
- Witnesses are people who may be able to supply information about the offence or offender.
- Complainants are the people who report the crime to the police.
- Suspects are the people whom the police believe may have committed the crime.

These categories are not mutually exclusive. For example, both victims and complainants may also be witnesses. As far as the police are concerned, the important distinction is between witnesses and suspects. A broad distinction may therefore be drawn between interrogations, where the purpose is to obtain a confession from a suspect and interviews, where the police attempt to obtain information from eye-witnesses. Eyewitness evidence is the mainstay of police investigations and most criminal trials. Accurate eyewitness evidence therefore improves the effectiveness of police investigations and serves the interests of justice. Psychologists have consequently investigated the ways that the police interview eyewitnesses and have sought to develop more effective techniques for eliciting such evidence.

The standard interview procedure

'Standard interview procedure' and 'standard police interview' are terms used to describe the way untrained police investigators typically interview witnesses (Geiselman et al., 1985). The aim of the standard police interview is to obtain as much specific information as possible about a crime from the witness. According to Gudjonsson (1996), a standard interview has four stages:

- Orientation. The purpose of the interview is stated and legal requirements are fulfilled, such as informing the witness of their rights.
- Listening. The witness is invited to give a free recall account of events, with minimal interruptions.
- Questions and answers. The interviewer asks questions with the aim of filling in gaps, reducing ambiguities and obtaining additional information.
- Advice. The finished statement is read through, final alterations made and the witness is informed of any further action (e.g. the police may wish to interview them again).

While this seems an intuitively reasonable approach, a great deal of research suggests that standard police interviews have features that act against the quality of testimony. Fisher et al. (1987a) analysed police interviews of child and adult witnesses and identified several significant problems. First, the sequencing of questions was determined by the desire for specific details, so questions were not asked in the order likely to help the witnesses access their memories effectively. Second, witnesses were frequently interrupted, which is likely to inhibit the recall process. When witnesses are frequently interrupted, they stop volunteering information spontaneously and wait to be asked things, often giving superficial answers (Fisher & Geiselman, 1992). Third, interviewers asked predominantly closed questions, often leading ones. These tend to bias witness statements in the direction of the interviewer's beliefs about the crime and can affect subsequent recall of the event (see Chapter 7). Fourth, interviewers did not use any strategies that might serve actively to enhance witness recall. While it is recommended that about 80% of interview duration should be given over to the witness speaking (Shepherd, 2008), a review of field studies by Launay and Py (2015) found that witnesses spoke for only 30 to 48% of the time so the process was dominated by the concerns of the investigator rather than the attempt to elicit accurate and detailed testimony. Where investigators did ask witnesses for their free recall of events, in 61% of cases it was interrupted by questions about specific issues and, in many cases, substantial numbers of leading questions were asked. All this suggests that the standard police interview is a poor way of obtaining good-quality evidence.

Cognitive interviewing

In response to the shortcomings of the standard police interview, Geiselman et al. (1985) developed a 'cognitive interview' (CI) procedure based on psychological principles. Research into cue-dependent forgetting has shown that memory traces contain many different types of information. Some internal factors such as mood and psychological state and some external cues such as smell and colour of surroundings are encoded in memory alongside other information about experiences. According to the encoding specificity principle, the retrieval of a memory trace is more likely if the cue information overlaps with the memory trace. One implication of this is that police should interview witnesses in ways that maximise the availability of retrieval cues whilst at the same time avoiding leading questions that may contaminate recall.

The CI requires investigators to use four retrieval strategies when obtaining information from witnesses:

- Reinstate the context. The witness is asked to imagine themselves back in the situation when the events took place, including the physical environment and their own emotional state.
- Report everything. The witness is asked to remember everything they witnessed, even only partially, and to report even things that seem irrelevant or insignificant.

- Change the order. The witness is asked to recall events in reverse order, starting with the last thing that happened and working backward.
- Change the perspective. The witness is asked to recall events from the point of view of someone else who was present or from a different angle of view.

Subsequent research has elaborated on Geiselman's original ideas to produce the Enhanced Cognitive Interview (ECI; Fisher & Geiselman, 1992). This has an additional focus on the social interaction between the interviewer and witness. For example, the interviewer must greet the witness, establish rapport with her and use her name. This helps reduce the anxiety that witnesses often feel that may inhibit recall. The interview process should be explained, stressing that the format is designed to help the witness recall as much as possible but also acknowledge that this might be difficult for her. The interviewer should then 'hand control' of the interview to the witness by stressing that the interviewer does not know what happened and therefore the witness is the important person in the process. After reinstating the context, the witness is asked for a free recall account of events, with no interruptions from the interviewer or other distractions, although the interviewer may give non-directive verbal prompts to keep the account flowing. Only once the detail has been exhausted should the interviewer start asking questions. During this phase, forced-choice and leading questions should be avoided.

Establishing the superiority of the CI over the standard interview depends on two questions: does it improve recall and does it reduce witness error? In a laboratory study, Geiselman et al. (1986) compared the CI, the standard interview and a hypnotic interview. The standard interview produced on average 29.4 correct witness statements, the CI an average of 41.1 correct statements and recall under hypnosis produced an average of 39 correct statements. So, under laboratory conditions, CIs produced a 30% improvement in recall with no increase in witness errors. However, Fisher et al. (1987b) found that an ECI led to a 23% improvement in correct witness statements but also a 28% increase in incorrect statements.

Memon et al. (2010) reviewed 65 experimental studies carried out over 25 years. Compared with standard interviews, the CI causes a substantial increase in recall of correct detail and a small but significant increase in errors. These findings strongly support the adoption of the CI in all investigations. The increase in errors with the CI might cause concern, but Memon et al. suggest that it might be countered through clearer instructions to interviewees, for example, stressing that they should not guess if they don't know something and that it is acceptable to say 'I don't know'. Unfortunately, despite the apparent benefits of the CI, there was little evidence in the 1990s and 2000s that police investigators were actually using the method. For example, Clarke and Milne (2001) found that 83% of interviews they studied showed no evidence of cognitive interviewing techniques. However, since cognitive interviewing was integrated more thoroughly into British police training as part of the PEACE model of interviewing (see below) there are indications that it has been more widely adopted in everyday policing.

Interrogation of suspects

The purpose of an interrogation is to extract a confession from a suspect. Many police forces use one of a number of manuals for interrogators. These tend to be based on the methods of experienced interrogators rather than on systematic research but they are psychologically sophisticated and may involve deception, manipulation, pressure and persuasion. One of the most influential interrogation manuals is by Inbau et al. (2011), who describe a nine-step process for inducing a suspect to confess (see Table 6.1).

Kassin and Gudjonsson (2004) identify three important processes: (1) custody and isolation, which puts the suspect under stress; (2) confrontation, in which the interrogator repeatedly accuses the suspect of the crime and blocks denials; and (3) minimisation, where the interrogator morally justifies the crime, making the suspect believe that he will be treated leniently. They argue that these increase the risk that an innocent suspect will make a false confession because he has been isolated,

TABLE 6.1 Interrogation techniques recommended by Inbau et al. (2011)

Step	Explanation
1 Direct positive confrontation	The suspect is told directly that he is considered to have committed the offence
2 Theme development	The interrogator suggests possible accounts of the crime that minimise the suspect's involvement or culpability. The aim is to show sympathy and understanding
3 Handling denials	The suspect is not allowed to repeatedly deny the offence. The interrogator interrupts denials to prevent the suspect from gaining a psychological advantage
4 Overcoming objections	The interrogator does not acknowledge reasons for the suspect's innocence. Once the suspect realises that objections get him nowhere, he stops making them
5 Procurement and retention of the suspect's attention	In order to avoid withdrawal on the suspect's part, the interrogator maintains physical proximity, good eye contact and uses the suspect's first name
6 Handling suspect's passive mood	The interrogator tries to facilitate a remorseful mood in the suspect, for example by focusing on the victim's distress
7 Presenting an alternative question	The suspect is presented with two accounts of the crime. Both are incriminating but one allows the suspect to explain why he committed the crime. Inbau et al. suggest that this alternative is more attractive to the suspect
8 Having suspect orally relate details of offence	Having accepted one of the accounts offered in step 7, the suspect gives an oral confession
9 Converting oral into written confession	The oral confession is put down in writing in order to overcome a later retraction by the suspect

intimidated, put under high levels of psychological pressure and then offered confession as a way out of the situation.

Research in the UK has shown that police interrogation tactics have changed since the second half of the 20th century. In the 1970s Softley (1980) found that persuasive and manipulative techniques were used in 60% of interviews. In the 1980s interview procedures were greatly affected by the Police and Criminal Evidence Act (PACE; 1984), which limited the use of coercive tactics. Since PACE, interviews are less likely to be conducted at night, are better recorded (using audiotape and, nowadays, video) and suspects are now more likely to consult a legal advisor before interrogation (Irving & McKenzie, 1989). Moston (1990) analysed 400 audiotaped interrogations carried out by the Metropolitan Police. Compared with earlier investigations there had been a dramatic fall in the use of manipulative techniques, presumably as a result of the increased legal restrictions on police behaviour. In the majority of cases, the police used an 'accusatorial strategy' in which the suspect was directly accused of the offence, the evidence against him was presented and the accusation was repeated. Pearse and Gudjonsson (1999) analysed interview recordings from 18 serious crimes and found that the most frequently used tactics were robust challenge (disputing the suspect's account and accusing them of lying) and intimidation (emphasising the seriousness of the suspect's situation). The use of these tended to increase throughout the interview until the suspect confessed. Of the 18 cases examined, 10 resulted in a conviction. Interestingly, it was found that the tactics used during interrogation were related to the chance that the confession would be ruled inadmissible by the court. In four out of six cases where intimidation had been used to an extreme degree, the court refused to admit the confession as evidence.

False confessions

The most serious problem with manipulative and coercive interrogations is the risk of false confessions. It is impossible to say with certainty how common false confessions are but Sigurdsson and Gudjonsson (1996) found that 12% of prison inmates claimed to have made at least one false confession in their life, usually in order to escape from police pressure or to protect another person. Among students who had been arrested at some point, 1.2 to 3.7% reported that they had made a false confession. The commonest reason was to protect someone else. In any case, there are sufficient numbers of wrongful convictions to show that there is a problem. In the UK, the cases of the Birmingham Six and the Guildford Four brought the issue into the public eye as individuals were convicted of terrorist offences on the basis of false confessions. In the US, Scheck et al. (2000) analysed the cases of 62 DNA exonerations, where convicted individuals were later shown to be innocent by DNA evidence, and found that, in 15 cases, a false confession had been made.

False confessions may be made for different reasons. Kassin and Wrightsman (1985) distinguish between voluntary, coerced-compliant and coerced-internalised confessions. Voluntary false confessions occur when a suspect confesses in the absence of pressure from the police. This could be because of a desire for notoriety, a wish to cause trouble by misleading the police or an inability to distinguish fantasy from reality (e.g. in the case of some mental illnesses). Coerced-compliant false confessions occur when a suspect admits to a crime they know they did not commit in order to escape the pressure of the interrogation, avoid a threat or obtain a reward of some sort. In the case of the Birmingham Six, four of the suspects signed confessions after being physically beaten, threatened with further violence and confronted with manufactured forensic evidence by the police officers interrogating them (Gudjonsson, 2003). Coerced-internalised false confessions occur when the suspect comes to believe that the version of events suggested by the police is correct and she actually did commit the offence. This occurs when a person distrusts her own memory and comes to rely on external sources like the police. It could happen, for example, because the suspect had amnesia caused by alcohol or head injury for the time of the alleged crime. Kassin and Gudjonsson (2004) give the example of Peter Reilly, who called the police when he discovered that his mother had been murdered. The police suspected him to be the killer and interrogated him, telling him that he had failed a lie detector test and that the test proved he was guilty despite his lack of memory. Reilly eventually accepted the police's account and spontaneously started 'remembering' committing the murder. Reilly was convicted on the basis of his confession but it was established two years later that he could not possibly have done it. The actions he 'remembered' were actually false reconstructive memories (see Chapter 7).

Some people are more at risk of making a false confession than others. Kassin and Gudjonsson (2004) identify characteristics that make people vulnerable including:

- Personality. People who score highly on the traits of compliance (being eager to please others and disliking confrontation) and suggestibility (having poor memory, high anxiety and a lack of assertiveness) are more likely to yield to pressure from interrogators.

- Age. Younger people are more at risk of making a false confession because they tend to be more compliant and suggestible and are more affected by the power and authority of the police than adults. They are also more likely to waive their legal rights, which makes them more vulnerable.

- Mental retardation. People with a low IQ are less likely to understand their legal rights and tend to be more compliant and suggestible, including a strong tendency to answer 'yes' to questions even when this is obviously inappropriate (Finlay and Lyons, 2002).

- Mental illness. Psychotic illnesses, where people lose the ability to distinguish between reality and ideas, may induce a person to confess falsely either spontaneously or under the influence of pressure from interrogators.

Ethical interviewing and the PEACE model

In the early 1990s an attempt was made by the UK authorities to improve the quality of all police interviews, including interrogation of suspects. The term 'interrogation' was dropped in favour of 'investigative interviewing' and a national standard approach, known as the PEACE model, was developed for all police interviews with suspects (Milne & Bull, 1999). The latest version is based on seven principles including that interviewers must approach every interview fairly and without prejudice and the interviewer must not be oppressive. The intention is to establish a true and accurate account of what happened, rather than to elicit a confession of guilt from the suspect. PEACE describes the phases involved in a good interview and stands for:

- Planning and preparation. The interviewer must collate the information already known before the interview, clarify what the aim of the interview is and develop a written plan for how it will proceed.
- Engage and explain. The interviewer establishes a rapport with the suspect, explains the purpose of the interview and the procedures that will be followed and encourage the suspect to say anything she feels is relevant.
- Account, clarification and challenge. The suspect is asked to give her account of events, in as much detail as possible. The interviewer takes an active listener role, allows the suspect to pause and take her time and uses open prompts to elicit more information. The suspect's account is not interrupted or challenged until she has told her story. Only then is the suspect's account challenged, with an emphasis on inconsistencies and conflicts with other evidence. Open questions are preferred and leading or forced-choice questions are discouraged. The active deception of the suspect is prohibited.
- Closure. The interviewer brings the interview to a planned conclusion rather than an abrupt end, with the suspect given the opportunity to clarify matters or ask questions.
- Evaluation. After the interview has finished, the investigator makes a decision as to whether any further action is required, assesses how well the suspect's account fits in with the rest of the investigation and reflectively evaluates her own performance during the interview (National College of Policing, 2016).

Investigators have sought to establish whether PEACE has achieved its aims of improving the evidence value of interviews with suspects. Early evidence suggested that training in PEACE techniques produced lasting changes to officers' interview techniques (McGurk et al., 1993) but a larger scale review by Clarke and Milne (2001) found that officers were finding it difficult to put their training into practice and that interviews were frequently marred by poor planning and poor communication skills. At the same time, however, Soukara et al. (2002) found indications that the introduction of PEACE had brought about a shift in the attitudes of experienced detectives, who emphasised the importance of good-quality training, planning and social skills and disapproval of the use of deception. Meissner and Russano (2003), comparing interrogations in the US and UK, noted that the move to ethical interviewing in the UK had not reduced the likelihood of obtaining a confession.

More recent evidence suggests that the PEACE model is now much more firmly embedded in UK policing. Soukara et al. (2009) used content analysis on audio recordings of 80 interviews covering a large range of crimes including violent, property and sexual offences. They coded the interviews for 17 different interview tactics including coercive/manipulative ones (e.g. intimidation and minimisation of the offence) and ethical interviewing practices (e.g. asking open questions and emphasising contradictions). They found very little evidence of problematic interview techniques. Most of the interviewing was consistent with the PEACE principles, although the use of leading questions was more prevalent than the model allows. Several investigations have addressed the issue of whether ethical interviewing is more helpful to investigations that the alternatives. Oxburgh et al. (2014) content analysed audio recordings of 59 police interviews with suspects of 'high-stakes' crimes (adult and child murder, sexual offences against children). They found that interviewers who showed more empathy also tended to ask more appropriate questions (i.e. less use of closed, forced-choice and leading questions) and elicited more information. This is broadly supporting of an ethical approach. Snook et al. (2015) interviewed 100 male prison inmates about the style adopted by the officers who interviewed them, the evidence that was presented during the interrogation and their own inclination to confess and cooperate with the enquiry. They found that the best predictors of self-reported cooperation were a humanitarian interviewing style and strong evidence, both of which significantly increased the chance of a confession. An accusatorial style and the use of deception by the interviewer reduced the suspects' preparedness to cooperate. Meissner et al. (2014) reviewed both observational field studies and experimental studies that compared 'accusatorial' with 'information-gathering' (i.e. ethical) interview strategies and found that the accusatorial approach increased the risk of a false confession whereas the information-gathering approach did not, suggesting that the ethical approach has the same benefits as the accusatorial one but without the drawbacks.

Kassin et al. (2010) compare the British approach favourably with the US and other countries in which the Inbau methods predominate, drawing attention to the role of PACE (1984) in ensuring that suspects are informed of their rights, allowed adequate rest and assessed as to whether their age or mental functioning requires the attendance of an 'appropriate adult' to ensure that the suspect is treated fairly. Kassin et al. argue for reform of US police interviewing practices in line with UK developments in order to reduce the risk of false confessions. In particular, they recommend that all police interviews should be recorded; time limits on interrogation should be imposed; the use of false evidence should be curtailed; the use of minimisation tactics should be limited; and police should receive better training on the identification and treatment of vulnerable suspects.

Offender profiling

It has been suggested that psychology could contribute directly to the apprehension of criminals through what is variously known as 'offender profiling', 'criminal profiling' or simply 'profiling'. The aim of offender profiling is to predict the characteristics of an unknown offender from the characteristics of the offence and the victims (Farrington, 2007). The basic assumption of profiling is that, just as offenders leave behind physical evidence in the form of fingerprints, fibres from clothes, bodily fluids and so on, they also leave *behavioural* evidence of how they acted during the offence. In a murder enquiry, this might include how the victim was killed and where and how the body was left. Physical evidence can be removed by a clever offender but it is much harder for the criminal to erase the traces of how they acted, especially if they were unaware that they were leaving such clues behind them. In principle, profiling could assist a police investigation in many ways. It might link crimes done by the same person, help predict future offences, allow police to target their resources and narrow down the pool of potential suspects. For example, the first use of DNA profiling in a murder investigation involved the DNA testing of all 4,583 men living in the town of Narborough in Leicester, UK. The offender, who had raped and murdered two young women, was identified and convicted but mass screening of suspects on this scale took months and was extremely expensive. Offender profiling might help police to prioritise some suspects, perhaps allowing offenders to be caught earlier and with less expenditure of resources. Profiling caught the popular imagination during the 1990s and the criminal profiler has since become a stock figure in police dramas. The media (and some profilers) present offender profiling as a highly accurate process that makes a significant contribution to the solution of complex cases. However, serious doubts have been voiced as to whether it has anything to contribute to conventional police investigative work.

Types of profiling

There are several different approaches to profiling. Ainsworth (2001) identifies four types, each with its own set of assumptions and methods. These are: crime scene analysis, clinical profiling, geographical profiling and investigative psychology.

Crime scene analysis

Crime scene analysis was originally developed in the US by agents of the Federal Bureau of Investigation's Behavioural Science Unit in the early 1970s. It is typically used only in serial violence and sexual crimes. The fundamental idea is that different types of offender have different characteristics and leave behind different types of crime scene. If the profiler can accurately diagnose the type of crime scene, they can work backwards from that to the type of offender and from there to the characteristics the offender is likely to have. The profiler starts by assembling as much information from the case as possible, including the crime scene, the forensic evidence, medical reports and the nature of the victim. This information is then used to make a judgement about whether the crime scene is organised or disorganised (Hazelwood & Douglas, 1980).

Organised crime scenes show evidence of planning, such as weapons and restraints being brought to the scene by the offender and the subsequent removal of evidence. Disorganised crime scenes have a more spontaneous character, with weapons being improvised from items found at the scene and little attempt to conceal evidence. According to Hazelwood (1987), the people responsible for the organised and disorganised crime scene would be quite different from one another. The organised offender is manipulative, cunning and capable of concealing a callous and sadistic personality beneath a mask of outward normality. He is socially and sexually competent, of at least normal intelligence and likely to be living with a partner. By contrast, the disorganised offender is likely to be experiencing severe mental illness, to be socially and sexually inadequate and to live alone, probably close to the scene of the attack. Although the distinction between organised and disorganised offenders remains fundamental to the FBI's approach, a number of additional typologies were subsequently developed to classify rapists according to their actions during their crimes. These are claimed to differentiate between different motives. For example, the 'power-reassurance' type is driven by a fear of sexual inadequacy, while the 'power-assertive' type is driven by a desire to assert his masculinity through power and dominance.

Clinical profiling

The clinical approach is not a uniform set of profiling techniques and clinical profilers may work in different ways. What they have in common is the use of clinical experience, often in forensic or clinical psychology or psychiatry, as a basis for understanding and making sense of the offender's actions. Clinical profilers may analyse violent crimes in relation to problems such as alcohol abuse and mental illness and try to 'get inside the head' of the offender to reveal insights that will allow his behaviour to be predicted. This approach is probably closest to the media portrayal of the offender profiler. The most well-known clinical profiler in the UK is probably Paul Britton, who has published best-selling accounts of his cases (Britton, 1998). His approach involves immersing himself in the evidence gathered by the police and generating intuitive insights about the offender by speculating about his thoughts, feelings and desires as he planned and carried out his crimes. Rather than working from formal theories and hypotheses about the nature of offenders generally, Britton prefers to treat each case as unique.

Geographical profiling

Geographical profiling starts with the observation that there are more crimes in some places and at certain times. Patterns in the location and timing of offences occur because criminals make choices about where to offend and those choices are shaped by their understanding of their environment. Their relationship with the environment shapes an offender's choices in all sorts of subtle, unconscious ways. Consequently, the distribution and timing of an offender's crimes may betray all sorts of other things about the offender. The basis of this approach is Cohen and Felson's (1979) Routine Activity Theory, which states that crimes occur where a motivated offender encounters a suitable victim in the absence of a capable guardian. Brantingham and Brantingham (1981) suggest that offending is an extension of the other things a criminal does in everyday life. The offender learns of opportunities for crime, potential victims and locations to dispose of evidence in the course of going to work, socialising, pursuing hobbies and other legitimate activities. Consequently, their criminal activities are shaped by their routine activities and so the location and timing of a series of offences may indicate where an offender lives or the type or location of his employment. Canter and Gregory's (1994) 'marauder' model of offending is based on this idea. They suggest that an offender has a home base and travels to find offence opportunities in the vicinity. Having offended, he returns home and subsequently sets out again to offend, this time travelling in a different direction so as to avoid the area in which the most recent offence took place. As more offences take place, the crime locations start to form a circular cluster. An investigator who identifies such a cluster of linked offences can draw a line between the two crimes furthest from one another and use this as the diameter of a circle; the offender's home base is likely to be within the circle.

Other patterns reveal other things, so while a circular cluster may imply that the offender is based within the area, crime locations strung out in a line along a main road might suggest that the offender's actions are shaped by a route he travels frequently, possibly between home and workplace. Although geographical profiling started out with pins stuck in a map, it now makes use of computers and sophisticated statistical analysis to draw inferences about where an offender may be located. The 'Dragnet' system (Canter, 2005) generates maps with coloured overlays, which indicate the relative probability that the offender is based in different locations. This can be used alongside other evidence to focus the investigation on some suspects rather than others or to concentrate police resources in particular areas.

Investigative psychology

Investigative psychology is not really a form of offender profiling; it is much broader than that, applying the methods of scientific psychology to the whole area of offending, police investigations and the prosecution of criminals (Canter & Youngs, 2010). It is most associated with David Canter, who became involved in police work in the mid-1980s when he was invited to provide psychological input into the investigation of a series of rapes and murders in the London area. The profile he drew was highly speculative (Canter, 1994) but contained a large number of suggestions that turned out to be correct, including the offender's home base, physical characteristics, employment and criminal history. Canter's profile allowed the police to focus their enquiry on John Duffy, who was subsequently arrested, tried and convicted. Being a research psychologist, Canter identified a number of hypotheses from his profile and set about testing them systematically. This developed into what is now known as investigative psychology.

At the centre of the approach is the 'criminal consistency principle' (Canter, 1995), which states that an offender's behaviour is consistent across offences and between offending and non-offending activities. Therefore, the way in which a crime is committed will reflect the everyday traits and behaviour of the offender. For example, in the case of male on female rape, the use of impersonal and degrading language would suggest an offender who objectifies women in everyday life; the profile would suggest failed domestic relationships or difficult relationships with women at work (Canter & Heritage, 1990). Warning a victim not to go to the police or destroying evidence would suggest knowledge of police procedures that might indicate a criminal record. Investigative psychology also draws on geographical profiling and the idea that a criminal's actions reflect his mental maps of the environment.

Since the early 1990s, investigative psychology has developed to encompass the idea that criminals organise their offending around personal life stories (criminal narrative themes) that give their criminal actions meaning, so an offender casts himself as a victim, a hero, a professional or as taking revenge. The narrative influences his criminal actions, for example, in his choice of victims and the way he interacts with them during offences. Another hallmark of current investigative psychology is the use of sophisticated statistical techniques to analyse data about offences. For example, Smallest Space Analysis and Facet Theory have been used extensively to analyse the relationships between different types of crime scene behaviour. This can be used to identify 'themes' in offending that are similar to the FBI typologies but that are derived objectively from data from a large number of crimes. For example, Salfati (2000) analysed 247 British homicides and found that the crime scene behaviours clustered around two styles. 'Instrumental' homicides are those carried out to fulfil a particular aim, such as getting money or sex; the victim as a person is incidental. Instrumental homicides were associated with neck wounds, the use of a weapon found at the scene and property being stolen. 'Expressive' homicides are those that are directed at the victim as a person. These crimes are more often associated with wounding to the face, head and torso and the use of a weapon brought to the scene.

Does profiling work?

Besides pervading popular culture, offender profiling in its various forms has had a substantial impact on law enforcement (Dowden et al., 2007). However, concern has mounted over the past decade that profiling does not enhance the effectiveness of police work and may, in some cases, derail it. The majority of criticisms have been aimed at the FBI's approach and at clinical profiling. The FBI's organised/disorganised typology was derived from interviews conducted with 36 incarcerated violent serial offenders who agreed to be in the study (Douglas & Olshaker, 1996). This is a questionable basis for a typology that has been widely applied. The sample was very small and included only those offenders who were willing to cooperate. There is no evidence that a systematic and agreed-on method for conducting the interviews or recording the data was used, making it difficult to establish exactly how the data were obtained and impossible to replicate the study to check reliability. Furthermore, among the informants were psychopathic and mentally ill offenders, all of whom had strong incentives to deceive and manipulate the investigators. In addition, no comparison group was used to check whether the characteristics found in the serial offenders were absent from other people (Devery, 2010).

Relatively little scientific work has been done to check the validity of the FBI categories. Snook et al. (2007) reviewed the published literature on offender profiling, identifying 130 articles. The majority of these offered nothing but anecdotal evidence and 'common sense' to support the claims they made about profiling. A minority of articles reports some sort of scientific evidence but this was frequently of poor quality and accompanied by errors of reasoning. A meta-analysis comparing the performance of expert profilers with non-profilers indicated that the profilers were no better than the comparison group at predicting the specific characteristics of offenders from crime scene evidence. Devery (2010) points out that FBI profilers have historically been reluctant to fully explain their methods and data on the grounds that this knowledge would be used by criminals. While this may be true, it means that the evidence base for crime scene analysis cannot be evaluated rigorously or its efficacy compared with alternative approaches. Consequently, the widespread belief in the virtues of FBI-style profiling is supported principally by anecdotal evidence and the mass-market 'true crime' books written by profilers and journalists, which may be inclined to present only those cases that appear favourable to profiling. Snook et al. (2008) argue that the apparent success of profiling stems in part from people's tendency to perceive information that is actually vague and very general as highly accurate. If a profiler correctly predicts that the offender is a white male in his 30s who drives a car this may seem remarkably accurate until one considers that the description could apply to an enormous number of people. Alison et al. (2003) gave police officers the same vague profile and one of two very different descriptions of the actual offender. The accuracy of the profile was rated highly, regardless of which description was given. Such a view of profiling positions it as closer to casting horoscopes than doing science.

Clinical profiling emerges as no better that the FBI's approach, for similar reasons. Clinical profiling is often described as a very intuitive process, making it difficult to describe objectively what is happening when a profile is drawn up and therefore hard to assess the validity of the process. Ainsworth (2000), commenting on Britton's approach, highlights the speculative nature of his inferences and his tendency to present questionable assertions about criminal behaviour as incontrovertible facts. Clinical profiling was significantly tainted by Britton's involvement with the investigation of the murder of Rachel Nickell in 1992. The police identified a suspect, Colin Stagg, and concocted a 'honey trap', whereby an undercover woman police officer befriended Stagg and tried to induce him to confess. Britton was involved as a consultant on the case. The profiling evidence was ruled inadmissible and Stagg was acquitted, the trial judge commenting scathingly on the abusive and unethical way in which psychology had been used in the case. Devery (2010) concludes that, while it is difficult to find any cases in which profiling has contributed decisively to the solving of a case, it is not difficult to find examples where profiles have sidetracked an enquiry, resulting in the arrest and even conviction of innocent people and allowing the actual offender to remain at large.

Geographical profiling and investigative psychology are regarded more favourably, although there remain questions about their usefulness to police investigations. One problem is that these approaches rely on accurate data. However, locations may be misreported by complainants or mis-recorded by police, or the systems used to report crime locations may not allow the user to specify exactly where a crime occurred. Similarly, the crime data relied on by investigative psychologists is subject to human error and distortion due to recording systems. Inevitably, some proportion of crime goes undetected so inferences based on the available data may be biased if certain offences are systematically overlooked. Some critics have suggested that investigative psychology is too data driven. While the use of statistical techniques helps to maintain objectivity, Copson et al. (1997) point out that analysis of data about the past does not necessarily predict the behaviour of future offenders because it cannot necessarily be assumed that similar offences are carried out by similar people for similar reasons.

Some attempts to replicate key findings in investigative psychology have failed. For example, Sturidsson et al. (2006) repeated Canter and Heritage's (1990) investigation of sexual assault motives with data from Sweden and did not find the same pattern. By the same token, such debates serve to illustrate the value of basing profiling on scientific methods. Geographical profiling and investigative psychology share assumptions about the need for objectivity, transparency about methods of data collection and analysis, the testing of hypotheses, the discarding of theories that are not supported by data and the open publication of findings. These features are what drives progress in scientific knowledge. In this light, arguments about the validity of data-gathering methods or analytical techniques are a positive thing.

Chapter summary

The prosecution of criminal suspects relies on evidence gathered by police and other investigators. Expert forensic testimony is widely assumed to be reliable evidence of guilt or innocence but research has shown that it can be affected by the biases of the investigator. Besides physical evidence, police obtain witness evidence by interviewing people. Cognitive interviewing, where the interviewer uses psychological techniques to increase the detail of witness statements, has consistently emerged as superior to standard police interviewing techniques, although it does cause a small decrease in accuracy. Interrogation of suspects is done with the aim of obtaining a confession. Widely used police tactics, such as intimidation and minimisation of the offence, have been shown to increase the risk of false confessions. In the UK, such strategies are now no longer allowed although they remain common in the US and elsewhere. The PEACE interview model, an information-gathering approach, has now been adopted in the UK. It appears just as effective for obtaining confessions as the accusatorial approach but the risk of false confessions is significantly lower. Offender profiling is the use of psychological techniques to identify suspects in criminal investigations. It was pioneered by the FBI in the US, but several distinct approaches to profiling exist. Typological and clinical approaches to profiling have been severely criticised as being no better than pseudoscientific guesswork but geographical profiling and investigative psychology, being rooted in sound scientific principles, hold the promise of contributing significantly to solving crimes.

Further reading

Canter, D. V., & Youngs, D. (2010). *Investigative Psychology: Offender Profiling and the Analysis of Criminal Action*. Chichester: Wiley. This textbook gives a comprehensive introduction to the fields of offender profiling and investigative psychology.

Gudjonsson, G. H. (1996). *The Psychology of Interrogations, Confessions and Testimony*. Chichester: Wiley. This is the classic text on interrogations and confessions.

7

Witness testimony

A person can become a witness to a crime in many ways, from being present at a minor altercation to being the bank cashier during an armed robbery. In an investigation, each witness may have important details of the event that may help the authorities apprehend the suspects and mount a prosecution. Witnesses may provide information in a number of ways. Apart from interviewing (see Chapter 6), police may ask witnesses to help generate images of suspects or identify an offender from an identity parade of possible suspects. In court, lawyers may ask the witness to repeat their testimony under oath, ask him questions or cross-examine him to identify weaknesses in his account of events. This chapter considers how attentional and memory process may affect a witness's capacity to give accurate testimony through weapon focus, the misinformation effect and the effects of emotional arousal. Finally, the special problems posed by child witnesses and the use of likenesses and identity parades are discussed.

Apply your learning

Witnesses to a crime have been called to give testimony in court. They were in a coffee shop when two men started arguing loudly. One pulled out a knife and threatened the other. While everyone was distracted one or more people removed purses/wallets/phones from the customers' pockets and bags. When challenged, the perpetrators ran out.

When the police arrived, an inexperienced officer started asking people who were still in the room what had happened. He took down notes of what the different witnesses said. Later on, some of the witnesses were interviewed, shown photographs of the suspects and asked if they recognised them. Subsequently, some witnesses were invited to an identification parade, where they were asked to pick some of the suspects out of the lineup.

How likely is it that the witnesses will be able to give accurate testimony in court? Identify the features you believe might affect the testimony. As you read this chapter, check whether the factors you have identified correspond with what the psychological research suggests.

Cognitive processes and witness testimony

Cognitive psychologists frequently compare the mind to a computer. Cognition (thinking) is imagined as information passing through a series of processing mechanisms. These translate and impose order on data coming from the outside world (perception), select and filter information for further processing (attention), temporarily retain information and perform mental operations on it (working memory) and store some of it in a more permanent form for later retrieval (long-term memory). A fundamental assumption of this view is that a person's capacity for processing information is limited. This means that a person's mental representation of the world around her is relatively impoverished compared with the infinite amount of data potentially available in her environment. This means that what a witness reports may differ markedly from what actually happened. However, this is not widely recognised. Most people imagine that memory is something like a video camera, in which remembering is akin to 'playback', providing a complete, accurate and objective record of events. In fact, witness memories may be incomplete, fuzzy, distorted or downright false, even if the witness is completely confident in their testimony. This occurs because of some fundamental features of human cognition.

Cognition is an active and selective process. Because our capacity is limited, most of the data about the people and events around us are simply not processed and never enter our awareness. This is vividly illustrated by a well-known demonstration in which around 50% of people focused on the task of counting basketball passes fail to register the presence of a person in a gorilla suit walking across the screen (Simons & Chabris, 1999). If a witness's attention is focused on something else then they may remain oblivious that a crime has occurred in their immediate vicinity. Consequently, they would be unable to offer anything of value to the police. Even assuming that a witness were attending to the events, she may be unable to offer an objective account of what happened. People bring different influences to any situation and these affect how the situation is perceived. This is the 'active' part of human perception: we are biased in the way we process sensory information. However, people are rarely aware of these biases as they operate automatically and outside conscious control. Several factors influence perception, including expectation, emotion, context and culture. For example, people tend to perceive 'TA13LE' as 'TABLE' because the context provided by the letters influences them to perceive the two digits as a letter. Similarly, a witness will not experience a crime completely objectively and it is likely to contain elements of their interpretation of the event.

Another issue is that memory is a reconstructive process. The fact that perception is selective means that there are inevitable gaps in people's memories. A fundamental feature of cognition is that we fill in these gaps with our existing knowledge (Bartlett, 1932). Bartlett's idea was that we can only understand new information by fitting it into our existing knowledge (or schemas). When this is difficult to do, for example, because it is new or complicated, information tends to be distorted or forgotten. The process of remembering involves reconstructing events out of encoded information and schematic knowledge, which may produce memories that are significantly different from what the person actually witnessed. However, the individual is unaware of any change. There is an ongoing debate about whether the original memory is completely lost or still exists somewhere in memory. In any case, reconstructive memory is sufficient for everyday life, where completely accurate and detailed recall is unnecessary. However, when details are important, as they often are in eyewitness testimony, reconstructive memory can become a problem. If a witness has gaps in their memory but is pushed to provide a comprehensive story, they could fill in the gaps with an imaginative reconstruction based on what they would usually expect or information taken in subsequently from media reports or suggested by an interviewer. Because of the automatic nature of much cognitive processing, they would be unaware that they were supplying inaccurate information. In fact, they could be very confident that their recall is good.

Weapon focus

'Weapon focus' refers to the tendency witnesses have, when a criminal is armed, to direct their attention towards the weapon. As a consequence, their capacity to encode other information, such as the criminal's physical appearance, decreases. Loftus et al. (1987) demonstrated this in a laboratory study where participants viewed a series of slides depicting a man in a restaurant obtaining some money from the counter. Half the participants saw the man holding a gun, the other half saw him holding a cheque. Recall of details from the slides was poorer in the 'gun' condition and participants were less accurate at identifying the target. Participants also focused their gaze for longer on the critical object when it was a gun. Similarly, Kramer et al. (1990) showed participants slides of a man carrying either a magazine or a bloody meat cleaver. The weapon lowered recall of the scene but increased recall of the weapon itself.

Although studies like these suggest that weapon focus affects memory, the use of slides under laboratory conditions does not directly resemble the conditions of real-world witnesses. Other studies have therefore used simulations, in which participants are exposed to events 'live'. For example, Maass and Köhnken (1989) recruited people to participate in what they were told was a study on sport and wellbeing. While waiting in an office, the participant was approached by a nurse carrying either a syringe (the 'weapon') or a pen. In the 'weapon' condition, some of the participants were told that they were about to receive an injection. Maass and Köhnken found that participants in the 'weapon' condition were less accurate in identifying the nurse from a lineup and showed greater recall of the weapon. However, neither the weapon nor the threat significantly affected recall of facial details.

Research based on witnesses to real criminal events has not produced the same clear-cut findings as artificial laboratory and field experiments. Fawcett et al. (2013) reviewed studies in which witnesses to real crimes were interviewed and archival studies based on analysis of police records. They found that the presence of a weapon during a crime was not associated with any decreases in descriptive detail or identification accuracy. This may be because watching slides or a video is inherently less personally relevant than being involved in actual events, especially since the witnesses to real crimes are also likely to be victims. However, the failure to find the weapons effect in the real world may also be due to the difficulty of assessing witness accuracy. Unlike experimental studies, where an objective record of what really happened exists, the 'ground truth' of most criminal events is unknown as no external verification of witnesses' reports is possible.

Two explanations have been offered for the weapon focus effect. One is that the presence of a weapon increases witnesses' anxiety levels, causing their attentional capacity to decrease. The witness focuses on the weapon as it is a threat and peripheral information receives relatively little processing. There is mixed support for this idea, as manipulating the level and direction of the threat does not affect witness accuracy (as in Maass & Köhnken, 1989). Alternatively, it could be that the weapon receives more attention because it is unexpected in the context. This view is supported by several studies in which an unusual object such as a rubber chicken had the same effect on witness accuracy as a gun or knife (e.g. Erickson et al., 2014). Further support comes from the finding that the weapon focus effect only appears when a weapon is unexpected. Witness accuracy is not affected, for example, when the target is holding a gun at a shooting range (Pickel, 2008).

One important question about weapon focus is whether it is under a witness's conscious control. Pickel et al. (2006) staged an incident in which a man burst into a lecture carrying either a book or a gun. The participants had first been given a lecture on either the weapon focus effect and the importance of attending to facial features or a lecture on another aspect of witness testimony. Those who had not been instructed about weapon focus showed poorer recall and more errors when a gun was present. However, in those who knew about weapon focus, the presence of the gun did not affect accuracy. This suggests that people can be taught to overcome the weapon focus effect.

Contamination by post-event information

Even if a witness's attention were directed to the right things they may still have inaccurate recall of events. Because memory is reconstructive, it is possible for information the witness encountered later to contaminate their memory of the event. This can happen when witnesses discuss the event with other people, including other witnesses. Alper et al. (1976) staged a theft in a lecture theatre and asked the students present to act as witnesses. Recall of events was tested individually. The witnesses were then invited to discuss the event with one another, following which recall was assessed again. After the discussion recall was more complete – a good thing – but, unfortunately, the witnesses also tended to report details that did not actually happen. In a similar study, Hollin and Clifford (1983) planted among the witnesses two confederates who were instructed deliberately to give wrong answers. When tested for individual recall, the participants tended to incorporate the misleading information given by the confederates into their answers.

Apart from influences from other witnesses, an important source of the misinformation effect can be the questions asked by investigators. An investigator may (unwittingly) include in their questions information that suggests to the witnesses what actually happened, who was responsible and so on. If information from leading questions is taken on board by the witness, they may subsequently produce memories that have been distorted by the investigator's questions. The classic demonstration of this is a study by Loftus and Palmer (1974). Participants were shown a video of a car accident. In the course of recalling the event, all were asked, 'How fast were the cars going when they ___?' The final word in the question was altered for different groups of participants so some were asked how fast the cars were travelling when they 'hit' while for other groups the words were 'smashed', 'bumped', 'collided' and 'contacted'. It was found that the word used had a significant effect on the estimates of speed. 'Smashed' produced an average estimate of 40mph, 'bumped' an estimate of 38mph and 'hit' only 34mph. It might be suggested that the participants' memories had not been affected and they were simply giving the answer that they thought the experimenters wanted. However, Loftus and Palmer later asked the participants whether they had seen any broken glass in the film (there was none): 32% of the 'smashed' group reported seeing broken glass, compared with only 14% of the 'hit' group. This suggests that the leading questions caused a lasting change in memory.

Subsequent studies have explored the effect of post-event information in some detail. A number of variables influence whether post-event information is likely to distort recall. These include:

- Time. Misinformation has a greater effect when there is a time lag between the original event and the presentation of the misinformation. This is because the memory for the original event has had a chance to fade (Loftus et al., 1978).

- Centrality. When misinformation concerns things that are central to the original event then misinformation has little effect but when it concerns peripheral details the misinformation effect is stronger (Sutherland & Hayne, 2001).

- Source reliability. When misinformation comes from a source that is distrusted it has a weaker effect than misinformation from a trusted source (Dodd & Bradshaw, 1980).

These variables have their effect because they influence the probability that the witness will detect a discrepancy between their memory of the original event and the misinformation supplied by another source (Tousignant et al., 1986). Other research has identified characteristics that make some people more susceptible to misinformation effects. Children and elderly people are more prone whereas those with higher IQs and good working memory appear less susceptible to the effect of post-event information (Nash et al., 2015).

Loftus originally suggested that the misinformation supplants the original memory in a way that makes it practically impossible to retrieve. However, others have argued that, provided that the original event was fully encoded, the memory trace persists unchanged somewhere in the memory system (McCloskey & Zaragoza, 1985). This implies that the misinformation effect can be overcome if suitable ways of accessing the original memory trace can be found. Cognitive interviewing (see Chapter 6) is consistent with this idea, using the reinstatement of the original memory context to provide retrieval cues and thereby enhance recall. It improves the amount of information successfully recalled but also leads to an increase in errors. It is sensible to warn witnesses of the potential effects of misinformation as doing so seems reliably to reduce the distorting effect of misleading information (Blank & Launay, 2014).

Real witnesses may experience fear and anxiety. Field studies have sometimes found high levels of witness accuracy. For example, Yuille and Cutshall (1986) interviewed 13 witnesses who had seen two people shot in broad daylight. They were able to supply high levels of detail and there was little change from the police statements they had given several months earlier. The researchers attempted to implant misleading information but were unable to. Similarly, Odinot et al. (2009) interviewed 14 witnesses to an armed robbery, three months after the event. There were CCTV recordings of the crime so it was possible to check the accuracy of the witnesses' recall. They found that 84% of the details provided by the witnesses were accurate. Odinot et al. were also able to assess the effect of misinformation as some of the witnesses had watched a television reconstruction of the crime, which contained several misleading details. These did not appear to affect the accuracy of those witnesses. Cases like these show that witness memory *can* be very accurate but relatively few violent, dramatic crimes occur and so the witnesses in these studies are not necessarily representative of the majority of cases. Furthermore, DNA exoneration cases suggest that eyewitness error is a significant problem in criminal cases: an analysis of 300 wrongful convictions found that 75% rested at least partially on mistaken eyewitness identification (Wells & Quinlivan, 2009).

Emotional arousal

It was previously believed that shocking and emotionally significant events (e.g. political assassinations, declarations of war) were encoded by a special memory system that is highly accurate and resistant to forgetting (Brown & Kulik, 1977). It has subsequently emerged that such 'flashbulb' memories are prone to forgetting and reconstructive errors, just like other memories (Hirst & Phelps, 2016). However, it remains a possibility that emotional arousal affects witness memory. In both Yuille and Cutshall (1986) and Odinot et al. (2009), witnesses to an unexpected and threatening event showed detailed recall, little forgetting, and resistance to misleading information. Similarly, Christianson and Hübinette (1993) found that witnesses to armed robberies had very accurate recall of central details of the event (e.g. actions, weapons and clothing) although their accuracy about the general circumstances (e.g. the date of the robbery) was lower. In studies in which people are simply asked to recall as much as they can about negative events in their life, researchers have found a correlation between the intensity of negative emotion and the amount of central detail recalled. For example, Wagenaar and Groeneweg (1990) compared testimonies from 78 survivors of the Nazi concentration camps and found great consistency between their accounts even after 40 years.

Laboratory studies have been less consistent and a number suggest that threat and emotional arousal impair recall rather than enhancing it. Clifford and Scott (1978) compared participants' recall of two films, one of which contained a scene of a physical assault. Recall was poorer for the violent film. Clifford and Hollin (1981) carried out a similar study but, as well as manipulating the level of violence, changed the films so that the perpetrator was either alone, with two companions or with four companions. Recall was worse when the film contained violence. The number of companions made no difference to recall of the non-violent incident but the addition of more companions made recall worse for the violent film. Deffenbacher (1983) reviewed 21 studies and found that, in half of them, emotional arousal increased accuracy and, in the other half, it got worse. Christianson (1992) suggests that the reason for these contradictory findings is that recall of emotionally arousing events tends to increase with time. Laboratory studies typically use fairly short retention intervals (hours or days) so recall accuracy of emotionally arousing events is lower. However, field studies tend to interview witnesses after intervals of weeks or months, during which time their accuracy has improved. Intuitively, it might be assumed that witnesses and victims should be interviewed as soon as possible after the event in order to record as much as possible before forgetting occurs but Christianson's interpretation implies that witness statements might be more informative if collected later. Overall, it does seem that witnesses have relatively accurate recall of the central features of emotionally arousing events because such events are distinctive and unusual, receive relatively more attentional processing and are elaborated on after the event (Christianson, 1992). Consequently, it should not be assumed that the testimony of victims and witnesses of violent crimes will be subject to the misinformation effect to the same degree as other witnesses.

Child witnesses

Historically, the legal profession has been suspicious of the testimony of child witnesses, suggesting at times that they are prone to fantasising and liable to be manipulative (e.g. Heydon, 1984). It is widely believed that children's memories are unreliable and that their statements should be treated with caution. Leippe et al. (1992) recruited three groups of people to take part in a study of skin conductivity: 5 and 6 year olds; 9 and 10 year olds and college students. During the procedure a female confederate entered the room, made an enquiry and left. Afterwards, the children and students were videotaped while they answered questions about the confederate: what had happened, what she looked like and what she said. They were also asked to identify the confederate from a range of photographs. Other college students were then asked to rate the videotaped testimony for believability.

Believability was much more dependent on age and speaking style than accuracy. Even though the children were as accurate as the college students, their testimony was rated as less accurate and less believable. Despite this common perception of child witnesses, they are capable of high levels of accuracy and detail, although the questioning of child witnesses needs to be handled carefully.

There are important differences between the memories of children and adults. Some of these are due to maturational changes in the brain. Others are to do with the child's capacity to interpret and organise information. According to Davies (1991) children's memories improve rapidly between the ages of 5 and 10 because:

- A growth in general knowledge helps children locate their experiences.
- Children learn 'scripts' or typical sequences of actions that allow memory to be used more efficiently.
- Children develop better strategies for encoding new information.

Because of these differences, child witnesses may need prompts or cues to elicit a complete account of events. Research has suggested that children are capable of 80–90% accuracy if questioned in a supportive manner soon after the event has occurred (Westcott, 2006). However, children are more suggestible than adults and so there is a danger that leading questions and other sorts of misinformation will result in inaccurate testimony. For example, Cohen and Harnick (1980) showed a 12-minute film to 9 year olds, 12 year olds and university students. The participants were then questioned about the film. Some of the questions were misleading (e.g. the question mentioned that a woman in the film was carrying a newspaper when she had actually been carrying a shopping bag). The 9 year olds were less accurate than the older participants on both the leading and neutral questions. Generally, it has been found that by the age of 12 children produce the same level of detail as an adult and are no more susceptible to leading questions than adults (Loftus et al., 1990)

Suggestibility decreases with age for several reasons. First, children may be less effective at encoding new information. Where there are gaps, misinformation from other sources may be used to reconstruct inaccurate memories (see above). Second, children may be more likely to take on board misleading information from figures of authority as their level of trust in these sources is higher than an adult's may be (cf. Dodd & Bradshaw, 1980). Third, children may register misleading information that comes from an adult and 'go along with it' because they believe it is expected of them (King & Yuille, 1986). This has important implications for children's testimony. According to Westcott (2006), young children's accuracy is typically highest in free recall, where they can give an account of events in their own words. However, the amount of testimony is typically limited so investigators then have to question the child about specifics and this is where most problems occur. Accuracy is highest when interviewers ask open questions that do not point the witness in a particular direction (e.g. 'What happened yesterday?') and when questions are about specific features of the child's account, provided they do not lead the witness. Two types of question that should be avoided are those that suggest the answer the investigator expects (e.g. 'You saw him take it, didn't you?') and those that limit the child to a range of responses, none of which may be correct. Questions like these are likely to elicit guessing or compliance, both of which reduce accuracy.

Because of its effectiveness in improving the quality of adult witness testimony, cognitive interviewing (see Chapter 6) has also been tested with child witnesses. The results have been favourable, with cognitive interviews producing around 20% more correct information than a standard interview and, particularly, more forensically relevant information about the people, locations, objects and actions involved in the event (Verkampt & Ginet, 2010). Cognitive interviewing with children is more effective when specific instructions are used, such as the interviewer telling the child that he, the interviewer, 'knows nothing' about what happened and stressing that it is acceptable for the child to say 'I don't know' in answer to any of the questions. Verkampt et al. (2014) involved 59 four and five year olds in a painting session during which student confederates performed 12 distinct actions (e.g. giving out a flower, a hat and some stickers). The children were subsequently tested using several variations on a cognitive interview strategy. The full cognitive interview produced 42% more correct information than a standard interviewer. However, when the 'interviewer knows nothing' instruction was omitted the amount of correct detail fell by 21% and fell still further when the 'can say I don't know' instruction was also omitted. Besides supporting the use of cognitive interviewing with children, these findings underline the importance of social interaction as an influence on the quality of children's testimony.

Identity parades (lineups)

Psychologists developed the cognitive interview in the 1980s as an aid to witness recall but other tools have been in use for much longer. In an ID parade (or 'lineup') a suspect stands in line with a number of innocent 'foils' who are usually drawn from the public because they fit the same general description of the suspect. The witness is asked to look at each person in turn and to make a positive identification if they recognise that person as the one originally seen committing or assisting the crime. The procedure may be done with a series of photographs, the suspect's photo placed among photos of foils. Researchers distinguish between *target-present* and *target-absent* lineups, depending on whether the suspect/target is in the lineup or not. The police may have identified an innocent person as a suspect, so the target for whom the witness is looking will not be in the lineup. A distinction is also made between *simultaneous* ID parades, where the witness views the target and foils all together and *sequential* ID parades, where the witness is shown one person at a time, with the target placed somewhere in the sequence.

The ID parade is intended to be a fair test of a witness's ability to recognise the culprit. The presence of the foils serves to make the witness's task difficult, so that strong evidence of guilt results from the witness's identification. Unfortunately, very confident witness identifications are frequently incorrect. Bruce (1988) describes several cases in which a witness has positively identified a suspect who has then produced an alibi. It subsequently emerged that the witness had been shown photographs of the suspect before the lineup. The witness identified the suspect on the basis of familiarity but could not distinguish whether they recognised the suspect from the original incident or the photographs (a 'source-monitoring error'). Because of the potential for misidentification, the variables that influence witness accuracy in ID parades have been extensively researched. Influences on witness identifications are generally divided into system variables (factors the criminal justice system has some control over) and estimator variables (those over which the system has no control).

Wells and Olson (2003) distinguish four categories of estimator variables:

- Characteristics of the witness. Very old and very young witnesses perform worse than young adults, and people are more accurate when identifying someone from their own ethnic group.

- Characteristics of the event. Viewing time and conditions affect accuracy, so if the light was poor and/or the suspect was only visible for a short time during the original event accuracy suffers. The use of disguises and increased age impair recognition.

- Characteristics of testimony. Witness confidence may indicate accuracy when viewing conditions are good (Brewer et al., 2002). The time taken to arrive at an identification may be a more useful variable as Dunning and Perretta (2002) found that witnesses who identified the suspect in under 10 or 12 seconds were 90% accurate whereas those who took longer were around 50% accurate.

- Lay observers' judgements of accuracy. Jurors and other non-experts are generally poor at judging the accuracy of witnesses' identification although this applies more when viewing conditions were poor, where jurors tend to overestimate accuracy.

Wells and Olson (2003) also distinguish a number of system variables. These are of greater interest than estimator variables as if they are properly understood steps can be taken to minimise sources of error in witness identifications. Important system variables include the giving of instructions, the content of the lineup and the presentation method. Instructing the witness that the target may be absent from the ID parade significantly reduces misidentifications. A meta-analysis by Steblay (1997) indicates that a warning of this type reduces misidentifications in target-absent lineups by 41.6% but accurate identifications in target-present lineups are hardly affected.

The content of the lineup is important as the foils used by the police must closely resemble the target. If they do not, then the suspect may be identified simply because they stand out from the others. In the UK, seven foils are typically used but Brigham and Pfeifer (1994) point out that it is not the number of foils that matters but the number of foils who actually look like the target. This is known as the 'functional size' of the lineup. In the UK, the majority of ID parades are now conducted by video (Horry et al., 2012). A head and shoulders videoclip of the suspect is taken and then a computer system such as VIPER™ or PROMAT™ is used. The basic characteristics of the suspect are entered and the system produces a pool of possible foils from a database of stored videoclips. Video ID parades have been shown to reduce incorrect identifications, are fairer to the suspect as misleading 'guilt' cues are reduced and save time and money, since the police no longer have to recruit foils for lineups. They also increase witnesses' willingness to take part in lineups because they worry less about not being anonymous or being threatened by the suspect (Dalton et al., 2013).

The simultaneous ID parade is believed to be the source of many inaccurate identifications. Part of the problem is that witnesses do not follow the instruction to study the individual faces of the people in the lineup and match them with their own memory. Rather, they view the parade as a whole, discount those who do not fit their memory and select from the remainder the person who most closely matches. The result is a probabilistic process of *recognition* rather than a positive *identification* (Thomson, 1995). Alternatives to the simultaneous lineup have been proposed. Wells (1984) argues for presenting a 'blank' lineup that does not contain the suspect. Witnesses who make a false identification are then discarded before the remaining witnesses are shown the real lineup. However, this method is not favoured by police. Another alternative is the sequential lineup. Cutler and Penrod (1995) describe a procedure in which the witness is shown faces one at a time and asked, after each, whether they recognise the face as the criminal. Importantly, the witness is not told how many faces they will see. This prevents the witness from making a probabilistic 'best fit' judgement. A meta-analysis of 72 studies showed that, compared with the simultaneous method, the sequential method caused a 22% reduction in mistaken identifications in target-absent lineups, although it also slightly reduced the number of correct identifications (Steblay et al., 2011).

As a result of psychological research into ID parade identifications, a number of recommendations are now made for the conduct of lineups, with the intention of reducing errors and misidentifications (Wells et al., 2012):

- Double-blind administration. The officer conducting the lineup (and any other official present) should not know who is the target and who are the foils. This is to avoid the conducting officer cuing the witness as to the identity of the target (e.g. through a change in voice when the target is referred to, hand gestures or direction of gaze). The double-blind procedure eliminates these cues.

- Unbiased instruction. The witness is clearly told, 'The culprit may or may not be present in the lineup.' This makes it easier for the witness to reject the entire lineup if she cannot make a positive identification. Without this instruction, there is a tendency for the witness to assume that the target is present and that it is her job to identify him (Clark, 2012).

- Lineup composition. The foils are selected because they plausibly resemble the target. If the foils are dissimilar from the target, the target is identified because he stands out rather than because the witness actually recognises him from the original event.

- Sequential lineup procedure. The lineup should be presented one at a time, with no indication of how many people the witness will be shown (see above).

Facial composites

Facial composites are impressions of an individual's appearance based on information provided by witnesses. They are produced to aid witness identifications and may be used in public appeals for information about crimes and in police investigations (e.g. making house-to-house enquiries). The earliest form of facial composite used was the artist's impression, which was used in the 1911 search for the murderer Dr Crippen, who was apprehended following the circulation of a sketch of Crippen and his companion (Davies & Valentine, 2007). Subsequently, police forces have adopted a series of aids to the construction of likenesses including Identikit, photofit, videofit and genetic algorithms.

An artist's impression involves an artist drawing a picture of the target based on information obtained from the witness or witnesses. There is no standard method for doing this but it commonly involves the artist interviewing the witness to establish the circumstances of the crime, constructing an initial sketch based on a verbal description and then gradually refining the image until the witness is satisfied that a good likeness has been achieved (e.g. Taylor, 2001). The lack of standardisation in the way that impressions are constructed makes it difficult to evaluate their effectiveness and so little research has been done in this area (Davies & Valentine, 2007). The construction of artist's impressions requires that the artist be skilled both in drawing and interviewing witnesses. Such people are rare so it is both time consuming and expensive for the police to use them. Consequently, mechanical and electronic systems have been adopted widely and artist's impressions are used only rarely.

Identikit and photofit were developed as methods for creating facial composites without the need for a police artist. The witness creates a facial likeness feature by feature, by choosing components until the face is complete. For example, the witness may be shown 40 different chins and asked to select the one that best matches their memory. This is then slotted together with the rest of the chosen features to create the composite. The earlier system, Identikit, used hand-drawn facial features. Photofit, developed later, used photographs of the different facial features. Kitson et al. (1978) surveyed police forces about the outcomes of cases involving 729 facial composites. While the photofits had been crucial in 5% of the investigations, in 45% of cases the composites were of little or no use. There are two main reasons why Identikit and photofit have been relatively unhelpful. First, these systems necessarily comprise only a limited number of face shapes and features and so witnesses are forced to choose from a selection that may not reflect what they actually remember.

There are limited options for varying the relationships between the positioning of the features and no options for varying their size. The result is that these systems simply cannot reproduce the possible range of faces the witness may describe. Second, and more fundamentally, Identikit and photofit are based on a misconception about how people encode and recall faces. Rather than processing the features of a novel face one by one (i.e. serially), people process facial features in parallel and encode the relationship between them as a 'gestalt' (Tanaka & Farah, 2003). Consequently, the whole process of building up a composite feature by feature works counter to the psychological processes of face memory, which impedes the construction of accurate likenesses (Davies & Valentine, 2007).

In the 1980s, personal computers became powerful enough to permit the use of software to constructive composite images. Early software essentially recreated the photofit approach on a screen, with some limited capacities for blending and editing features. Although capable, in principle, of creating highly recognisable composites, it performed no better than photofit in tests, as it was based on the same 'serial' approach (Kovera et al., 1997). The E-Fit software (Aspley Limited, 1993) adopted by many British police forces in the 1990s was more flexible than earlier systems and was designed to accommodate a 'figural' approach more closely aligned with the gestalt process of facial recognition in humans. E-Fit is often used alongside cognitive interviewing (see Chapter 6) to maximise witness recall. The witness's responses to a series of questions are used to construct a composite image from a database of features and the witness can then refine the image by altering features or their configuration until it matches what they remember. Unfortunately, E-Fit performs only marginally better than its predecessors. For example, Davies and Oldman (1999) asked witnesses to work with an experienced E-Fit operator to construct facial composites of famous people either from memory or from photographs. When these were shown to others to judge, only 10% of the composites created from photographs were correctly identified and only 6% of the composites created from memory.

More recently, researchers have developed software capable of representing faces in a holistic way by analysing the relationships between facial features in a sample of people using a statistical technique called principal components analysis. Based on information provided by the witness, this software can generate a range of candidate facial composites. The witness can then reject some of these and a 'genetic algorithm' can be used to 'breed' the remainder to create a new generation of composites. This process can go on and on through many generations until a composite image is produced that the witness is satisfied with, but without the process of selecting individual facial features. One such system, EvoFIT (EvoFIT Limited, 2001), has been adopted by a number of UK police forces. A meta-analysis of 23 evaluation studies found that EvoFIT composites were around four times more identifiable than composites generated using feature-based systems like E-Fit (Frowd et al., 2015). This type of system, which aligns with the processes of human facial recognition more closely than its predecessors, will probably become more widely adopted in the near future.

Chapter summary

Laypeople frequently believe that human memory preserves a full and accurate record of events, but it does not. People encode relatively little information about the events they witness and this is then subject to forgetting and reconstructive errors. This has consequences for the quality of witness testimony. A weapon used during a crime attracts attention and so witnesses often have poor recall of other things. Memory can be contaminated by post-event information, as people have difficulty distinguishing between what they encoded during the event and what they learned later. Misleading information introduced by other witnesses or by leading questions can alter witness testimony. Strong emotional states increase witness accuracy for central details of events. In all these areas, there is conflict between the findings of laboratory and field studies. It is widely believed that child witnesses are inherently unreliable but research suggests otherwise, although young children do have limited recall and are liable to be influenced by adults who ask leading questions. Identity parades (lineups) and facial composites are used by police to enhance witness testimony. Lineups are liable to produce false identifications if strict procedures to avoid bias are not followed. Facial composites generated by Identikit, photofit and videofit have been of limited use to investigations as they frequently fail to resemble their target, although new systems based on genetic algorithms show more promise.

Further reading

Loftus, E. (1997). *Eyewitness Testimony*. Cambridge: Harvard University Press. An overview of the topic by the researcher who defined the field. The fact that it is still in print 20 years after publication is testament to its influence.

Courtroom processes

In principle, the outcome of a criminal trial is decided by the evidence presented to the court. In reality, courtrooms play host to a complex web of people, roles and relationships, influencing one another both intentionally and unwittingly. The evidence is only one factor that determines whether a defendant is found guilty or not guilty. This chapter examines some of the psychological processes that influence a trial, starting with a consideration of different types of trial procedure and how the strength of a case may be affected by the strategies used by legal professionals. There is then a discussion of some of the legal and extralegal factors that influence jury decisions including the composition of the jury, group processes of deliberation and the impact of pretrial publicity and juror bias on the outcome of trials.

Trial procedures

In most places, trial procedures take one of two forms, adversarial or inquisitorial. In an adversarial system, such as the UK or US, criminal cases are contested between the prosecution and defence, who take opposing positions. Each side tries to establish a preferred version of events by presenting facts in a particular way and discrediting the arguments and witnesses of the opposition. In this system, the judge takes a passive role, ensuring that legal procedures are followed correctly, ruling on the admissibility of evidence and interpreting the law, but not influencing the way cases are developed or presented. In an inquisitorial system (such as in France or Italy), the judge takes a more active role in determining the conduct of the case, preparing evidence and questioning witnesses. Rather than winning the case regardless, inquisitorial systems see their aim as establishing the truth; a biased presentation of the facts is discouraged.

Research since the 1970s has addressed the question of whether one system is better than the other. Thibaut and Walker (1978) investigated this using mock trials. They found that participants tended to favour the adversarial system as the participants were more satisfied with the verdicts, the procedure was considered fairer and perceived bias was reduced. Thibaut and Walker conclude that the adversarial system is objectively superior to other systems but this has been disputed. Hayden and Anderson (1979) argue that although many people subjectively *prefer* an adversarial system, it does not follow that the adversarial approach is objectively better, especially since an adversarial system entails monetary and social costs that should be considered when evaluating systems of justice. Stephenson (1992) adds that Thibaut and Walker's mock trials used civil cases where the facts were not in question, whereas in many criminal cases the facts themselves are disputed, so the findings may not generalise well. Subsequent research has suggested that non-adversarial procedures are favoured under some circumstances, such as in collectivist, communitarian cultures (MacCoun, 2005).

Juries

With very few exceptions (e.g. highly complex financial fraud cases), the more serious criminal trials in the UK are conducted with a jury. The role of members of a jury is to listen to the arguments presented by the prosecution and defence and to decide, collectively, whether the prosecution has proved the defendant's guilt 'beyond a reasonable doubt'. The legal system operates on the assumption that juries are rational and unbiased in their deliberation and that, therefore, the trial will be fair. In reality, the jurors may understand neither the evidence presented to them nor the legal instructions given by the judge (Monahan & Loftus, 1982) and they may be unable to separate the courtroom evidence from their own biases and their other knowledge of the case. Psychologists have investigated a number of processes that may affect jury decision making.

Jury size and composition

In the UK and US, juries typically have 12 members but some US courts have experimented with smaller juries. Saks (1977) reports that juries of five or six members tend to reach their verdict more quickly than do 12. However, they are also less likely to examine all the evidence in detail, tend to favour the prosecution and are less representative of society (Hans & Vidmar, 1986). A meta-analysis of 17 studies by Saks and Marti (1997) concluded that larger juries deliberate for longer, are more likely to contain members of minority groups, more frequently fail to reach a unanimous verdict and may recall trial proceedings more accurately. On balance, it would seem sensible to remain with 12-person juries.

A jury is meant to be representative of the community in which the trial takes place. In the UK, anyone over the age of 18 and under 70 who is eligible to vote may be called for jury service and may be fined if he refuses. There are exceptions, including court staff and legal professionals and others may be disqualified if they have served a prison sentence in the previous 10 years. In both the UK and US, legal counsel may reject jurors they regard as unsuitable. This right is not much used in the UK but in the US, where lawyers are given much more information about prospective jurors, the selection of the jury is a distinct phase in the trial process (the *voir dire*) and can take a great deal of time. In the US, unsuitable candidates are screened out using several criteria:

- Knowledge of pretrial publicity.
- Attitudes towards the offence.
- Personal acquaintance with anyone involved with the case.

Some US courts have used a controversial process called 'scientific jury selection' (or 'systematic jury selection') in which data from attitude surveys are used to try to predict the likely biases of potential jurors. A sample of people similar to the juror pool is questioned on issues believed to be pertinent to the trial, such as their authoritarian attitudes, religious beliefs, assumptions about criminal behaviour and so on (Seltzer, 2006). This is then used to produce a profile of the 'ideal' jury, allowing legal teams to screen out 'unsuitable' candidates during the *voir dire*. Both sides in the case may do this, so the *voir dire* can be lengthy. Seltzer (2006) identifies four major criticisms of systematic jury selection. First, it favours rich defendants, as only they have the money to pay for the process, so equality before the law is undermined. Second, it undermines the representativeness of juries because jurors will be dropped simply because they do not fit the legal team's profile. Third, it tends to remove the more intelligent jurors, resulting in a 'dumbing down' of the jury. Finally, the predictive power of the data used in scientific jury selection is typically rather low. Overall, there are too few consistent relationships between the attitudes of mock jurors and the outcomes of trials to justify the time and effort involved in systematic jury selection.

Jury deliberation

Once both prosecution and defence have presented their case to the jury, deliberation can start. Before this happens, the judge sums up the case for the jury and may explain the range of verdicts they are allowed to reach and the key questions they need to decide on. The jurors are then sent to a private room to deliberate and are kept from outside influences (e.g. in most jurisdictions they must surrender their mobile phones). In England and Wales, juries are directed to reach a unanimous verdict. If this proves impossible, then the judge may allow a majority verdict of 11 to one or 10 to two. In the event that the jury is 'deadlocked' (the jury is split between 'guilty' and 'not guilty'), then the judge may discharge the jury and the case may be retried.

According to Hastie et al. (1983), jury deliberations go through three stages (see Table 8.1).

Because jury decisions are made as a group, they are subject to the effects of group dynamics. These include: normative influence, where those in the minority feel pressured to go along with the majority even if they do not agree; leadership, where one member of the group has additional influence over the group's direction; and group polarisation, where the collective decision of the group is more

TABLE 8.1 Stages in jury decision making (Hastie et al., 1983)

Stage	Characteristics
Orientation period	Relaxed and open discussion Set agenda Raise questions and explore facts Different opinions arise
Open confrontation	Fierce debate Focus on detail Explore different interpretations Pressure on minority to conform Support for group decision established
Reconciliation	Attempts to smooth over conflicts Tension released through humour

extreme than that which the individuals would have arrived at alone. Because deliberation is private, it has not been possible to study these processes directly (in the UK, it is illegal to enquire about what happens in the jury room) but there is no compelling reason to believe that juries are much different from groups that have been studied in other contexts. According to Bornstein and Greene (2011), about 90% of the time the majority verdict of individual jurors before deliberation is the same as the jury's group verdict after deliberation. This suggests that social processes within the jury have some impact on the eventual verdict, but not an enormous amount. There are also some indications that, where minority jurors change their decision to the majority verdict, this is usually because they become convinced during discussion that the majority is correct (Salerno & Diamond, 2010), which would suggest that informational influence is more important than normative influence.

Research using mock juries has shed some light on the processes of jury decision making. Hastie et al. (1983) observed two distinct approaches to reaching a verdict:

- Verdict driven. The jury takes an early vote on the guilt or otherwise of the defendant and discusses which of the verdict options open to them is most acceptable to the jurors. They vote frequently as different options are discussed.

- Evidence driven. The jury focuses on evaluating the evidence and attempting to reach a consensus about the truth from the conflicting facts. They vote on the verdict relatively little.

Hastie et al. found that each approach was used about one-third of the time; in the remaining third no clear strategy was discernible. Evidence-driven juries deliberated for longer, spent more time discussing the legal guidance they were given and reached more of a consensus on the evidence. Subsequent research has shown that an evidence-driven approach is more likely when a unanimous verdict is required (Bornstein & Greene, 2011).

Influences on jury decisions

In principle, the outcome of a trial should be decided by the evidential factors: the jury's assessment of the evidence presented in court and the legal guidance given by the trial judge. However, the outcome of a criminal trial may also be influenced by extralegal factors. These include the persuasion skills of the trial lawyers, jurors' beliefs about the types of evidence presented, publicity surrounding the trial and the characteristics of the defendant.

Persuasion by trial lawyers

In an adversarial system, the prosecution and defence compete to establish their version of events as the true one. Consequently, alongside knowledge of the law, persuasion is an important capacity for a lawyer to have (Walker, 1980). Relatively little research has directly examined the effectiveness of courtroom advocacy but a well-developed research literature exists on persuasion and attitude change. Argument-based persuasion is usually conceptualised as a cognitive process. In order for an individual to adopt the arguer's point of view she must pay attention to the argument, comprehend it and accept it (Jonas et al., 1995). Ideally, every jury would consist solely of attentive individuals with the intelligence and knowledge to understand the case. However, jurors, being a representative sample of the general public, vary widely in these capacities. The first task of an effective lawyer is therefore to secure the jurors' attention and present the case to them in ways that they are likely to understand.

The Yale Model

Assuming that these conditions are met, the 'Yale Model' of persuasive communication (Hovland & Janis, 1959) describes a number of factors that affect the persuasiveness of an argument. These include the source, the message, the recipient and the situation in which persuasion occurs. Kapardis (2002) suggests that attempts to persuade a jury (or judge or magistrate) are more likely to succeed when the source:

- Is perceived as objective and knowledgeable.
- Appears to support a position against their own interests.
- Is familiar or similar to the recipients in background and attitudes.
- Is perceived as likeable and physically attractive.

Attitude change research has suggested that the message itself is more likely to persuade if it is not structured as an attempt to influence the target (Walster & Festinger, 1962) although it is difficult to see how a trial lawyer could avoid this, given her role in proceedings. Perhaps more usefully, arguments are more persuasive if the source acknowledges both sides of the argument and admits to the weaknesses in her position while remaining confident of her own case. Admitting to weaknesses (sometimes termed 'stealing thunder') serves to inoculate the recipients against counter-arguments raised by the opposing side (Dolnik et al., 2003).

Systematic versus heuristic processing

McAuliff et al. (2011) distinguish between two ways in which jurors process the arguments a lawyer presents in court. When jurors process arguments systematically, they analyse information in a comprehensive and effortful way, thinking in depth and carefully assessing the validity of the argument. When they process arguments heuristically, they rely on 'rules of thumb' when making their judgements. Such rules might include 'experts are usually right' or 'the majority opinion is usually the correct one'. With heuristic processing, the content or logic of the argument is not processed very deeply. McAuliff et al. suggest that, when their case is strong, lawyers should prompt the jurors to process their argument systematically. They can do this by selecting jurors likely to be systematic processors, by ensuring that witness evidence (especially from experts) is comprehensible by all the jurors and even by testing out arguments on mock juries to check whether the real jury is likely to adopt systematic processing in response. Systematic processing is preferred here because it tends to produce more stable attitude change and it is important that the persuasion of the jury lasts until they start deliberating their verdict, which may be days or weeks later. However, if the case is weak, then systematic processing should be discouraged as it means the jurors are more likely to identify flaws in the argument and are therefore less likely to be persuaded. One way to encourage heuristic processing is to present the case in a difficult and confusing way. This increases the cognitive load on the jurors, who adopt heuristic processing in response.

Storytelling in court

Some research has focused on how lawyers structure their presentation of cases. Legal professionals often assume that jury decisions are based on an assessment of the probability of each event presented in evidence (Yovel & Mertz, 2004). However, Pennington and Hastie (1990) have found instead that, as they form their decision about the case, jurors summarise the case around what they take to be the pivotal facts and fit these into a story that makes sense to them. Different jurors may tell different stories about the same facts. One may decide that the defendant in a murder trial was frightened by an altercation with the victim, another that the defendant was angered. The juror chooses a verdict that matches the story he has constructed about the case. This could mean the difference between guilty of murder, guilty of manslaughter or even not guilty on grounds of self-defence, depending on the story. This implies that lawyers should present their arguments to capitalise on the jurors' stock of culturally acquired narratives. Pennington and Hastie (1988) conducted mock trial studies in which juries were presented with cases organised in either 'witness order', where the evidence was sequenced in terms of which evidence seemed the most compelling, or 'story order', where the evidence was organised to present a coherent narrative of events. When both prosecution and defence used the same order, the jury convicted the defendant around 60% of the time. However, when the prosecution used story order and the defence used witness order, the conviction rate rose to 78% whereas when the defence used story order and the prosecution witness order, the conviction rate fell to only 31%. It appears, therefore, that lawyers should lead the jurors to adopt compelling narratives of the case that support their position. It also seems that the side that 'gets there first' in telling the story has a distinct advantage. Once a juror has adopted one particular story he tends to evaluative each new piece of evidence in terms of how well it fits his preferred narrative, assigning more weight to information that is consistent (a confirmation bias). Consequently, a relatively insignificant fact entered into evidence early on may have a disproportionate effect on the case if it prompts the juror to adopt the right kind of story (Kahan, 2015).

Courtroom evidence

In reaching their verdict, jurors are expected to assess each piece of evidence, weighing up its credibility and importance to the case as a whole. It has been suggested that jurors are swayed more by some types of evidence than others.

A confession by the defendant is probably the most influential piece of evidence the prosecution can present to a jury (McCormick, 1972). Kassin and Neumann (1997) presented mock juries in a murder trial with different forms of evidence including a confession, eyewitness identification and negative character witness. The confession produced the highest conviction rate. However, it is recognised by legal authorities that confessions are problematic and so most legal systems require that they are corroborated by other evidence (Kassin & Gudjonsson, 2004). While it is fair to say that, in the majority of cases, the defendant is guilty of the act to which they have confessed, there is a significant number of cases in which the confession is false (see Chapter 6). Nonetheless, jurors tend to discount evidence that suggests a confession is false. Bornstein and Greene (2017) give the example of Chuck Erickson, who was convicted of murder on the basis of a coerced-internalised false confession. The jury convicted Erickson despite the fact that none of the forensic evidence recovered from the murder scene matched him and despite having seen videotape of the interrogation in which police investigators fed him key details about the murder. Miscarriages of justice, such as that of the Birmingham Six, show that Erickson's case is not an isolated one. Fundamentally, jurors do not understand why a defendant would admit to a crime she did not commit, as they lack an insight into the types of social and psychological process that might induce her to do so. Even when a confession shows evidence of being coerced and when a judge instructs the jury that it should be discounted, it still increases the jury's tendency to convict the defendant (Kassin & Sukel, 1997).

Research has shown that eyewitness evidence, including descriptions of events and identification of suspects, can be unreliable (see Chapter 7). However, jurors typically take a 'common sense' view of eyewitness testimony, believing it to be an accurate record of events and not appreciating the factors that can make it unreliable. According to Bornstein and Greene (2017), part of the problem is that the way witnesses are prepared before trial makes them very confident and jurors assume that confidence is strongly related to accurately. Penrod and Cutler (1987) found that witnesses who spoke clearly and without hesitation were perceived as more convincing, competent, trustworthy, intelligent and truthful. Unfortunately, the relationship between confidence and accuracy is not strong (Leippe & Eisenstadt, 2007) and the consequence of this is a large number of wrongful convictions made on the basis of mistaken eyewitness testimony.

The use of expert witnesses presenting forensic evidence has grown substantially in recent years. Some have suggested that the unrealistic portrayal of forensic investigators on the TV and in films has influenced the beliefs of jurors about such evidence. Jurors may expect that forensic evidence will always be presented, even though this might be impractical or the case may not require it. On the one hand, jurors might acquit guilty defendants because their expectation of forensic evidence was not met. On the other hand, valid defence arguments about the limitations of forensic evidence may be ignored because jurors assume it is infallible (Cooley & Turvey, 2014). Jurors do seem to place a high degree of trust in forensic evidence. Lieberman et al. (2008) asked people to rate the accuracy of nine different forms of evidence. DNA evidence was rated as the most accurate, with confessions and eyewitness testimony rated least. In line with the Yale Model, expert witnesses are largely perceived as high-credibility sources of information, especially if they are also confident when they testify (Brodsky et al., 2010). However, it is a mistake to assume that jurors automatically accept and overvalue expert testimony. Statistical evidence, for example, is often given less weight than it deserves (Martire et al., 2013). Bornstein and Greene (2017) conclude that jurors generally assume that an expert witness is credible, a rational view given their status as experts. However, they do think critically and where they perceive that the expert is biased or when they cannot understand the evidence, they tend to discount the testimony. Consequently, anxiety about the 'CSI effect' is probably unwarranted.

Apply your learning

Prianca Patel, a fashion model, and Nigel Bentley, a businessman, are both charged with separate offences of financial fraud. Each is to be tried by jury in different courts in London. All other things being equal, do you believe that one is more likely than the other to be found guilty? Make a note of your views and justifications, then compare your ideas with what research into jury decisions has found.

Pretrial publicity

When jurors deliberate their verdict, they are instructed to confine themselves to the evidence presented to the court and to put aside any other knowledge of the case. Unfortunately, this does not seem to be possible. In a high-profile case, there may have been considerable media coverage before the trial, particularly in the US, where there are fewer legal restrictions on what the media may report than in the

UK. What the jurors learn from newspapers and television may affect their interpretation of the courtroom evidence. Because media coverage is likely to favour one side of the case, this has the potential to bias the jury's decision making. In an early study by Padawer-Singer and Barton (1975), mock jurors were played tapes of a criminal trial and asked to reach a verdict. Prior to this, one group of participants was given newspaper cuttings about the defendant's criminal record and confession, while another group read newspaper stories that omitted these details. Participants exposed to negative pretrial publicity convicted the defendant 78% of the time, compared with only 55% of the time for the control group. A meta-analysis by Steblay et al. (1999) shows that this finding is reliable. Exposure to negative pretrial publicity increases the probability of a guilty verdict, especially in murder, sexual and drug cases. The effect is cumulative, so more exposure is associated with more guilty verdicts and the strength of the effect increases with time between exposure to pretrial publicity and the trial. However, the overall influence of pretrial publicity is relatively small. Steblay et al. suggest, following Pennington and Hastie (1990), that pretrial publicity influences the story that jurors tell themselves about the case, feeding into an overall belief framework about the defendant's innocence or guilt.

Subsequent research has suggested that pretrial publicity need not be specific to the case being tried to have an effect. Kovera (2002) exposed participants to a television news programme about a rape case. Different groups saw either a version biased in favour of the defence or one biased towards the prosecution. A control group saw no news story. The participants were then given a different rape case and asked about the evidence they would require before returning a guilty verdict. Compared with the pro-prosecution and control participants, those who had viewed the pro-defence news story reported needing more corroborating evidence before they would find the defendant guilty. Kovera's study is unusual in also showing that pretrial publicity can work in favour of the defence. Interestingly, exposure to the pro-prosecution version of the news story had no effect. Kovera suggests that, since the TV news predominantly report rape trials in a prosecution-oriented way, the control participants had already been exposed to pro-prosecution media via their usual media consumption, which eliminated the difference between the pro-prosecution and control conditions in the study.

Daftary-Kapur et al. (2010) consider a number of strategies for reducing the biasing effects of pretrial publicity including delaying the trial, screening potential jurors and admonishing the jury to disregard negative publicity. None of these is likely to be effective. Steblay et al. found that the effect of negative pretrial publicity increases with time, so delaying the trial may make matters worse. They also found that asking jurors to form a verdict before the case – as may happen during *voir dire* – may backfire, increasing the impact of pretrial publicity. Admonitions to the jurors apparently have little impact in reducing bias (Sue et al., 1974), although changing the trial venue can be a useful measure as surveys have found that, except in very high-profile cases, knowledge of pretrial publicity is typically confined to one community (Nietzel & Dillehay, 1983).

Defendant characteristics

In an ideal world, juries would be made up of unbiased and unprejudiced people. However, juries represent the general public and people hold stereotypes and prejudices about the people around them. This creates the potential for jury verdicts to be affected by irrelevant aspects of the defendant such as their physical attractiveness, gender or ethnicity.

Attractiveness

In general, physically attractive defendants are treated more leniently than their unattractive counterparts. This is principally due to the 'halo effect', whereby people with one positive attribute are assumed to have other positive attributes, so people who are physically attractive are also assumed to be more successful, happier, more socially competent, intelligent and so on (Dion et al., 1972). In a jury trial, this can give rise to the 'attractiveness-leniency effect' whereby jurors' decisions about guilt or innocence are affected by the stereotypes they hold about attractive and unattractive people. Castellow et al. (1990) asked mock jurors to judge a case in which a 23-year-old woman accused her male employer of sexual harassment. It was alleged that he had made sexual remarks, attempted to kiss and inappropriately touch her and described to her sexual acts in which he wanted to engage with her. The participants were shown combinations of attractive and unattractive photographs of both the complainant (the woman) and the defendant (her employer). With an unattractive complainant and an attractive defendant the jurors convicted 41% of the time. However, with an attractive complainant and unattractive defendant this rose to an 83% conviction rate. This shows that jurors' judgements about the motives and character of defendants are affected by physical appearance. A meta-analysis by Mazzella and Feingold (1994) examined 25 studies in which defendant attractiveness was a variable. Unattractive defendants were more likely to be found guilty. Other studies have confirmed that attractiveness is usually an advantage to the defendant except where jurors suspect that the defendant used their attractiveness to aid their crime.

Gender

Evidence for an effect of defendant gender on jury decisions is mixed. Ragatz and Russell (2010) gave participants a scenario in which someone had killed a partner in a 'crime of passion' and asked them to judge how guilty the defendant was and what the resultant sentence should be. Some participants were told the defendant was male, some female. The researchers also varied the reported sexual orientation of the defendant. They found that, compared with other defendants, heterosexual women were judged as less culpable and were more likely to be found guilty of manslaughter (a lesser crime) than murder. However, not all studies have found this. Cruse and Leigh (1987) gave mock jurors a case in which a defendant was alleged to have attacked a former partner with a knife. Some participants were told that 'Jack Bailey' had attacked 'Lucy Hill' whereas others were told that 'Lucy Hill' had attacked 'Jack Bailey'. When the defendant was male he was found guilty 43% of the time but when she was female this rose to 69%. The overall picture is that gender does not systematically affect jury decisions. Mazzella and Feingold's (1994) meta-analysis found no general effect of gender on judgements of guilt.

It is probable that the defendant's gender, the type of crime and the jurors' attitudes and beliefs about gender interact to influence the verdict. In Ragatz and Russell's study, heterosexual females benefitted from 'benevolent sexism' that inclined the jurors towards leniency. By contrast, Cruse and Leigh's participants' may have perceived the female defendant more negatively because her violent act violated gender role stereotypes ('double deviance'; see Chapter 12). This is supported by Wiest and Duffy (2013), who gathered data from media accounts of 81 cases of filicide (i.e. the killing of a child by a parent). Content analysis was used to code each case for a number of features such as the offender's marital status, whether they were the child's primary caregiver, their employment and their history of mental health problems. Male offenders were more likely to be found guilty of murder, whereas women were more likely to be found guilty of lesser crimes or to be found not guilty by reason of insanity, even though rates of mental illness were similar between the male and female offenders. The men also received harsher sentences than the women. However, Wiest and Duffy also found that the treatment of the female offenders depended on how closely they conformed to the 'traditional' gender role stereotype. Apart from illustrating the complexity of potential interactions between different factors in jury decisions, findings like this underline the importance of considering the attitudes and beliefs of the jury alongside the characteristics of the defendant.

Race/ethnicity

Many people harbour prejudiced attitudes against members of other ethnic groups. Because juries are a representative selection of community members it follows that prejudiced people end up on juries. This raises the question of whether members of minority ethnic groups are at a disadvantage when tried by a jury likely to consist mainly of members of the majority ethnicity. It is not difficult to find individual examples of prejudiced language and attitudes in English courtrooms (Daly & Pattenden, 2005), but it is more important to establish whether there is evidence of a systematic race/ethnicity bias among jurors. Some mock jury studies have found that white defendants are treated more leniently than black ones. Pfeifer and Ogloff (1991) found that white university students rated black defendants as significantly more likely to be guilty than white ones. This effect was more pronounced when the victim was also white but the difference disappeared when the participants were reminded that all elements of the crime needed to be proved beyond a reasonable doubt. These results suggest that jurors' racial biases may affect their verdicts but also that the legal instructions given by a judge before deliberation may prevent jurors from acting on their biases.

Meta-analyses of studies of jury decisions have reached different conclusions about the role of race/ethnicity in verdict and sentencing decisions. Mazzella and

Feingold (1994) analysed 29 studies looking at verdicts among both black and white jurors. There was no general effect of race on judgement of guilt. Mitchell et al. (2005) took a different approach, classifying defendants in terms of whether they were members of a juror's racial ingroup or outgroup, thereby allowing for bias by both white jurors against black defendants and black jurors against white defendants. Their meta-analysis of 34 studies showed that jurors were more likely to find members of other ethnic groups guilty than members of their own. As in Pfeifer and Ogloff's (1991) study, the level of bias was reduced when participants were reminded to consider all the evidence fully and when participants had to give a clear-cut verdict of guilty or not guilty, rather than indicating probability of guilt on a scale. Since these conditions more closely resemble what happens in a real trial it is likely that courtroom decisions are less affected by racial bias than mock jury studies but, given the consistency of the effect found by Mitchell et al. it is unlikely that trial procedures eliminate racial (or other biases) completely.

Death penalty decisions

In UK courts, the jury has no involvement in determining the sentence an offender receives once convicted. The sentence is decided by the trial judge. The same is largely true for the US but one exception is in states that retain the death penalty. Following a guilty verdict, the jury may then be called on to decide whether an offender who fits the eligibility criteria is sentenced to execution. This takes place in a separate 'sentencing phase' of the trial. The jury hears arguments from the prosecution and defence regarding whether the death penalty should be imposed and then returns a collective decision following deliberation. The jury *must* agree unanimously. Jury selection in capital cases is a somewhat unusual process as the trial jury must be 'death qualified'. During the *voir dire*, any juror who states that he would never impose the death penalty under any circumstances is screened out (Haney, 2008).

The requirement for death qualification means that some groups (e.g. members of certain faiths) are systematically excluded from juries in capital cases. It has been asked whether death qualification biases the jurors' judgements of guilt or innocence. Death-qualified juries tend to contain a disproportionate number of white men and are more likely to contain people with a conservative religious outlook (Summers et al., 2010). By default, death-qualified juries contain more individuals with pro-death-penalty attitudes and this appears to make them more likely than other groups to convict the defendant (Bornstein & Greene, 2017). This is probably due to the tendency of people with pro-death-penalty attitudes to side with the prosecution. It may be exacerbated by the fact that the process of death qualification requires jurors to consider *before* they hear the case how they would act if they found the defendant guilty. This may serve to increase the jurors' belief in the defendant's guilt at the outset of the trial (Haney, 2008). It may legitimately be asked whether it is possible for the defendant in a capital case to receive a fair trial at all.

It was noted above that the ethnic background of a defendant influences the risk of being found guilty. This tendency carries over into death penalty decisions. Mock jury studies have found a tendency for black defendants to be given the death sentence more frequently than white (Lynch & Haney, 2009), although the race of the *victim* is more of an influence than the race of the defendant. Analysis of actual cases indicates that death sentences are imposed more often when the victim is white than when black, particularly when the defendant is black and the victim white. This reflects a tendency to overlook mitigating circumstances and identify aggravating factors in the cases of black defendants (Baldus et al., 1998). The unrepresentative nature of death-qualified juries seems to contribute to racial bias in imposition of the death sentence, since the greater the proportion of white members on the jury, the greater the probability of a death sentence, especially if the defendant is black. However, at the time of writing, the Supreme Court of the United States retained the view that racial bias in death penalty decisions is not a cause for concern (Bornstein & Greene, 2017).

Issues arising from mock jury research

The majority of the studies used to understand jury decisions have used the 'mock jury' paradigm, in which research participants are recruited, presented with information about a hypothetical trial (often in the form of a written case summary) and asked to make judgements about the culpability of the defendant. The researchers manipulate one or more variables (e.g. the ethnic group or gender of the defendant or victim or some salient feature of the evidence) in order to estimate their impact on the participants' judgements. These studies are carried out on the assumption that the research situation sufficiently resembles that of a real trial to generalise from one to the other. This needs critical examination, as mock jury studies differ from real jury trials in a number of ways. Real jurors hear the case from lawyers, witnesses and judges whereas mock jurors may just read a summary or watch a video. Real juries deliberate their decisions before reaching a verdict whereas mock jurors frequently give individual decisions. Real jurors are also aware that their decisions can have enormous consequences for defendants, whereas little is at stake in a mock jury study. Some researchers have assessed the impact of differences like these in order to evaluate the validity of mock jury studies.

Wiener et al. (2011) argue that, on the one hand, mock jury studies have many features that increase researchers' ability to draw valid conclusions from their data (internal validity) including random assignment of participants to conditions, control of potential confounding variables, standardisation of procedures and instructions to participants and sophisticated statistical analyses. On the other hand, such studies generally lack external validity due to their reliance of samples of students. They also lack construct validity. Features like the use of case summaries, multiple assessments of the verdict and no opportunity to deliberate are unrepresentative of real jury decision making. Wiener et al., suggest that the emphasis on internal

validity means that researchers can be less confident that they have learned anything meaningful about actual jury behaviour. The courtroom is a complex system
in which juror characteristics, legal counsel, judges, evidential factors, the nature of
the crime and victim and so on all interact and attempts to break it down into independent variables whose effect can be isolated from all the others arguably results
in studies that mislead us about the behaviour of actual juries.

Against this view, a meta-analysis of mock jury studies by Bornstein et al. (2017)
looked for evidence that student samples reached verdicts differently from more
diverse samples. Analysing 40 studies using criminal cases they concluded that
using students did not affect verdicts and ratings of culpability. The only significant
effect was that students gave slightly harsher sentences. This would suggest that the
external validity of mock jury findings is sound. In relation to the construct validity
of mock jury studies, Devine et al. (2016) collected self-report data from judges,
lawyers and jurors in 114 criminal trials to identify the factors that influenced the
verdict. They found that the strongest influence on the verdict was the strength of
the prosecution case. The effect of extra-evidential factors on verdicts was relatively
small. Taken together, variables such as pretrial publicity, defendant attractiveness
and ethnicity and jury diversity explained some of the variation in verdicts but few
of them had a significant influence on their own. The exception to this was jury
diversity: juries that contained more women and more non-white people were less
likely to convict the defendant. This suggests that mock jury studies tend to exaggerate the effect of extra-evidential factors due to a lack of construct validity.

Chapter summary

Criminal trials take place under either an adversarial system, where prosecution
and defence compete to establish their version of events and the judge plays a passive role, or an inquisitorial system, in which the judge plays a more active role.
Broadly, people are more satisfied with the adversarial system in the UK and US,
although there are exceptions. Serious criminal cases in the UK and US are decided
by a jury, whose task it is to weigh up the evidence presented in court and decide
whether the defendant is guilty or not. Juries usually have 12 members. Smaller
juries tend to favour the prosecution and spend less time considering their verdict.
Trial lawyers have the right to exclude potential jurors from a trial but this right
is used much more often in the US than the UK and there are questions about the
effect this may have on the fairness of the justice system. Juries reach their verdicts
as a group and it is possible that group dynamics affect the verdict although the
deliberation process has only a limited impact on the jurors' individual decisions.
Jurors can be affected by the strategies used by trial lawyers. These include presenting themselves and the case in line with the Yale Model of persuasion and constructing cases in ways that allow jurors to tell compelling stories about the motives
and actions of the defendant. Some forms of evidence are more influential on juries
than others, particularly confessions and eyewitness accounts but, surprisingly,

jurors tend to give less weight to forensic evidence than it deserves. Mock jury studies suggest that jury verdicts are also influenced by pretrial publicity and by the characteristics of the defendant. Pretrial publicity is usually negative about the defendant and therefore tends to increase the probability of a conviction. Physically attractive defendants are less likely to be found guilty than unattractive ones, except when the jurors suspect that their attractiveness helped them commit the crime. Defendant gender does not appear to have a clear effect on juror decisions. Race/ethnicity of the defendant, however, does seem to influence verdicts, with jurors tending to treat defendants more leniently when they come from the juror's own ethnic group. This bias is also present in death sentence decisions made by juries and may be exacerbated by the process of selecting 'death-qualified' jurors. Finally, it should be noted that the majority of research findings in this area have been based on mock jury studies. While these typically have good internal validity, there are concerns about how well the results generalise to jury decisions in real criminal trials.

Further reading

Bornstein, B. H., & Greene, E. (2017). *The Jury Under Fire: Myth, Controversy, and Reform*. Oxford: Oxford University Press. A comprehensive, up-to-date and fascinating analysis of research into the jury trial process.

Judicial responses to offending

This chapter discusses some of the ways in which the judicial system may deal with offenders. Imprisonment is the most obvious way offenders are punished and the chapter starts with an examination of the purposes of imprisonment, its impact on the individual and its effect on reoffending. There is then a discussion of some of the main alternatives to imprisonment including fines, probation, community punishments and restorative justice. Psychological interventions for offending, which may be offered alongside judicial punishments, are discussed in Chapter 10.

Apply your learning

Marco has admitted a number of credit card fraud offences. The judge is considering possible sentences of a prison sentence, a suspended prison sentence or a period of probation. List the possible arguments for and against each and decide which is the most appropriate sentence. After reading this chapter, review your decision and reasoning in the light of what you have learned. Would you still recommend the same sentence?

Imprisonment

When an offender is imprisoned, he is deprived of his liberty and confined in an institution maintained for that specific purpose. In the UK, male prisoners are classified as category A to D, with 'category A' denoting those who pose the greatest risk of escape and harm to others. This determines the type of prison to which an offender is sent. The main distinction is between closed and open prisons. Inmates of open prisons, who must be in category D, are permitted to leave the prison grounds in order, for example, to work in the community. The purpose of open prisons is to reintegrate offenders into law-abiding society.

About 8% of the UK prison population are 'on remand'. They have not been convicted of an offence but are awaiting trial and are considered a sufficient risk for them not to be allowed to remain at liberty. However, the majority of prisoners have been convicted of one or more offences and have been sentenced to imprisonment for a specified period of time. The UK prison population has been growing steadily since 1940 and, at the end of 2017, was around 94,000. This partly reflects growth in the population of the country as a whole, but the proportion of the population in prison has also increased. In England and Wales in 1901 there were 86 male prisoners for every 100,000 people in the population. By 2016 this had increased to 182 per 100,000. The majority of prisoners are men. In 2016 the rate of female imprisonment was 16 per 100,000 population. About 75% of UK prisoners in 2016 were serving a sentence of more than four years. The most common offences for which people were imprisoned were violence against the person, sexual offences, robbery, theft and drug offences (Allen & Watson, 2017).

The UK's incarceration rate is high compared with other Western European countries. In broader comparisons, the UK has a moderate rate of imprisonment, substantially higher than Finland (54.4 per 100,000), although much lower than Lithuania (295.6 per 100,000). The US has seen an explosion in imprisonment since the 1970s as the US has pursued a programme of mass incarceration. Until the 1970s the US rate of imprisonment was around 110 per 100,000 (Wood, 2009). Over the following decades it rose sharply to peak at 755 per 100,000 in 2008 and in 2015 stood at 666 per 100,000 population (World Prison Brief, 2017). There are several reasons for this rise including a shift in social attitudes away from rehabilitation and towards retribution and a substantial rise in the number of people imprisoned for non-violent drug offences under the aegis of the US government's 'war on drugs'.

Does prison work?

Imprisonment can serve a number of purposes including:

- Retribution. Making the offender 'pay' for their offence by subjecting him to an aversive environment.
- Incapacitation. Preventing the offender from committing further offences by isolating him from potential victims.
- Deterrence. Making potential offenders 'think twice' about committing an offence because of the potential consequences.
- Reform. Bringing about a change in the offender so that, on release, he does not commit further offences.

Different people emphasise different functions of imprisonment, often depending on their political outlook. Conservative commentators tend to emphasise retribution, while more liberal ones stress the potential of imprisonment to reform the offender. The question of whether 'prison works' is not easy to answer because it depends heavily on what is meant by 'working'. Those whose priority is retribution may judge prison in terms of how unpleasant it makes life for prisoners whereas those who are more concerned with reform are likely to focus on the rate of reoffending.

Retribution

The rationale for retribution is that an offender has inflicted pain on other individuals or on the wider society and that it is therefore necessary to inflict pain on them in return. As a form of retribution, prison is unpleasant for those who experience it. Sykes (1958) identifies five 'pains of imprisonment':

- Loss of liberty. The inmate is confined in the prison, removed from contact with friends and family, loses civil status and is rejected by the community.

- Deprivation of goods and services. The inmate loses her material possessions and may no longer make choices about most things in her life.

- Frustration of sexual desire. The inmate is deprived of her intimate relationships.

- Deprivation of autonomy. The inmate must submit to the prison regime and must work, associate with others and engage in other activities at the time specified by the regime.

- Deprivation of security. The inmate is surrounded by unpredictable and potentially violent others, resulting in fear and anxiety.

These pains are common to prisons everywhere but prison regimes vary considerably between different countries and states. In Finland, even the highest security closed prisons have a relatively non-oppressive regime with many opportunities for work and study. At the other extreme are the 'supermax' prisons operating in the US, in which inmates are kept in conditions of near complete isolation and sensory deprivation, confined to small concrete and steel cells for 23 hours a day and communication with others, including staff and other inmates, is forbidden (Kurki & Morris, 2001). In the UK, the popular press frequently expounds the view that prisons are 'too soft'. Given that two men may be sharing an 8x10 feet cell without 24-hour access to toilets, the view that British prisons are akin to 'holiday camps' is a misrepresentation (Jewkes, 2011). Some have nonetheless argued that prisons should be made more unpleasant ('penal harm'). This opens up a debate about human rights and humane treatment that will not be pursued here. However, making prisons harsher may undermine their capacity to reform offenders. Drago et al. (2011) used data from the Italian prison system to create a measure of prison harshness derived from the degree of overcrowding, the death rate of prisoners and the level of support and assistance available to inmates. They found that harsher prison conditions were associated with an increase in criminal behaviour after release.

Incapacitation

In terms of incapacitation, prison works to the extent that the 94,000 people currently imprisoned in the UK are therefore not out in the community committing further offences. It is difficult to quantify how much crime is thereby avoided. Spelman (2000) estimates that incapacitation reduces serious offending by between 10 and 20 offences per prisoner per year, although Lofstrom and Raphael (2016) point out that studies like these rely on data gathered in the 1970s, when the US incarceration rate was much lower. Research in Italy and the Netherlands has found a similar effect but there is a diminishing return. As the imprisonment rate rises there is a reduction in offending but once it exceeds around 200 per 100,000 further reductions are minimal (Buonanno & Raphael, 2013). Lofstrom and Raphael (2016) examined the effect of reducing the prison population in California as the result of sentencing reforms. They found that imprisoning fewer people had no effect on violent crime but was associated with a modest increase in property crimes. Cullen et al. (2011) acknowledge the existence of an incapacitation effect but point out that analyses like these 'rig the data' (p.S51) as they compare the effect of imprisonment with the effect of doing nothing, whereas a fair analysis of the effects of imprisonment would compare it with other, non-custodial sentences.

Deterrence

Claims about the deterrent effect of prison rest on the idea that there are individuals who *would* commit crimes but do not because the threat of imprisonment is sufficiently great. A distinction is made between specific and general deterrence. Specific deterrence refers to the effect on the individual who has been punished and is discussed below in relation to reform. General deterrence refers to the effect prison (or another punishment) has on people in general. General deterrence is allied to social learning theory (see Chapter 5) since those who observe a model may learn from both the model's actions and their consequences. Potential offenders who learn of others who have been sent to prison experience their punishment vicariously. This increases their own expectancy of punishment should they commit the same type of crime, so they become less likely to imitate criminal acts.

In practice it is very difficult to obtain clear-cut evidence for a general deterrence effect. Ross (1973) studied the effect of increasing the severity of punishment for drink driving offences in the UK. A deterrence effect was found, as there was initially a reduction in alcohol-related driving fatalities. Unfortunately, the effect disappeared quickly. Sherman (1990) suggests that people who are motivated to offend initially reduce their criminal activities in response to the increased threat of punishment but learn (through trial and error and the reports of others) that they are unlikely to be caught and so soon feel able to resume acting on their criminal impulses.

Some researchers have compared offending rates between areas and time periods with different law and order policies to see if changes in the severity of punishment (e.g. increased prison terms) correlate with differences in the crime rate. Donohue (2009) found a negative correlation between imprisonment rates and crime rates, so as the prison population grows, the crime rate decreases. While this is consistent with a general deterrence effect, it is equally consistent with an incapacitation effect, as higher imprisonment rates remove more offenders from circulation. Nagin (2013) argues that, where deterrence effects are found, it is the *certainty* of getting caught that deters potential offenders, not the *severity* of the punishment that follows. Consequently, it is better for policymakers to focus on policing than imprisonment as policing is more visible to potential offenders and consequently increases their perceived risk of getting caught.

Reform

If prison is evaluated in terms of its potential to reform the offender, then the key measure of its effectiveness is the recidivism rate. Recidivism is a return to offending following punishment. The claim that prison has a specific deterrent effect can be understood in relation to two general theories of offending. Rational choice theory (see Chapter 4) suggests that offending is the outcome of a rational process where the individual weighs up the costs and benefits of offending and acts accordingly. The threat of imprisonment is a cost of offending and is weighed against the potential gains, such as money and enhanced status. Imprisonment can be understood in terms of behaviourist learning theory. Behaviourism holds that behaviour is shaped and maintained by its consequences. If a behaviour is reliably followed by a punishment, it becomes less likely in future. The pains of imprisonment should, in principle, act to either increase the perceived costs of offending (RCT) or to weaken offending actions (behaviourism).

If so, we might expect that those who have been imprisoned would be less likely to reoffend than those who have had an alternative, non-custodial sentence. The evidence suggests that imprisonment does not have a specific deterrent effect. In the UK, about 59% of those released from prison reoffend within two years (Fazel & Wolf, 2015). This figure has been stable for some time and is similar to that recorded in many other countries. Bottomley and Pease (1986) found a UK reconviction rate of around 60% and some estimates suggest that reoffending among young male offenders in the UK is as high as 82% (Home Office, 1994). Figures from the US paint a similar picture. Langan and Levin (2002) traced US prisoners released in 1994. They found that, within three years of release, 67.5% were rearrested, 46.9% were reconvicted and 25.4% were sentenced to another prison term.

These data do not obviously suggest that prison is an effective deterrent against further offending. However, even if the recidivism rate is high it might still be that prison is a more effective deterrent than other punishments (e.g. fines, probation or community punishment). How does prison compare with the alternatives? Gendreau et al. (2000) reviewed studies comparing prison with community-based punishments and concluded that prison resulted in a 7% increase in recidivism. Smith et al. (2002) reported that the recidivism rate was 8% higher in imprisoned offenders. Villettaz et al. (2006) reviewed 27 studies comparing imprisonment and community-based sanctions. Prison emerged as superior in only two studies. Fourteen studies found no difference between prison and non-custodial sentences and 11 found that non-custodial sentences had a lower recidivism rate. These findings are consistent with survey data indicating that some offenders find community-based punishments more aversive than short-term imprisonment because of the degree of supervision and requirement for change involved (Moore et al., 2008).

It has been claimed that the experience of imprisonment makes people more likely to commit subsequent offences. Social learning theory (Chapter 5) suggests that criminal behaviour results from the learning of pro-crime attitudes and behaviours from others. If so, the wisdom of confining a novice offender with hundreds or thousands of experienced criminals might be questioned. It may also be that the labelling that occurs as a consequence of imprisonment may militate against reform. The 'colleges of crime' view has had mixed support. Walker et al. (1981) compared first offenders given a variety of sentences and found that those given prison or a fine were less likely to be reconvicted than those given probation or a suspended sentence, suggesting that imprisonment does not increase subsequent criminality. However, offenders are not a homogeneous group and neither are prisons, so it may still be that some types of prison increase criminality in some types of offender (Mears et al., 2015). Cid (2009) compared recidivism rates in 241 offenders sentenced to prison and 304 given a suspended sentence (i.e. they were released under the threat of imprisonment if they committed any further offences during a two-year period). The offenders were followed up for eight years. Cid found that imprisoned offenders were significantly more likely to be re-imprisoned than those given suspended sentences. He suggests that this is due to the effect of imprisonment on offenders' self-definitions, in line with labelling theory (see Chapter 5).

A limitation of this study is that the offenders were assigned their sentences by judges, whose sentencing decisions might well reflect their knowledge of reoffending risk in each case. The 'prison' group might always have been at a higher risk of reoffending than the 'suspended sentence' group (a selection bias). Ideally, in a study of this sort, offenders should be randomly assigned to different punishments as this ensures that other risk factors average out between the groups and the only systematic difference between them is the type of sentence they are given. For obvious reasons, this rarely happens in the disposal of real criminal cases. However, Gaes and Camp (2009) report a study in which inmates in California who were designated 'Level III' (medium-high risk) were randomly assigned to either Level III or Level I (lower security) prisons. They found that Level III inmates who served their sentence in a Level III prison had a 31% higher risk of returning to prison than those who had been in a Level I prison. Since all the inmates had the same risk rating, this suggests that the environment of the higher security prison increased the tendency to reoffend. Gaes and Camp suggest that a higher security prison exposes the offender to a harsher environment where violence is valued by the peer group, resulting in social learning of pro-violence attitudes.

Why does prison not reform offenders?

The failure of imprisonment to reform offenders can be understood in a number of ways. Behaviourist theory holds that, in order to be effective, punishment needs to be probable, prompt and aversive. That is, the punishment must (1) reliably follow the target behaviour; (2) occur soon after the target behaviour; and (3) be unpleasant. Imprisonment does not fulfil these requirements. First, an offender may commit many offences but be punished only for one or a few of them, so imprisonment is not a reliable consequence of offending. Second, a long time may separate the offence from the imprisonment as the offender must first be caught, then charged and tried, so in many cases punishment is not prompt. Third, prison is already unpleasant and making it more so does not make it any more effective (see above). It should also be considered that research from the biological tradition has shown that a significant proportion of offenders are impaired in their capacity to learn from punishment (see Chapters 3 and 4). In addition, an offender may acquire benefits from his crimes (e.g. cash, goods, enhanced social status) so the reinforcements available for offending in the short term can outweigh the longer term negative consequences. Cognitive factors may also be relevant, as the offender, rather than interpreting prison as a consequence of his crime, may instead interpret prison as a consequence of getting caught. What he learns is not that he should stop offending but that he should be more careful. An analysis based on rational choice theory would be very similar. In many cases, the potential offender reasons that although imprisonment is a severe consequence, it is also an unlikely one and therefore it does not outweigh the anticipated benefits of committing the crime.

Effects of imprisonment

Imprisonment inevitably affects those who experience it, especially if for the first time. The exact effects depend on the characteristics of the offender, the offence, the length of the sentence and the prison regime.

Some research reports significant psychological effects of long-term imprisonment including depression, apathy, emotional instability, changes in cognition and personality, and early onset dementia (Rasch, 1981). However, influential studies by Zamble and Porporino (1988) and Zamble (1992) found that, while prisoners on remand and early in their sentences show high levels of anxiety, hopelessness and depression, these effects decline with time. Zamble (1992) reports that, longitudinally, psychological symptoms decrease and there is an increase in prisoners' capacity for structured activity. Other longitudinal studies have reported mixed findings. Brinded et al. (1999) found that imprisonment resulted in increases in major depression and alcohol and drug abuse but Dettbarn (2012) found that mental health among long-term prisoners actually improved over time. She analysed data from psychiatric examinations of prisoners taken, on average, 14 years apart. At the first examination 69% of the inmates were diagnosable with psychological disorders but by the time of the second examination, this had reduced to 48.3%. Most of the reduction was in personality disorders. Many of these inmates had received psychotherapy while in prison (which is unlikely to be the case for many prisons) and the prevalence of psychological problems remained very high in comparison with the general population. It may also be that longitudinal studies of the effects of imprisonment depict them as more benign than they actually are because of selective attrition: those most negatively affected by imprisonment do not appear in the final data set because they have died (through illness, drug use and suicide) or been transferred to other prisons or hospitals (Liebling & Maruna, 2005).

Prisoners run a higher risk of suicide than members of the general population. Between 2007 and 2016 the number of self-inflicted deaths in British prisons rose steadily, reaching an all-time high of 119 people in 2016, meaning that the suicide risk in UK prisons is now around eight times that in the general population (Ministry of Justice, 2017b). Liebling (1992) identifies several risk factors for suicide in prison. Many of these are the same as those that exacerbate suicide risk in the general population: adverse life events, poor education, unemployment, drug and alcohol problems, and mental health problems. Prison-specific factors include overcrowding, which is also associated with poorer mental health and higher risk of drug problems. Suicide risk is highest among prisoners on remand or awaiting sentencing. Self-report data from prisoners who attempted suicide in prisons in England and Wales found that 84% had experienced anxiety and/or depression in the previous year, 57% had a personality disorder and 48% had problems with drug use. Inmates reported a variety of triggering events including transfer to another prison, loss of custody of children and bullying by other inmates (Liebling, 2007). The increased suicide risk of prisoners extends beyond their release. Pratt et al. (2006) found that the suicide risk in prisoners within one year of release was eight times that in the general population for men and around 36 times the general population risk for women. The greatest risk period is in the first 28 days after release. Pratt et al. suggest a number of contributing factors including drug use, exclusion from the community, lack of housing and poor access to mental health support services.

Liebling and Maruna (2005) argue that psychological research into the effects of imprisonment has used rather limited ways of measuring the harm that prison inflicts. They identify a number of areas that have been neglected until relatively recently including:

- Physical health. As a result of high levels of intravenous drug use, unprotected sex and tattooing, prisoners run an increased risk of diseases such as hepatitis B and C and HIV.

- Post-traumatic stress disorder (PTSD). Some groups of prisoners, including those who have been wrongly convicted and those who have witnessed violence while inside, show a pattern of symptoms and personality changes that include difficulties forming close relationships, anxiety, depression, anger and difficulty concentrating. Symptoms of PTSD may serve to make adjustment to both imprisonment and subsequent release very difficult.

- Effects on prisoners' families. The children of prisoners experience sudden separation from an attachment figure, which may have developmental consequences, especially since the imprisonment of a parent may also result in a deterioration of the material and social support available to the family.

Wood (2009) observes that the use of mass incarceration in the US has resulted in nearly 3% of children having had a parent in prison, rising to nearly 10% of BME children. Imprisonment puts a severe strain on spousal relationships, frequently resulting in the breakup of families and loss of contact with children. Even if the human cost is ignored, strong relationships with partner and children are reported to be a factor in avoiding recidivism, and good family networks increase the probability of employment on release (since many released inmates in the US are employed by family members), which also helps reduce recidivism. Beyond the family, there is some evidence that high levels of imprisonment disrupt communities. Imprisonment disproportionately removes individuals from poor, urban neighbourhoods with a high proportion of minorities. Up to a point, this reduces the local crime rate as offenders are incapacitated. However, as the number of people incarcerated climbs it becomes difficult for residents of the neighbourhood to maintain the informal mechanisms that preserve social organisation (see Chapter 5). Consequently, high rates of imprisonment may, ironically, contribute to an increased crime rate (Renauer et al., 2006).

Imprisonment: general considerations

Overall, there are relatively few arguments for imprisoning significant numbers of offenders. On the one hand, it does serve the functions of retribution and incapacitation. On the other hand, it is no more effective than non-custodial sentencing at reforming the offender and may sometimes increase recidivism. It is also potentially damaging to offenders, their families and communities. Alongside this, it is worth considering the financial costs involved in imprisoning large numbers. The UK government reports a cost per prisoner of around £35,000 a year for imprisonment (Ministry of Justice, 2017a). Since most alternatives are substantially cheaper, there is a strong economic argument against imprisoning offenders who pose a low risk to society. Marsh and Fox (2008) reviewed studies of imprisonment and non-custodial sentencing in relation to their cost to the UK government over the lifetime of an offender. They estimated that, compared with 'standard' prison (i.e. the offender is simply confined for the duration of her sentence), both prison with added elements (such as educational input, drug treatment and sex offender treatment) and community-based sentences (such as intense surveillance in the community) were significantly more effective at reducing recidivism. They found that alternatives to 'standard' imprisonment saved significant amounts of public money, between £19,000 and £88,000 per offender.

Non-custodial sentencing

Besides imprisonment, legal systems have a variety of other means of punishing and reforming offenders. In the UK and the US, the commonest forms of non-custodial sentence are fines, probation and community punishment, which are discussed below. In addition to these, courts in England and Wales may impose other sentences (Ashworth, 2010):

■ Absolute discharge. The offender is released with no conditions attached. This is only very rarely applied, typically for the most minor of offences.

■ Conditional discharge or 'bind over'. The offender is released on the condition that, should they commit another offence within a specified time period (up to three years), they will be sentenced for both that offence and the original one. It is used as a threat to maintain good behaviour.

- Compensation order. The offender is required to pay a specified sum of money to her victim(s) to recompense for her offence. This is different from a fine, which is paid to the authorities.

Fines

A fine is a sum of money paid to the authorities by an offender as restitution for her offence. The amount is set by the trial judge but must be within limits laid down by law. Caldwell (1965) suggests that fines have a number of advantages over other forms of punishment. First, the system is economical as it costs little to administer, since it does not require outlay on the maintenance of the offender (unlike prison or probation) and provides a source of revenue for the state, country or city. Second, fines do not stigmatise the offender or expose her to the adverse effects of imprisonment and can be adjusted to reflect her financial circumstances. Third, fines can be imposed in situations where other punishments are impossible, such as when a business rather than an individual has broken the law. Ashworth (2010) adds that, unlike other punishments, fines are reversible if it emerges that the individual was wrongfully convicted.

Evidence on the effectiveness of fines in reducing recidivism is mixed. Feldman (1993) states that, for first offenders, fines are more effective than imprisonment or probation in preventing reoffending and Walker et al. (1981) found they led to lower reoffending rates than probation or a suspended sentence. One problem with this evidence is selection bias. The courts decide which offenders get fined and which receive other sanctions and the two groups may differ in a number of ways. For example, a judge may be more likely to impose a fine on someone whose life circumstances are stable, has a job and a family, all of which would give them a lower risk of reoffending, so it is difficult to conclude that fines are responsible for the lower reconviction rates. Unfortunately, relatively few well-controlled studies of the comparative effectiveness of fines have been conducted (Weatherburn & Moffatt, 2011). Bouffard and Muftić (2007) compared recidivism rates in low-level offenders sentenced either to community service or given a fine. They found that the community service group were less likely to reoffend, even though they had more serious criminal histories. However, in relation to general deterrence, a review by Wagenaar et al. (2007) concluded that areas in which mandatory fines were introduced for drink driving offences had a greater reduction in fatal vehicle crashes than areas where mandatory prison terms were introduced.

Evidence aside, there are a number of arguments against the use of fines. First, the fine may be paid by the offender's family or friends, lessening its impact on the actual offender. Second, for many offences, such as prostitution and possession of drugs, fines are used in a routine way with no intention to reform the offender. Third, fines can come to be seen as an 'operating cost' of offending. For example, some companies whose activities pollute the environment have pursued a policy of paying fines for breaking environmental protection laws because this is cheaper than making the necessary changes to ensure that pollution does not take place.

Fourth, there are arguments about whether fines are a just punishment. A fine has a greater impact on a poorer person. This could be perceived as unjust, as poorer people are disproportionately punished. Judges can adjust the size of a fine (within limits) to reflect the financial circumstances of the offender but imposing bigger fines on richer offenders is also arguably unjust, because a judicial sanction should be based on the nature of the offence and the offender's degree of culpability, not her life circumstances. Finally, there are offences for which a fine is obviously inappropriate, such as any offence where there is a risk to the public if the offender is not incapacitated.

Probation and community sentences

When an offender is placed on probation he is released into the community on the condition that he submits to the supervision and guidance of a probation officer. Typically, the offender is under threat of imprisonment if he fails to comply with the probation order. Depending on the offence, a range of conditions might be specified. In England and Wales, probation orders are subsumed under the general category of 'community sentences'. A community sentence can require an offender to:

- Do unpaid work ('community service').
- Undertake specific activities (e.g. restorative justice; see below).
- Attend a rehabilitation programme.
- Refrain from specific prohibited activities.
- Obey a curfew that restricts their movements and times of activity.
- Stay out of specified places.
- Reside in a particular area.
- Receive treatment for mental health problems.
- Receive treatment for drug or alcohol problems.
- Submit to regular supervision by a probation officer.

A community sentence may be used as an alternative to imprisonment but probation and other conditions may also be imposed where an offender has been released from prison but is expected to complete a period of probation before being discharged completely.

Probation has a number of obvious advantages over imprisonment. As with fines, the offender remains in the community, meaning he is not stigmatised or exposed to the adverse effects of imprisonment. In addition, a community sentence does not disrupt the offender's employment or family ties, both of which help to protect against recidivism. Probation is also substantially cheaper than prison, costing around a tenth of the cost of imprisonment. For example, the UK Ministry of Justice (2011) calculated the annual cost of an intensive probation programme at between £4,000 and £7,000 per offender. At the time, the estimated annual cost of keeping an offender in prison was around £40,000.

Although the financial advantage is clear, the key question is whether community sentences are at least as effective as prison. Broadly, the answer seems to be yes. For example, Oldfield (1996) tracked the reoffending rate among 857 offenders sentenced to either imprisonment or to probation with a requirement to (1) attend a day centre or (2) attend a group work programme. Over a five-year period, 63% of the imprisoned offenders were reconvicted. For those on probation, the reconviction rate was 63% for the 'day centre' group but 41% for those given 'group work'. This shows that community sentences can be significantly more effective than prison but also that it depends on the content of the community sentence. Further support comes from Roshier (1995) who found two-year reoffending rates of 64% for imprisonment, 41% for probation and 37% for probation with a community service/unpaid work requirement. Wermink et al. (2010) compared short-term imprisonment with community service in a study of 4,246 Dutch offenders. Importantly, they matched the prison and community service offenders to control for the possibility that the imprisoned group had a higher general risk of recidivism. Over a five-year follow-up period, the average offender sentenced to imprisonment received 1.21 more convictions than the average offender given community service. That is, community service led to a 46.8% reduction in recidivism. Wermink et al. were unable to draw conclusions about why community service performed so much better than prison but they point out that, in the Netherlands, community service is performed in the offender's spare time and is not scheduled to interfere with their usual activities or social networks. This makes it unlikely that the effectiveness of community service is due to its aversive nature.

Not all research has supported the superiority of community sentences. Killias et al. (2010) compared 123 Swiss offenders randomly assigned to either community service or a short prison sentence (maximum 14 days). Over the following 11 years no significant differences were found in the recidivism rates of the two groups. Killias et al. suggest that imprisonment is less disruptive to employment and social relationships than is often assumed. This may be true for the extremely short prison sentences studied, but once a prison sentence exceeds a few weeks its detrimental effect may become more marked. It should also be noted that the small sample used by Killias et al. makes it hard to draw firm conclusions. By the same token, this study does have a significant strength in that the offenders were randomly assigned to the different punishments. This helps to rule out selection bias, whereby the offenders assigned to the community sentence were those with the lowest risk of recidivism. The danger of selection bias is highlighted by a large-scale review of studies comparing custodial and non-custodial sentences by Villettaz et al. (2015). They found, overall, that non-custodial sentences were associated with lower recidivism. However, the difference was more marked in the quasi-experimental studies than the true experiments. When offenders were randomly assigned to different punishments, the differences between prison and non-custodial sentences were not significant. Villetaz et al. identify a number of other limitations with the research evidence in this area: the follow-up periods are too short (usually two years); measures of recidivism are relatively poor (over-reliance on official statistics and under-use of offender self-reports); and the effects of different types of sentence on areas such as health, employment, and social and family relationships are rarely investigated. Overall, then, it is possible that the superiority of community sentences over imprisonment has been exaggerated by the methods chosen to investigate it. That said, even if community sentences are only as effective as imprisonment, the cost-effectiveness aspect of the community option is difficult to argue with.

Restorative justice

Restorative justice is a set of ideas and practices that represent an alternative to the 'punitive' model of justice that predominates in the Western world. In the punitive model, justice is served by taking retribution on the offender. In the restorative model, justice is served by healing the harm (to victims and the wider society) that the offence caused (Bazemore, 2009). Restorative justice takes many different forms, but the key elements are (1) that offenders, victims and other stakeholders in the offence voluntarily agree to participate; (2) that the offender must take responsibility for the harm he caused and be willing to discuss it honestly with victims and the community; and (3) that offender, victims and others meet face to face to agree on an appropriate way of repairing the harm (Llewellyn & Howse, 1998). The outcome of a restorative justice approach is typically that the offender is required to make amends for his offence. This could include apologising to the victim(s), unpaid work for the community or the victim, or entering into an agreement about future behaviour (Bazemore, 2009). Restorative justice is not necessarily an alternative to other judicial sanctions and could be employed at many points in the criminal justice system. It can be used instead of charging individuals and trying them in court but equally might be used with a convicted offender as part of a community sentence or as a condition of parole after a prison sentence (Latimer et al., 2005).

A number of claims are made about restorative justice. First, it is beneficial to victims, as recognition is given to the harm they have personally suffered and redress is received from the offender(s). Second, it encourages the reintegration of offenders into the community after their offence, which may reduce recidivism. Third, it is perceived as fairer and more just than the punitive model by victims, offenders and communities, leading to greater satisfaction with justice. There is evidence to support these claims. For example, Maxwell and Morris (2001) report two schemes run with adult offenders in New Zealand. The schemes mainly dealt with property offences and minor acts of violence and the victims were principally friends, family and local businesses. The restorative programmes included a range of requirements including paying reparations, engaging in therapy for drugs, alcohol or violent behaviour and attending driving or parenting courses. Compared with matched offenders who were processed by the standard judicial trial process, those on the restorative justice programme were less likely to be reconvicted. Qualitative self-report data gathered from the offenders showed that some welcomed the opportunity to make things right with their victims and that many felt that the experience had been a positive one.

A substantial body of research into restorative justice has grown up since the 1970s. Latimer et al. (2005) reviewed 35 studies in which restorative and non-restorative justice programmes were compared. Restorative justice resulted in greater victim satisfaction, greater compliance with sanctions by offenders and lower recidivism rates. No difference was found for offender satisfaction. However, Latimer et al. noted that in many of the studies reviewed involvement in a restorative justice programme was voluntary – as its principles require – and so there is a danger that the apparent superiority of restorative approaches is due to selection bias. Additionally, many of the programmes reviewed by Latimer et al. were aimed at younger offenders, so it is not clear whether adult offenders respond similarly. A more recent meta-analysis by Sherman et al. (2015) addresses some of these concerns. They reviewed 10 studies involving both juvenile and adult offenders and in which offenders were randomly allocated to receive restorative justice or not, thus avoiding selection bias. With the proviso that restorative justice is only appropriate when both offender and victim are willing to participate voluntarily, Sherman et al. found that restorative justice was associated with a small but statistically significant reduction in reoffending, especially when used to supplement conventional justice (as opposed to replacing it, where the evidence is equivocal). It remains unclear why restorative justice should have a greater effect on recidivism than the conventional approach. Sherman et al. connect the emotional intensity of restorative justice meetings with the triggering of 'turning points' in a criminal career, when an offender makes a commitment to the idea of desisting from crime. In support of this, they indicate that restorative justice has a stronger effect on violent recidivism than in property offences, where the degree of emotional intensity is typically lower.

Chapter summary

The judicial system responds to offending with a range of sanctions including both custodial and non-custodial sentences. Imprisonment is the most serious sanction available in most Western democracies but its use varies widely. In the UK and US, there was a substantial growth in imprisonment between the 1940s and the present day. Prison serves a number of functions including retribution, incapacitation, deterrence and reform of the offender. Although it is painful for the offender in a number of ways and may affect her physical, psychological and social wellbeing, there is little evidence to suggest that it reforms criminals and some that suggests it makes offending worse. However, it does incapacitate offenders for the duration of their sentence and is a necessary measure in the case of those who pose a significant risk to society. Imprisonment is comparatively costly and there are economic arguments for avoiding it in favour of non-custodial sentences when the risk to the public is low. Non-custodial sentences include fines and community sentences. Fines have advantages in that they do not disrupt the offender's life in the same way as prison and they may generate revenue for the authorities. The evidence for their effectiveness is not strong, although they do have a deterrent effect on some offences. Community sentences involve releasing an offender into society but imposing requirements (e.g. community service) or restrictions (e.g. a curfew) on her, under threat of more serious sanctions. Evidence suggests that those who serve community sentences have a lower recidivism rate than those who are imprisoned and there are substantial monetary savings. Restorative justice involves offenders, victims and other stakeholders voluntarily devising ways for offenders to repair the harm they have caused. It appears to produce better outcomes than conventional justice both in terms of recidivism and victim satisfaction. However, much of the evidence in the area of non-custodial sentencing is affected by selection bias, as only in a few studies are offenders randomly assigned to different punishments. Consequently, the evidence base exaggerates the difference in effectiveness between prison and the alternatives.

Further reading

Liebling, A., & Maruna, S. (2006). *The Effects of Imprisonment (Cambridge Criminal Justice Series)*. London: Routledge. An authoritative edited volume on the effects of imprisonment with contributions from a number of influential researchers.

10

Crime prevention

The goal of crime prevention is to reduce the amount of criminal activity and the harm that it causes along with the number of criminal offenders and their victims. Crime prevention strategies are used by individuals, communities, businesses and government to target those factors that are known to cause crime in order to facilitate a reduction in crime. This chapter surveys some of the ways in which psychology can contribute to reducing crime. It starts by distinguishing between different types of crime prevention and then discusses how crime can be prevented by altering the environment, intervening with people at risk of involvement in criminal activity and by helping to rehabilitate offenders.

Approaches to crime prevention

The Public Health Model is an approach to crime prevention adopted from the medical profession. The medical approach to, for example, heart disease is not solely based on emergency procedures that occur once someone has already had a heart attack, but on ways in which people can reduce their risk of developing heart disease in the first place (e.g. adopting a healthy lifestyle). In the Public Health Model of crime prevention there are three interrelated and coordinated approaches for reducing the seriousness and incidence of criminal behaviour: primary, secondary and tertiary (Mackey, 2012). Primary and secondary preventions are forms of deterrence; they try to encourage people not to commit an offence. Tertiary prevention aims to reform offenders so that they do not reoffend (see Chapter 9).

Primary crime prevention refers to proactive attempts to prevent crime before it happens. These include strengthening resiliency factors that help individuals to avoid criminal behaviours, and reducing risk factors that increase the likelihood of criminal behaviour. Such programmes could include those in schools designed to reduce risk factors in children and adolescents that might lead to more serious criminal activity later in life such as drug and alcohol use, carrying a knife and joining a gang (Regoli et al., 2010).

Secondary interventions refer to attempts to change those people who run a high risk of offending but are not yet involved in serious criminal activity. These programmes target a narrower group of individuals than primary prevention programmes. In young males, the main risk factors for criminality are hyperactivity, poor concentration, poor academic achievement, an antisocial father, a large family size, low income, poor parental supervision and parental disharmony (Farrington, 2000). Thus, secondary programmes might specifically target such individuals in early adolescence to provide appropriate mentors, role models and additional academic support in order to divert them from criminal trajectories.

Tertiary interventions are those that involve working with known offenders already in the criminal justice system to prevent them from reoffending. These can include drug and alcohol treatment, further education and training and psychological interventions such as anger management programmes. The aim is to rehabilitate offenders and provides a somewhat different approach from that of penal harm. Penal harm works on the principle that if prison is made sufficiently unpleasant (Spartan living conditions, little contact with other people, reduced access to books, TV and games, etc.) the person will be motivated to avoid further offences (see Chapter 9). Tertiary interventions work on the principle that incarceration on its own may not be sufficient. For instance, if someone is convicted of assault and spends time in prison, he may continue to commit further offences of assault if he does not believe that he has actually done something wrong. Indeed, he may even feel justified in committing further assault against those responsible for his incarceration. There is a need to change how that person thinks not just to incarcerate him.

Situational crime prevention

Situational crime prevention is based on the understanding that certain crimes are more likely to occur in some areas than others (sometimes referred to as crime 'hot spots'). In the United States, for example, 60% of crimes occur within the same locations (Eck, 2006). Situational crime prevention is underpinned by Rational Choice Theory (Clarke, 1997; see Chapter 4). Rational Choice Theory proposes that offending behaviour results from a series of decisions (e.g. effort required, moral costs, severity of punishment, etc.), background factors (e.g. upbringing, previous experience of crime, etc.) and environmental cues (e.g. opportunity to commit crime).

The general approach adopted by situational crime prevention is to the reduce the opportunity for people to engage in criminal behaviour by changing the physical environment in ways that increase the effort required to commit a crime, enhance the risk of detection, reduce the gains associated with crime, remove the excuses for committing a crime and reduce factors that prompt criminal behaviour (Cornish & Clarke, 2003). Changes to the physical environment to reduce crime are sometimes referred to as crime prevention through environmental design (CPTED) strategies. These include improved street lighting, the use of closed-circuit television and creating defensible space.

Improved street lighting

The idea behind improved street lighting in city and town centres, residential areas and public housing communities is that natural surveillance is improved. This makes it easier to see and identify criminals and encourages more pedestrians to use those areas. The increased risk of being recognised or interrupted while attacking people or property reduces the likelihood of someone choosing to offend. In a review of 13 studies from the US and UK, Welsh and Farrington (2009) found an average reduction in crime of 21% although it was more effective in reducing property crime than violent crime. In nine of those 13 studies, both daytime and night-time crimes were recorded and showed a 30% reduction in crime. The remaining four studies only measured night-time crimes and showed no statistically significant reduction in crime when compared with a control condition with no improved street lighting. Since surveillance conditions are good in the daytime, this analysis suggests the effect of improved street lighting may not actually be due to improved natural surveillance at night but other related factors such as increased social pride resulting from investment from local authorities and the increased collective efficacy that results from this (see Chapter 5).

The best evidence for an improved street lighting scheme comes from Stoke-on-Trent. An experimental area, with improved street lighting, was compared with a neighbouring area and a control area with no improved street lighting (Painter & Farrington, 1999). The incidence of crime, based on victim surveys rather than police records, showed a reduction of crime by 43% in the experimental area, by 45% in the neighbouring area and 2% in the control area. This suggests that the benefits of improved street lighting may not be limited to the area in which they are introduced, but diffuse to surrounding areas, too. A financial cost-benefit analysis of schemes in Stoke-on-Trent and Dudley showed the investment on installing the new street lighting resulted in substantial saving for victims and the local council. Every £1 spent resulted in a saving of £6.12 in Dudley and £5.43 in Stoke-on-Trent (Painter & Farrington, 2001).

Closed-circuit television

Closed-circuit television (CCTV) is another form of surveillance designed to increase the risk of detection and reduce the likelihood of offending. In a review of 44 studies in which CCTV was installed in towns and city centres, the use of CCTV had no statistically significant effect on crime (Welsh & Farrington, 2009). However, CCTV may be effective under limited conditions, for instance, to reduce vehicle crime in car parks. One evaluation compared car parks in Coventry, Hartlepool and Bradford where CCTV was installed (along with notices about the CCTV and the presence of security personnel) with car parks where CCTV was not installed (Tilley, 1993). After 24 months there was a 59% reduction in car crime in the car parks where CCTV was installed compared with a 16% reduction in the car parks where CCTV was not installed. CCTV in towns and city centres might be more effective if it is targeted at crime 'hot spots' and for specific types of crime (e.g. property crime). Mobile CCTV facilities could make this a feasible and cost-effective solution.

Defensible space

The model of defensible space is derived from research into the failure of high-rise, high-density housing projects in the United States where communal space was vandalised, littered and rendered unusable, and violence, prostitution and drug dealing were commonplace (Newman, 1972). Newman suggested that the responsibility for maintaining and securing a public space and for establishing common rules for its use was proportional to the density of people living in an area. The more people, the less responsibility is taken. Similar problems have been found in urban projects in the UK such as Hulme area of Manchester where high-density blocks built in 1972 were demolished in 1996. Newman's solution was to create mini-neighbourhoods to create a sense of community with clearly delineated boundaries through the use of fences, landscaping and creating cul-de-sacs by breaking up roads with large ornamental gates. Police presence and law enforcement was enhanced and a home ownership scheme was encouraged in order to reinforce a sense of neighbourhood identification. In the Five Oaks area of Dayton, Ohio, where Newman's ideas were put into effect, violence decreased by 50%, traffic was lowered by one-third, and two-thirds of residents reported it to be a better place to live in.

These studies have shown that situational crime prevention can be a cost-effective approach in reducing crime by making changes to the environment that influence perceptions of the risks of offending or encourage civic ownership and responsibility. Each type of environment, however, presents unique issues and challenges. For example, in small commercial premises, such as newsagents and petrol stations, the placement of the till can be critical in preventing robbery (Crowe, 1991). The cashier should be able to observe the entry point to the premises and have good lines of sight throughout the shop or store. For maximum visibility, windows should not be blocked with adverts or product displays and there should be only one access point to monitor people entering and leaving.

Developmental crime prevention

Developmental crime prevention involves identifying individuals who are at risk of becoming involved in crime and diverting them before they get involved in the criminal justice system. It is based on identifying those factors that increase the likelihood of offending and taking action to counteract them and identifying those factors that prevent offending and taking action to boost them. Although many studies identify risk factors in offending, it is not often clear whether they directly influence the onset, frequency, persistence or duration of offending or merely correlate with it (Kazdin et al., 1997). For instance, coming from a large family is correlated with the likelihood of offending and is therefore a risk factor (Farrington & Loeber, 1999). It is not clear, however, how coming from a large family is causally related to being an offender. Is it because antisocial people have more children, because parental supervision is poorer in large families, or is it a consequence of poverty? Programmes designed to reduce risk factors and boost resilience factors will only be effective if they target those factors that are causally related to offending. There are many types of developmental crime prevention programme. These include those designed for parents (e.g. effective parenting strategies and improving parental education), pre-school and day-care settings (e.g. to boost cognitive stimulation or reading skills in young children) and secondary school and community programmes (e.g. academic support, anti-bullying and mentoring).

School-based programmes

School-based programmes can be effective in helping students to manage their behaviour in school and stay out of trouble, improve their study skills and learning behaviours. In one such multi-component study, children aged 6 were randomly assigned to an experimental condition designed to enhance parental attachment and bonding at school or a control condition (Hawkins et al., 1991). The experimental group intervention involved training for parents on how to identify and reinforce socially desirable behaviour, training for teachers on classroom management and training for students in socially desirable methods of problem solving. By the age of 12 years, children in the experimental group were less likely to have engaged in criminal activity or used drugs (O'Donnell et al., 1995). By the age of 18 years children in the experimental group were less likely to abuse alcohol, were less violent and had fewer sexual partners (Hawkins et al., 1999). A cost-benefit analysis showed that for every $1 spent on the programme, $3 were saved in the cost to crime victims and the US government (Aos et al., 2001).

Community-based programmes

An example of a community-based programme is the 'Big Brothers, Big Sisters of America' (BBBS), a national mentoring organisation founded in 1904 dedicated to improving the life chances of adolescents at risk of offending. In this programme, adolescents are paired with an adult mentor who meets with them for three or four times per month for at least one year. One evaluation compared 1,100 adolescents who were randomly assigned either to the BBBS mentoring scheme or to a control group that received no mentoring. Those who received mentoring were 32% less likely to have engaged in violent behaviour, 46% less likely to have used drugs, 27% less likely to have used alcohol and 30% less likely to have been absent from school without permission (Grossman & Tierney, 1998). Aos et al. (2004) estimated that $3 were saved in the cost to crime victims and the US government for every $1 spent on the programme. A review of 18 mentoring programmes concluded that mentoring programmes were effective in preventing future offending behaviour (Jolliffe & Farrington, 2004). On average, participants in mentoring programmes were 10% less likely to become offenders than individuals who did not participate. However, the effectiveness of the interventions depended on the amount of contact between the mentor and mentee. Programmes with greater contact were, on average, more effective.

Family programmes

Family programmes are typically designed directly to provide support for parents, teach effective parenting skills and/or teach children social skills. One such programme, designed for children aged 6 years who were identified as disruptive (aggressive and hyperactive), combined parental and child training (Tremblay et al., 1995, 1996). Children received training in social skills and self-control through coaching and roleplay of scenarios such as 'how to react to teasing' and 'what to do when you are angry'. Parents received training in how to reinforce desirable behaviour, discipline children without punishment and manage family crisis situations. Compared with a control condition in which no training was provided, children aged 12 in the experimental condition (child and parent training) committed fewer burglaries, were involved in fewer fights and got drunk less often (Tremblay et al., 1992). By the age of 24, persons in the experimental condition were significantly less likely to have a criminal record (Boisjoli et al., 2007).

These studies have shown that developmental crime prevention can be a cost-effective approach to reducing crime. The particular challenge for studies evaluating this type of crime prevention is that intervention programmes are often run in childhood or adolescence and beneficial effects may not been seen for many years until the participants in those programmes are late adolescents or adults. Nonetheless, longitudinal studies that follow individuals over a period of time have shown how it is possible to successfully intervene during childhood or early adolescence to create a beneficial long-term outcome.

Offender rehabilitation

Recent statistics from the UK showed that from 2014 to 2015 the overall reoffending rate for persons who had already had contact with the criminal justice system was 25 to 27% (Ministry of Justice, 2017a). This need not necessarily be a prison term but can include those cautioned, convicted or released from custody without serving a prison term. For adults, the reoffending rates were between 24 and 25% and for young offenders 29 and 37%. Clearly, contact with the criminal justice system in itself is not sufficient to prevent recidivism (see Chapter 9). Attempts to rehabilitate offenders, especially those serving a prison sentence, were commonplace in many countries throughout the 20th century. A now famous report in 1974 reviewed 231 studies of offender rehabilitation programmes, including counselling, probation and parole, from 1945 to 1967 concluded that they were largely ineffective (Martinson, 1974). The findings of this report were seized on by those who were sceptical about the philosophy of rehabilitation. Offender rehabilitation, however, continues to be the official policy of many governments, including that of the UK, as complementary to incarceration (Ministry of Justice, 2017b).

In the years since the Martinson report, there has been an accumulation of evidence that rehabilitation programmes can reduce offending if they incorporate the following principles (Vennard & Hedderman, 1998):

1 Individuals are classified on their risk of reoffending and more intensive programmes given to those at high risk.

2 Factors that lead to criminal behaviour are targeted, such as antisocial attitudes, drug dependency, a low level of education and skills, and poor interpersonal skills.

3 Programmes have high integrity; that is, staff are properly trained and do not deviate from the aims and methods of the programme.

4 Teaching methods match the learning styles of offenders.

5 Programmes challenge the attitudes, values and beliefs of offenders that support criminal behaviour; offenders learn how to challenge their own pro-crime attitudes, values and beliefs.

Psychologists have been prominent in developing, delivering and evaluating a wide range of offender rehabilitation programmes. Such programmes include treatment for alcohol and substance abuse, support for mental health conditions and cognitive-behavioural programmes for offending behaviour (e.g. sex offenders and anger management), developing and enhancing family relationships and reducing negative peer relationships.

Anger management programmes

Many types of offending (e.g. rape, assault, bodily harm, manslaughter and murder) are linked to or directly involve aggression and violence. Although there are many causes of aggression and violence, one common predisposing factor is an inability of the person to effectively deal with feelings of anger. Most people experience anger at varying times and at varying degrees of intensity, but can keep their anger in check and do not resort to physical violence.

Novaco (1975) argued that cognition plays a central role in the emotional arousal that precedes aggressive and violent behaviour. Anger arises quickly in situations in which a person feels threatened or insecure because of existing emotional distress about other things in that person's life. Those feelings are then transferred to an available target (who may or may not be related to the anger-provoking situation). Expressing and directing anger towards that target then provides a sense of control that reinforces the aggressive behaviour. Novaco's approach was not to try to prevent anger from arising in the first place but to teach the person to monitor, control and manage her reactions to anger. This involves teaching new strategies for regaining self-control and techniques for resolving conflict without resorting to violence. Novaco's anger management programme has three phases:

1 Cognitive preparation.

2 Skill acquisition.

3 Application practice.

In the first phase, the person is taught to reflect on and analyse her own patterns of thought and behaviour when she becomes angry. First, the offender has to identify episodes in the past when she became angry and responded with violence and then to examine what the triggers were. The idea is that people learn to identify those situations that are high risk for their becoming violent. Second, the offender is asked to recall what her patterns of thought were during those violent episodes and, with the help of a psychologically trained counsellor or therapist, identify and then challenge irrational thoughts and assumptions about others. For instance, the offender may have shown patterns of thought that signify a hostile attributional bias, that is, a tendency to interpret the ambiguous or benign actions or speech of others as being indicative of a hostile intent. The offender, for example, might have responded with anger and violence to someone she thinks might have looked at them in a 'funny way'. In this way, the offender can break automatic cycles of violent behaviour by changing her beliefs and attitudes towards others. Third, the offender reflects on the consequences of anger (e.g. alienating friends, losing her job or being incarcerated).

In the second phase, the person is taught new skills to allow her to deal with anger-provoking situations in a more effective way. Cognitive skills can involve learning to say 'stop' to herself when automatic and irrational thoughts about others arise (e.g. 'that person is looking at me in a funny way'). Social and communication skills involve learning how to interpret and respond to others in ways that do not escalate aggression. Problem-solving skills involve learning how to identify alternative solutions to resolve conflict situations with others without becoming violent.

In the third and final phase, the offender is given the opportunity to practise the new skills she has learned in a safe and controlled environment. This could be done by roleplaying situations with a counsellor or therapist or with other offenders on group anger management programmes. The roleplay situations would be those that have triggered violent behaviours in the past. These would be practised in a hierarchy, starting with situations that were only slightly problematic and gradually working up to more problematic situations as the offender became more practised and confident in using her new approach.

Apply your learning

Jim describes how he came to commit a violent assault in a bar:

> *The pub was pretty full and this idiot walked into me as I came back from the bar and spilled my drink. I said to him, 'Watch what you're doing' and he was like 'Yeah mate, whatever', like he thought I was just nothing. I walked away but I couldn't stop going over what he'd said in my head and I could see his face, like he was laughing at me. Next thing I knew, I've gone over to him and picked up a glass and stuck it in his face. He wasn't laughing then.*

> Identify from Jim's account the cognitive processes that may have contributed to his offence. Suggest how a therapist could attempt to reduce Jim's risk of violence as a response.

Between 1999 and 2001 20 courts in Washington, USA, dealing with juvenile offenders implemented an anger management programme called anger replacement therapy (ART). This resulted in 1,500 offenders participating in these programmes. Eighteen months after participating in ART reoffending rates were down 24% compared with a control group that did not receive the therapy (Barnoski, 2004). Although this may not sound like a large reduction, a cost-benefit analysis estimated a saving of $6.71 to crime victims and the US government for every $1 spent (Aos et al., 2006). This figure rose to a saving of $11.66 where the programme was delivered more competently.

Sex offender programmes

Core Sex Offender Treatment Programme (SOTP) is a cognitive behavioural therapy-based programme used with imprisoned men in England and Wales since 1992. It is based on the principle of identifying and addressing criminogenic needs. These are traits or characteristics that influence the person's likelihood of reoffending. It is offered to men who have been sentenced to a minimum of 12 months in prison, who are willing to engage in treatment and who are not in denial of their offending. It is used to treat a wide range of offences including rape, sexual assault, sexual offences with children and the possession and distribution of banned material. SOTP includes cognitive restructuring to challenge the thoughts, beliefs and attitudes that support or permit sexual offending, changing previous dysfunctional behaviours by building new skills and increasing victim empathy. There is a basic programme with 'booster' sessions prior to release and an extended programme for high-risk offenders.

In an evaluation of SOTP, 647 convicted adult sex offenders who participated in SOTP from 1992 to 1994 were compared with a similar group of 1,910 sex offenders who were not treated (Friendship et al., 2003). After two years, those participating in SOTP were less likely to commit a further sexual or violent crime (4.6%) than those who had not participated in SOTP (8.1%). While these results are promising, the largest study of SOTP is less so. Mews et al. (2017) compared 2,562 convicted adult sex offenders from 2000 to 2012 who underwent treatment with 13,219 convicted sex offenders who had not undergone treatment. The majority of offenders had committed an offence related to sexual contact with a child aged under 16 years (58%) or rape/serious sexual assault of an adult (28%). Offenders who had and had not undergone treatment were matched on 87 factors (including age, ethnicity, length of sentence, type of offence, gender of victim and so on). Offenders who had undergone SOTP were more likely to engage in at least one further

TABLE 10.1 Meta-analyses of CBT programmes for sex offenders

Author	Number of studies reviewed	Reduction in reoffending
Gallagher et al. (1999)	25	8%
Hanson et al. (2002)	43	4.5%
Lösel & Schmucker (2005)	69	6%
MacKenzie (2006)	28	10%

sexual offence (10%) than those who had not (8%) and were more likely to reoffend in relation to child images (4.4%) than those who had not (2.9%). There were no differences between those who had and had not undergone SOTP treatment on a range of other outcomes including prostitution, non-sexual violent offences and non-sexual non-violent offences.

These two studies provide mixed evidence for the effectiveness of SOTP. As these studies were quasi-experimental and did not randomly assign participants to treatment and control groups, there is a risk of selection bias. It is possible that difference between the two was confounded by factors that were not included in the matching process such as risk of reoffending, sexual deviancy or participating in other forms of treatment. For instance, those at a higher risk of reoffending or with sexual deviancy might have entered the treatment programme and those in the control group might have participated in other forms of treatment to SOTP. Several meta-analyses of other forms of CBT-based programmes for sexual offenders do suggest a reduction in offending following treatment (Table 10.1).

The reasoning and rehabilitation programme

Reasoning and rehabilitation (R&R) is a CBT-based rehabilitation programme developed in Canada that aims to teach the cognitive skills, social skills and values that are required for prosocial competence (Ross et al., 1988). It is based on the principle that offending behaviour is underpinned by deficits in cognitive skills resulting from problems in the environment, poor parental supervision or ineffective education, rather than low intelligence. As a result, individuals with cognitive deficits have difficulties with self-control, empathy, taking on the perspectives of others and values. Through teaching offenders these skills, the R&R programme aims to equip former offenders to be able to successfully avoid reoffending in the future. R&R is delivered in 35 two-hour sessions for groups of between six and 12 adults, with between two to four sessions per week. It includes roleplay, thinking games, learning exercises, dilemma puzzles and problems. The programme is now used in over 20 countries, including the UK, and represents the most widely disseminated and frequently evaluated offender rehabilitation programme. The nine elements of R&R are:

1   Self-control. To stop and think about the consequences of an action before making a decision.

2 Metacognition. To understanding that how we think influences how we feel and behave.

3 Critical reasoning. How to think objectively and rationally without distorting the facts or blaming others.

4 Social skills. How to interact with others effectively in social situations.

5 Problem-solving skills. Analysing problems to understand and consider the values, behaviour and feelings of others and how one's own behaviour can affect others.

6 Creative thinking. How to find prosocial, rather than antisocial, solutions to interpersonal problems.

7 Social perspective taking. How to consider the thoughts, feelings and views of others.

8 Value enhancement. How to adopt prosocial views.

9 Emotional management. Learning how to control anger.

A meta-analysis of 26 studies based in Canada, the United States, UK and Sweden found that R&R reduced reoffending by an average of 14% in those who completed the programme compared with those who did not participate (Tong & Farrington, 2006). The programme was equally effective whether delivered in a prison or community setting and for both low- and high-risk offenders. A cost-benefit analysis estimated that for every $1 spent on the programme, $8 were saved to the victims of crime (Aos et al., 2001). Although the programme is effective in reducing reoffending behaviour it is not without critics. One problem is that it focuses solely on the cognitions of the offender and ignores the social and environmental factors that increase the risk of reoffending such as drug use, poor living conditions, low income and unemployment (May, 1999).

Crime prevention: general considerations

Psychologists, along with criminologists, the police and other professions in the criminal justice system, have been instrumental in researching the reasons why people commit crime, developing theoretical models to explain criminal activity and then using those theories to create interventions and applications designed to reduce criminal activity and offending behaviour. The studies described in this chapter suggest that crime reduction is indeed possible using theoretically informed interventions. Furthermore, many studies evaluating the outcome of interventions have been accompanied by cost-benefit analyses that show that the financial benefit to victims and authorities outweighs the costs of implementing those interventions. These achievements are results of a slow accumulation of evidence over a number of years. The need for an evidence-based approach to policy decision making around crime, policing and the justice system highlights the need for continuing high-quality research capable of rigorous evaluation of crime reduction programmes. Psychologists are well placed to be able to continue to contribute to these developments in the future.

Chapter summary

In crime prevention, psychologists distinguish between primary, secondary and tertiary prevention. Primary prevention involves intervening in ways that stop crime before it happens, by changing the environment. Improved street lighting, CCTV and defensible space have all be shown to reduce offending in the areas where they are implemented, although they are more effective against some types of offence and in some areas than others. Secondary prevention involves targeting individuals who run an increased risk of becoming involved in crime and diverting them before this happens. School-based programmes, mentoring and family-based programmes have all been shown to reduce offending in high-risk groups although their impact is hard to evaluate since the beneficial effects may not become apparent until many years later. Tertiary prevention aims to reduce reoffending among those who have been convicted. Given that approximately 25 to 27% of offenders reoffend, in the UK, attempts to reduce reoffending through rehabilitation are vital. Psychological approaches to rehabilitation focus on changing thoughts and cognitions that may contribute to reoffending, teaching offenders new skills to help them deal with situations in ways that will not lead to reoffending, and helping offenders to identify and break ingrained and destructive cycles of behaviour. Three such programmes are anger management, the Core Sex Offender Treatment Programme and the reasoning and rehabilitation programme. Outcome studies that compare offenders who have and have not participated in rehabilitation programmes have largely shown positive results in reducing reoffending.

Further reading

Robinson, G., & Crowe, I. (2009). *Offender Rehabilitation: Theory, Research and Practice*. Thousand Oaks, CA: Sage. A comprehensive introduction to offender rehabilitation, including explorations of the history of the field and the issues that surround implementation and evaluation.

Wortley, R., & Townsley, M. (Eds.) (2016). *Environmental Criminology and Crime Analysis*. London: Routledge. An edited text covering environmental approaches to crime prevention and many related topics, including offender profiling (see Chapter 6). It includes contributions from many well-known and influential researchers.

11

Contemporary topics: terrorism and cybercrime

The core topics of criminology and criminological psychology have not changed much in the past few decades: offending, victimisation, policing, courtroom processes, punishment and rehabilitation. However, societal change brings with it changes both in criminal activity and people's concerns about crime. This chapter outlines two areas that have generated interest in recent years: terrorism and cybercrime.

Apply your learning

Before reading any further, list the characteristics you associate with (1) a terrorist and (2) a cybercriminal. Give as much detail as you can. After reading the rest of the chapter, come back to your lists and assess how accurate your idea of these two types of offender was.

Terrorism

The term 'terrorist' broadly denotes individuals and groups who use violent means to bring about societal change. There are, however, difficulties surrounding the term (Schmid, 2004). Terrorism covers an enormous range of actions, including religiously, politically and nationalistically inspired violence that may, beneath the surface, have little in common. It also embodies a judgement about the legitimacy of violence, so what is condemned by some as terrorism may be lauded by others as an act of warfare or a blow for freedom. Nonetheless, terrorism is a major public concern in Europe and the US. This is reflected in media coverage of terrorist incidents such as the suicide bombing of the Manchester Arena in May 2017, which killed 23 people and injured over 500 more. Anxiety currently focuses on Islamic-inspired terrorism but throughout the 20th and 21st centuries Western states have been subjected to terrorist acts informed by many causes including nationalism (e.g. the Provisional Irish Republican Army and the Ulster Defence Regiment in Britain and Northern

Ireland) and political extremism from both the left (e.g. the Red Army Faction in Germany) and right wing (e.g. Timothy McVeigh, the 'Oklahoma City Bomber' in the US).

Worry about terrorism is understandable, given the horrifying nature of such attacks. However, while it is widely perceived as a major threat, in the West, terrorism actually carries a low risk to the individual and does not threaten social order (Bakker, 2015). Outside Europe and America, terrorism presents a much greater danger. The Global Terrorism Database (GTD) held by the University of Maryland has compiled records of terrorist attacks since the early 1970s. By the end of 2017 it contained information about 170,000 incidents. In 2016 13,400 terrorist attacks were logged resulting in 34,000 deaths (a 10% reduction from 2015). The vast majority of attacks, deaths and injuries were in the Middle East, Africa and South Asia, which together accounted for 97% of the total deaths. By contrast, attacks in Western Europe accounted for 1% of the total and the US for even less than this (National Consortium for the Study of Terrorism and Responses to Terrorism (START), 2017). In 2016, by far the deadliest terrorist organisation was Islamic State in Iraq and the Levant (ISIL), responsible for 11,700 deaths in 1,400 attacks with more attributed to associated groups and individuals. Outside the West, terrorism poses a significant risk of death and injury and a credible threat to the social order. Besides the damage inflicted by terrorism itself, insecurity is further heightened by violent antiterrorist countermeasures by the authorities.

Psychological effects of terrorism

Any shocking and terrifying event that involves significant threat or loss of life is likely to affect those exposed to it. Terrorist attacks are no exception and some research has suggested that disasters in which human actions are to blame have an increased psychological impact (Norris, 2005). In many cases, those directly exposed to terrorist attacks develop PTSD (see Chapter 2). Two months after the 9/11 attacks on the World Trade Center in New York, Schlenger et al. (2002) carried out a survey of 2,273 US adults. As might be expected, the incidence of PTSD symptoms was substantially higher in New York (11.2%) than in the rest of the US (4%). Those who were directly exposed to the attack had a higher incidence of PTSD, as did women, younger people and those who had watched more TV coverage of the attacks in the immediate aftermath. The impact of terrorist attacks diminishes with time but the effects can be long lasting. Scrimin et al. (2011) found that 29.3% of a sample of children exposed to a hostage-taking attack in Beslan, Russia, in 2004 met the criteria for PTSD three years after the event. Consistent with other research, those directly involved as hostages were most likely to have PTSD. Longitudinal studies of people affected by the 9/11 attacks found that levels of PTSD generally declined in the years following the attacks. The exceptions were the emergency services and recovery workers where, after three years, PTSD symptoms started to rise significantly. The reasons for this are not clear but it could be the result of under-reporting of symptoms by these groups in the immediate aftermath (Lowell et al., 2017).

Who becomes a terrorist?

It is tempting to believe that only highly disturbed individuals are capable of terrorist acts. However, the evidence suggests that terrorists are, as a rule, psychologically normal. Silke (2008) reviewed evidence in this area, finding no evidence that terrorism is associated with personality disorder or mental illness. Terrorist organisations undoubtedly contain such individuals, but they are the exception and some studies suggest that terrorists are more psychologically healthy than non-terrorists (Lyons & Harbinson, 1986). Although psychopathic individuals (see Chapter 4) might be drawn to terrorist activities, Borum (2008) observes that they make poor terrorists as they typically lack commitment to ideals and organisations and are not inclined to act in self-sacrificing ways.

Attempts to profile the 'typical terrorist' have failed because they are too vague to be useful. Terrorists are a remarkably heterogeneous group although young males predominate, consistent with the heightened risk taking and delinquency in this group (Silke, 2008; see Chapter 2). In other ways, terrorists are unlike typical criminals. Sageman (2004) surveyed members of extremist Islamic organisations and found that the majority (60%) had some higher education, 75% were from a middle or upper class background and many were in professional occupations. The majority were married, which again is unlike the typical criminal as marriage is often associated with a move away from delinquent peers and desistance from crime. They typically had a very strong affiliation with a Muslim identity but this was not as a result of a highly religious upbringing or education (83% had gone to secular schools). Rather, they had experienced an intensification of their faith prior to their involvement in violent activities. Bakker and De Bont (2016) confirmed many of these findings. Their sample typically had lower SES and educational attainment but only 2% showed any sign of psychological disorders. Most had increased their commitment to their faith (e.g. through clothing and religious observances) shortly prior to any terrorist involvement.

These demographic profiles offer few clues about motives for terrorist involvement but other characteristics may be more significant. A sense of being marginalised and discriminated against has commonly been found to be associated with pro-terrorism attitudes. For example, Catholics in Northern Ireland in the 1970s suffered from the effects of economic deprivation, poor education and a lack of political representation that led to increased sympathy with Irish republican terrorist groups (O'Leary, 2007). Horgan (2009) interviewed 60 former terrorists and identified several common themes in their thinking. Those open to violent extremism tended to feel angry and alienated, felt that legitimate political processes did not represent them or their group, identified strongly with members of their group who had been the victims of injustice and had social networks containing others (e.g. peers and family members) who were sympathetic to terrorist causes. Similarly, Silke (2008) observes that Muslims in the UK, compared with other groups, have higher unemployment rates, poorer educational outcomes and are under-represented in politics, a pattern that is repeated throughout Western Europe. As such, Muslims could justifiably see themselves as unfairly marginalised as a group, which may be a predisposing factor towards involvement with extremism.

Explanations of terrorism

One influential theory of terrorist involvement is the 'staircase model' proposed by Moghaddam (2005). This describes how an individual may become increasingly enmeshed in a set of psychological processes that culminate in terrorist acts. It is a progressive model in which many people start out on the lower floors but some climb upwards to higher levels of involvement. The number doing so gets fewer as they climb higher until only a few individuals are left who actually commit terrorist acts (see Table 11.1).

Moghaddam sees the potential terrorist as making rational choices (see Chapter 4) guided by his perception of the world. Most significant is the perception that the group he belongs to has suffered an injustice. This makes the decision to engage with extremism seem logical to him, although it might not appear so to others. At the higher steps, moral disengagement strategies (see Chapter 4) are used to justify violent acts and affiliation with the extremist group promotes a social identity that exaggerates the differences between the extremist and his 'enemies' (see Chapter 5). Most terrorist organisations use a 'small cell' structure in which each member only knows a small number of other members, to reduce the threat of infiltration by counterterrorist forces. The small group fosters close relationships that strengthen the 'us versus them' worldview, leading to increased acceptance of terrorist ideas. Once the individual is fully immersed in the terrorist world, the final step is the sidestepping of inhibitions against killing. Moghaddam identifies two mechanisms for this. First, terrorist training encourages recruits to view anyone not actively opposing the authorities as an enemy ('anyone not for us is against us') so there are no innocent victims. Second, terrorist methods often serve to increase the psychological distance

TABLE 11.1 Steps in the 'staircase model' of terrorist involvement (Moghaddam, 2005)

Step	Explanation
Ground floor	The individual experiences feelings of injustice and relative deprivation leading to a sense of grievance
First floor	He looks for ways of changing the situation to achieve justice
Second floor	Feeling powerless to effect change, he becomes frustrated and angry. At this point, he is open to influence by leaders who direct his aggression towards an 'enemy'
Third floor	He adopts pro-terrorism moral values and starts to believe that violence is justified to achieve justice
Fourth floor	He is recruited into a terrorist organisation; the 'us versus them' worldview solidifies
Fifth floor	The individual is given training to overcome his final inhibitions against violence

between aggressor and victim. Reactions of fear and horror and behaviours like pleading serve to inhibit violence so many terrorist acts are planned to be sudden, with no warning to or interaction with victims (e.g. bombing).

Lygre et al. (2011) reviewed studies relevant to Moghaddam's framework to assess its empirical support. By searching the available literature they identified 38 research studies covering a variety of processes in the model, finding substantial support. For example, van Zomeren et al. (2008) found that perceived injustice has a moderately strong relationship with collective action, which supports the first step in the staircase model. The role of displaced aggression in step two is well supported by Berkowitz (1959) and others. In step three, support was found for the use of moral disengagement strategies (Bandura, 1990) and indoctrination (Grimland et al., 2006). The processes of conformity and obedience that allow inhibitions against violence to be sidestepped are very well researched (e.g. Milgram, 1963). Overall, Lygre et al. conclude that the staircase model is based on plausible psychological mechanisms that are supported by empirical evidence. However, they note that there is a relative absence of studies directly related to terrorism and there are very few investigations that have tested the proposition that the processes in the model chain together as Moghaddam describes.

Although it oversimplifies the relationship between pro-terrorist attitudes and violent behaviour (McCauley & Moskalenko, 2017), the staircase model has made a significant contribution to the psychology of terrorism by helping the field move beyond the ultimately fruitless search for personality and psychopathological correlates of terrorist activity. It provides an explanation of extremist thinking and behaviour rooted in well-understood psychological mechanisms. It also has important implications for reducing terrorism. Moghaddam's framework stresses that terrorist acts are only the final step in a process that starts much earlier. Prevention of terrorism should focus on people at the bottom of the staircase by supporting justice and participation in democratic society by people who feel that their group has been marginalised. Education should be targeted to undermine rigid, categorical ways of thinking about 'us and them'. Finally, the authorities should be prepared to engage in dialogue with extremist organisations. Although this might seem unpalatable to some, the success of the Northern Ireland peace process, which resulted in former extremists on both sides participating in democratic government, suggests that dialogue has a vital role to play in addressing the roots of terrorist engagement.

De-radicalisation

While the problem of terrorism ultimately requires political solutions, psychology may contribute at an individual level by diverting extremists and terrorists away from violent activities through the process of de-radicalisation. Kruglanski et al. (2007) suggest that an effective de-radicalisation programme requires three components:

- A cognitive component addressing the beliefs that support terrorism.
- An emotional component addressing the anger and frustration that underlie radicalisation.

- A social component addressing the possibility that former terrorists will become re-radicalised on re-entering their communities.

Kruglanski et al. (2014) have developed programmes informed by the idea that commitment to violent extremism is based on a quest for personal significance. They argue that people have a basic human need to matter to other people and that experiences of loss or humiliation can arouse the goal of achieving significance in the eyes of others. If they are exposed to an ideology that articulates a grievance, a culprit to blame and a moral warrant for violence then radicalisation is the likely outcome. Kruglanski's programme was implemented with detained members of the Liberation Tigers of Tamil Eelam (LTTE) in Sri Lanka. It had three strands: (1) disconnecting extremists from their leaders, to diminish their sense of group identity as LTTE members; (2) developing individual identity through activities such as art and yoga; and (3) providing vocational education to facilitate both economic success and to provide a legitimate route to a sense of personal significance. Compared with a matched control group, those who completed the programme showed significant decreases in support for violent political actions.

Such interventions provide evidence that de-radicalisation is possible although it is not clear how long the effects last following release. In the UK, de-radicalisation is a significant strand of government counterterrorism policy but its success has been mixed. In line with the staircase model, the 'Prevent' strategy was implemented with the goal of detecting the early signs of radicalisation and diverting people before they break the law. Prevent is predicated on community involvement since community members are best placed to detect problems and to contribute to the diversion process. A key component is 'Channel', wherein people of concern are referred to the authorities for assessment by community members or others (e.g. teachers). If assessment indicates that intervention is warranted, this is carried out by community partners and typically involves counselling, mentoring and theological support aimed at countering extremist ideology. The whole process is monitored by the police.

It is unclear how many individuals have successfully been diverted from radicalisation by Prevent and Channel, partly because this is inherently difficult to assess and partly because planned evaluation studies were abandoned due to government budget cuts (Griffith-Dickson et al., 2014). Critics have raised several concerns. Powell (2016) argues that Prevent is counterproductive because it focuses on Islamist religious ideology without addressing the socio-political concerns that fuel a sense of grievance and injustice. Consequently, it over-emphasises the role of faith and underestimates the role of economic and social marginalisation of Muslims and the effects of British foreign policy in the Middle East. Although Prevent is nominally aimed at addressing all types of extremism, the focus has been on Islam and the policy is perceived as stigmatising Muslims. Community members have also voiced suspicion that it is involved in intelligence gathering by the security services (House of Commons, 2010). Mastroe (2016) suggests that Prevent has acted to alienate the community support on which it relies. The Channel programme has also suffered from substantial over-reporting of concerns by teachers, who are instructed to treat any possible sign of radicalisation as a child safety concern. This risks overstretching the already limited resources available for assessment and intervention.

Government de-radicalisation programmes are in their relative infancy and it is currently not clear whether they do more good than harm. The success criteria for such programmes have rarely been made explicit (Horgan, in DeAngelis, 2009). If an individual desists from terrorist activities but retains their extremist beliefs, does this count as a success or a failure? Assuming that de-radicalisation programmes remain a fixture of government policy then systematic research into the effectiveness of such initiatives to identify what does and does not work is a clear priority.

Cybercrime

There are few aspects of 21st century life that have not been affected in some way by computers. Around 50% of the people on Earth now have access to the Internet and this number will inevitably grow. Just as the Internet has created new opportunities for communication, commerce and social contact, so, too, it has created new opportunities for criminal activity. Cybercrime is a term used loosely to describe crime in which computers play a role. It includes:

- Hacking: gaining unauthorised access to data.
- Malware: writing or distributing software that disrupts or damages computer systems.
- Distributed denial of service (DDoS) attacks: disrupting an Internet service by flooding it with data requests.
- Fraud (e.g. credit card fraud or other online 'scams').
- Piracy of music, video and games.
- Spamming: sending bulk unsolicited messages via Internet or mobile phone.
- Harassment, bullying and 'trolling'.
- Stalking.

The majority of cybercrimes are old crimes committed in new ways, but there are some offences that would not exist in the absence of the Internet. Therefore, Clough (2015) distinguishes between cyber-enabled crime (e.g. illegal pornography, stalking) and cyber-dependent crime (e.g. hacking, DDoS attacks).

Besides causing the same types of problem as offline offending, cybercrime presents a number of additional challenges. In order for a crime to occur, an offender must come together with a victim. Because of the scale of Internet use and the fact that a user's physical location is largely irrelevant, there are consequently many more opportunities for crimes to occur. Policing cybercrime is difficult since it may be hard to establish whose jurisdiction an offence falls within and offenders in many cases are located in a different country from victims. Its technical nature also requires new knowledge and skills for law enforcement agencies used to dealing with 'real-world' offences and it creates new risks for law enforcement personnel, such as the traumatic stress and burnout that may be suffered by those whose work exposes them to very disturbing material such as child pornography. The Internet also makes it relatively easy for offenders to maintain anonymity, allowing them to cover their tracks or even hide the existence of their crimes completely. Cybercrime also presents problems for the courts, as criminal laws may not be applicable to online offences and juries in cybercrime cases may have poor understanding of the technical nature of the evidence presented to them.

Measuring cybercrime

Measuring the extent of any type of crime is difficult (see Chapter 2) but this is especially the case for cybercrime. Clough (2015) identifies several issues. First, there is no widely agreed definition of cybercrime, so different authorities count different acts and therefore arrive at different estimates. Second, cybercrimes that are reported to the police are often recorded under 'traditional' offence categories so the 'cyber' element is lost, making it difficult to know what proportion of recorded crimes involved computers, phones or the Internet. Third, cybercrime is likely to be under-reported because the victim may fear the reaction of the police or may not think that the police can do anything about it. In addition, some victims may not realise they have been victimised or may not categorise what happened to them as a crime.

Large-scale victimisation surveys have recently started to include cybercrime. In the US, the National Crime and Victimisation Survey has included a question about cybervictimisation since 2006 but it does not distinguish between different types of offence, so it only offers rather limited data. In the UK, the CSEW introduced questions on fraud and damage caused by viruses in 2015. However, while stalking offences are recorded by the CSEW, cyberstalking is not covered as such. In relation to offender self-reports, Diamond and Bachmann (2015) conclude that data on cyberoffenders are 'virtually non-existent' (p.27). The Survey of Inmates in State and Federal Correctional Facilities collects data on the use of computers by offenders for a variety of crimes. Beyond this, the majority of data on the prevalence of offending come from surveys of college students for minor offences like music piracy.

Involvement in cybercrime

The popular stereotype of the cybercriminal is the 'lone hacker', often imagined as a young male with limited social skills and a high level of technical knowledge. The pervasiveness of this stereotype masks the fact that a great variety of people are involved in cybercrime for a range of reasons. One obvious motive is financial gain. However, McAlaney et al. (2016) suggest that many individuals get involved in cybercrime primarily because they enjoy it. Cybercrime might also be motivated by political or ideological concerns and revenge.

TABLE 11.2 Typology of cybercriminal groups (McGuire, 2012)

Type	Explanation
Type I	(a) Short-lived 'swarms' with no leadership structure who are involved mainly in ideologically driven offending such as hate crime or politically motivated activities
	(b) Stable and organised groups with a clear leadership structure that are involved in a wide variety of offences such as piracy, 'phishing' scams, malware and online sexual offending
Type II	Groups that switch seamlessly between online and offline offending, frequently centred on large-scale and systematic card fraud
Type III	'Traditional' organised criminal groups that have moved into online offending, generally in the same areas as their existing activities (e.g. pornography, gambling and blackmail)

Whatever the goal, cyberoffending is exacerbated by anonymity, since the offender calculates that the chances of being caught are low (as in rational choice theory; see Chapter 4). Disinhibition may also play a role, since online acts may not feel 'real' to the offender and, where offending is a group activity, de-individuation may also occur, where the offenders partially lose their sense of self awareness and, with it, their inhibitions against harming others.

The majority of cybercrime is carried out by groups rather than individuals and is mainly profit oriented. McGuire (2012) estimates that 80% of online criminal activity is of a group character. McGuire distinguishes three types of group (see Table 11.2).

While financial gain predominates as a motive for organised online offending, there is increasing awareness that some organisations are allied with and/ or sponsored by nation states. While their organisation and methods parallel the profit-driven groups, their choices of target (e.g. political figures and parties, military systems) mark them as distinct. It is not clear whether state-sponsored cyber attacks should be considered cybercrime as such or as espionage or warfare.

Explanations of cybercrime

Because cybercrime on a large scale is a relatively recent phenomenon, a number of basic questions have yet to be resolved. One question is whether those who commit cybercrimes would otherwise commit offline offences or does cybercrime offer opportunities for criminal behaviour to people who otherwise would not have offended. A related question is whether the theoretical approaches developed to explain offline offending are suitable for explaining online offences or whether new theories need to be devised to explain cybercrime. So far, it appears that some theories transfer fairly well to the online world albeit with some modification.

Personality

Chapter 4 discussed the relationship between personality and offending. In relation to cybercrime, Rogers et al. (2006) found an association between cyber-offending and an amoral outlook and low levels of extraversion (which partly coincides with the stereotype of the cybercriminal) but much stronger links have been found with psychopathy and related traits. Research has focused on three interrelated characteristics, psychopathy, narcissism and Machiavellianism, collectively known as the 'dark triad' of personality traits (or the 'dark tetrad' if sadism is also included). Williams et al. (2001) found that hacking was associated with high levels of dark triad traits. Seigfried-Spellar et al. (2017) recruited 235 online volunteers and collected self-reports of personality and a range of computer-based misbehaviour ranging from the fairly trivial (e.g. guessing passwords) to the more serious (e.g. identity fraud) as well as self-reports of offline criminality. Of the sample, 57% reported some degree of online criminality. There was a negative correlation between online criminality and the personality traits of agreeableness and openness and a positive correlation with psychopathic traits. They also found a strong correlation between online and offline offending, both violent and non-violent. This suggests that there is an overlap between online and offline offending and that computer crime may be an index of general criminal behaviour.

This view is supported by research into trolling, defined by Buckels et al. (2014, p.97) as 'behaving in a deceptive, destructive or disruptive manner in a social setting on the Internet with no apparent instrumental purpose'. Trolling, while clearly antisocial, is not specifically an offence in most jurisdictions but has been prosecuted successfully in the UK under various laws including the Communications Act (2003). Buckels et al. collected self-report data from 1,215 respondents about their personality traits and a range of online behaviour, some of it innocuous (e.g. chatting, debating issues) and some antisocial. They found a positive association between trolling, psychopathic traits and sadism. There was no relationship between these traits and other types of online activity. Lopes and Yu (2017) asked 135 participants, also recruited online, to view two fake Facebook profiles, constructed so that one appeared more popular than the other. Respondents were asked how far they would agree with a range of trolling comments on each profile. Personality measures were also taken. Lopes and Yu found a strong association between dark triad traits and trolling. They also found that the respondents with higher levels of psychopathy were more likely to troll the popular profile, possibly because there is more to gain by inflicting harm on a high-status victim. Buckels et al. found that online antisociality was related to how much respondents used the Internet. It could be that the online environment, which creates opportunities both for anonymity and for the construction of new identities, is attractive to people who wish to be unpleasant to others but feel inhibited from doing so in the 'real' world. Alternatively, it may be that over-immersion in the online world can have an antisocial influence.

Social learning theory

Chapter 5 discussed social learning as an explanation of criminal behaviour. There are indications that social learning is also an important process in some types of online offending. Involvement in hacking, piracy and online harassment is associated with delinquent peers. Morris and Blackburn (2009) recruited 600 college students to supply self-report data on cyberoffending. They were asked how often they had committed four types of online crime (guessing passwords, attempted hacking, file manipulation and malware) in the previous year. They also reported how often their friends engaged in the same sorts of activity and gave details of their level of computer knowledge and how much time they spent online. Respondents also completed a set of attitude scales to assess whether they had definitions favourable to computer crime, some questions to assess their perceived likelihood of being caught for online criminal acts and some questions about sources from which they had learned about different types of cyberoffence. They found that social learning variables predicted involvement in cybercrime although not to the same extent for all types of offence. Guessing passwords was most dependent on holding pro-cybercrime definitions/attitudes whereas attempted hacking and malicious file manipulation were most strongly influenced by association with peers involved in the same activities. Malware, by contrast, depended more on exposure to models outside the peer group. Interestingly, Morris and Blackburn found no gender differences in online criminality, although this might be due to the unrepresentative nature of their sample. Holt et al. (2010) carried out a similar study but with a broader conception of 'cyberdeviance', which included software and media piracy, viewing pornography, online plagiarism, illegally accessing WiFi and hacking. They found that involvement in such activities was quite strongly influenced by social learning but, unlike Morris and Blackburn, found that men were more likely to be involved than women. Both studies found that white respondents were more likely to commit offences online than black. It is difficult to say whether the association between delinquent peers and cyberoffending represents a direct influence of the peer group on the individuals or whether individuals attracted to cybercrime seek out people with similar interests.

Studies like these suggest both that cybercrime is influenced by social learning processes and, as a corollary, that social learning theory appears to transfer quite well from the physical to the digital world. However, it should be noted that these studies, and others like them, have a number of significant limitations. First, they rely entirely on self-reports, which are subject to many types of bias and it would be desirable to confirm these findings with more direct observations of behaviour. Second, the samples are unrepresentative of the broader population, being young and university educated and with plentiful access to computer networks and opportunities to acquire computer skills, so it is unclear how far these findings generalise. Third, the offences studied represent the less serious end of the spectrum of computer crime, omitting both more serious property crimes (e.g. card fraud) and personal crimes (e.g. harassment). Nonetheless, it is reasonable to conclude that social learning has at least a modest effect on cybercrime alongside other influences including personality.

Routine activity theory

One criminological theory that has been very influential in understanding 'real-world' offending is routine activity theory (RAT). RAT is an interesting contrast to most psychological theories of crime in that it does not speculate about the motives of offenders. Rather, it takes as given that the population contains a certain proportion of people who wish to commit offences. It focuses instead on the fact that, for a crime to occur, (1) a motivated offender must (2) encounter a suitable victim or other offending opportunity (3) in the absence of a capable guardian who would otherwise act as a deterrent (Cohen & Felson, 1979). RAT has influenced the development of geographical offender profiling (see Chapter 6) and situational crime prevention (see Chapter 10). It has also been suggested as a theoretical framework for understanding cybercrime.

One area to which RAT has been applied is in understanding the growth of cyber-harassment and cyberstalking. These terms refer broadly to activities like threatening, insulting and otherwise harming victims through electronic means. It generally denotes more sustained victimisation than the comparatively transient 'trolling'. It often has a sexual element (e.g. unwanted sexual advances, sexual harassment and the sending/posting of obscene comments and images) (Wick et al., 2017). Cyberstalking and harassment may be perpetrated by strangers, as when public figures on social media platforms such as Twitter are targeted, but is also associated with former and current intimate partners and acquaintances. These behaviours appear to be growing in prevalence. Finn (2004) found that 10 to 15% of student samples reported some degree of victimisation, whereas Melander (2010) found about double this. Wick et al. (2017) suggest, using RAT, that the growth of these crimes results from steadily increasing take-up of the Internet, which creates more opportunities for offenders to encounter victims. They surveyed 298 US university students about their experiences of online harassment victimisation. They also asked about respondents' online exposure (e.g. how much they used online shopping, banking, dating etc.), their level of online disclosure (i.e. the extent to which they shared personal information through photographs on social media etc.) and their own involvement of the victimisation of others. Of respondents, 80% reported some degree of both victimisation and perpetration. Those who had the highest level of online exposure had the highest risk of victimisation. Findings like these broadly support the idea that cybervictimisation is primarily due to situational factors rather than individual ones and suggest that RAT may have some utility as an approach to explaining cybercrime.

However, critics have pointed out that the transfer of RAT to the online world may not be as straightforward as it initially appears. RAT is rooted in the relationship between offending, space and time: offenders and criminal opportunities come together at particular times and in particular places; understanding how time and place influence offending is what gives the theory its power. However, the online world renders physical location largely irrelevant and places far fewer constraints on the timing of activities (Yar, 2005), which raises questions about whether RAT is capable of predicting cyberoffending in the same way as 'real-world' offending. Other aspects of RAT transfer to the cyber realm only with difficulty. For example, offline offending is influenced by the fact that some physical objects are easier to steal/damage than others by dint of being smaller/lighter/less durable and so on. Digital targets do not have the same properties, except perhaps metaphorically. Similarly, real-world targets vary in terms of their visibility and accessibility to potential offenders but visibility and accessibility in the online world need to be understood differently. There is also the question of 'capable guardians'. In RAT, this refers both to authorities such as the police but also to informal surveillance and enforcement of law-abiding norms by members of the public (this is a similar idea to collective efficacy; see Chapter 5). Again, it is not clear how the notion of the capable guardian applies in the online world. So while RAT offers an attractive set of metaphors for discussing cybercrime, there are clearly some ways in which its core concepts will need to be reformulated. It may yet emerge that theoretical approaches that view cyberoffending as a distinct category of crime (as opposed to 'old wine in new bottles'; Grabosky, 2001) may ultimately be more useful.

Future developments

Although research into cybercriminology is at a comparatively early stage it has generated a great deal of interesting debate and findings. Ngo and Jaishankar (2017) identify a number of priorities for the emerging field. First, there is a need for work on defining and classifying cybercrime. There is a proliferation of definitions, which inhibits communication between scholars. Greater clarity would improve communication and make it easier to start understanding the scale and scope of cyberoffending. Second, the measurement of cybercrime is still in its infancy. Although moving in the right direction (e.g. through the recent inclusion of cyberoffending in the CSEW), there is still far to go in the acquisition of valid data on the incidence and prevalence of online offending. Third, the development of knowledge of cybercrime has only just started. Part of the problem is the apparent lack of interest in cybercrime from 'mainstream' criminology and criminological psychology. Given the opportunities the Internet creates for a single offender to reach more victims with less risk of detection than in the 'real world', this is unfortunate. Finally, Ngo and Jaishankar point to the need to develop practical applications for cybercrime prevention. Currently, there is very little systematic knowledge of what works, what does not and why. However, the existence of so many gaps in what is undoubtedly an important area seems likely to generate a great deal of research in the near future, so it is probable that knowledge of online offending will grow markedly over the next few years.

Chapter summary

Changes in society are reflected in the concerns of psychologists and criminologists. Two topics of contemporary interest are terrorism and cybercrime. Terrorism is the use of violence to bring about political change. High-profile terrorist attacks have made terrorism a significant concern in the West but the majority of terrorist victims currently are from the Middle East, Africa and South Asia. Terrorist attacks have lasting psychological consequences, including PTSD. Those most at risk are those directly exposed and emergency services and recovery workers are particularly affected in the long term. Contrary to stereotypes, terrorists are a diverse group and attempts to establish a 'terrorist profile' have been unsuccessful. The staircase model of terrorism views the development of violent extremism as rooted in a sense of injustice, marginalisation and collective injustice. These thoughts and feelings may be held by many people in a given community with progressively fewer people advancing towards more direct engagement with radicalism and very few progressing to actual terrorist acts. There have been some promising attempts to de-radicalise terrorists but not all have been successful because they do not adequately address the social and political concerns that drive extremist involvement.

Cybercrime is crime in which computers play a role. It covers a range of activities, some of which are dependent on computers (e.g. hacking) and some of which are enabled by computers (e.g. fraud). Cybercrime presents new challenges to law enforcement because of its technical nature and the opportunities it creates for offenders to target victims anywhere in the world. The scale of cybercrime is currently unknown. The stereotype of the 'lone hacker' is misleading since the majority of cybercriminals offend in groups. Theories from 'traditional' criminological psychology have had some success in explaining cyberoffending. Personality research has identified traits of psychopathy, narcissism, Machiavellianism and sadism as significant influences on cybercrime. Social learning theory has highlighted the role of the peer group in activities like hacking and software piracy. Routine activity theory has been used to predict victimisation in online stalking and harassment. However, it is currently unclear whether new theories will be required to adequately understand offending in the online world.

Further reading

Horgan, J. (2012). *The Psychology of Terrorism*, rev. 2nd ed. London: Routledge. A comprehensive overview of research in the field by an acknowledged expert.

International Journal of Cybercriminology publishes academic research into cybercrime and is open access. It makes fascinating reading. http://www.cybercrimejournal.com/.

Kirwan, G., & Power, A. (2013). *Psychology of Cybercrime*. Cambridge: Cambridge University Press. Although a few years old in a field that changes rapidly, this is the standard introductory text to the field.

National Consortium for the Study of Terrorism and Responses to Terrorism houses the Global Terrorism Database and publishes regular bulletins and articles on the subject. http://www.start.umd.edu/.

12

Critical perspectives: crime, gender and race

The view of criminological psychology presented in this book could be regarded as the mainstream of theory and research in the field. However, there is a long tradition of critical thinking in research into crime, victimisation and criminal law that calls into question the assumptions, methods of enquiry and conclusions of the dominant view. This chapter explores some of the themes and ideas developed by critical researchers into criminology and criminological psychology. The term 'critical perspectives' covers a great range of viewpoints and it would be impossible in a single short chapter to do justice to this diversity. Consequently, what is presented here should be taken only as a very general introduction to the area. The chapter starts by identifying key features of the majority view and contrasting this with some of the assumptions critical perspectives tend to share. There is then an exploration of how critical thinking about gender and race has led to conceptions of crime, criminality and victimisation that contrast with those of the mainstream.

The mainstream view

The majority of criminological psychology is based on a philosophical viewpoint called positivism. Essentially, positivism claims that there is an objective, physical world 'out there' and that it is possible to establish what it is like and how it works using the methods of science. As applied to the study of crime, positivism assumes that there are people in the world who do things called 'crimes'. Crimes have an objective existence that makes them different from other acts that are not crimes. Positivism further assumes that crimes are done by a distinct type of person we call a criminal, who is measurably different from other people who are not criminals. It also holds that the things that happen in the world have causes and that it is possible, using objective methods, to establish which causes have which effects. The positivist approach to understanding crime is, broadly, to establish (1) what makes criminals different from non-criminals and (2) how they come to be that way. To illustrate, recall the biological view of criminality presented in Chapter 3.

Biopsychologists argue that there are detectable differences between the brains of criminals and non-criminals in areas such as the frontal cortex and the amygdala. The consequence of these differences is that affected individuals either have abnormal emotional responses to others or are unable to restrain themselves in acting in ways that violate the moral consensus of society. These brain differences are thought to have a variety of causes, including genetic influences, physical damage to the brain and stress resulting from childhood adversity. The methods chosen to investigate the area aim to establish objective facts about the causes of crime, for example, by comparing people with and without criminal convictions on measures of brain structure and functioning, such as data from brain imaging studies. These are selected to avoid subjectivity or interpretation, as this may result in a loss of objectivity. The biopsychological view of crime conforms to the positivist model very closely in its emphasis on an objective, knowable reality underlying criminal acts.

Critical perspectives on crime

Collectively, critical perspectives on crime, psychology and criminology challenge the mainstream, positivist view. Chapter 2 discussed how the socially constructed nature of the phenomenon makes crime difficult to define in the clear and objective terms required by scientific enquiry. While mainstream criminological psychology has acknowledged a difficulty here it has tended to sidestep the problem and focus on crime as legally defined nonetheless. In contrast, critical perspectives have opened up debate about the implications of the socially constructed nature of crime. For example, Becker's (1963) labelling theory (see Chapter 5) asserts that no behaviour is inherently criminal; rather, acts become criminal when defined as such by society. Some groups in society have more power than others to influence which acts are defined as criminal and hence which acts are policed and punished. A critical perspective on crime might ask, therefore, whether the psychological study of crime, criminals, policing and justice really only serves the interests of a powerful few, even though it is presented as an objective description of reality.

Critical perspectives are plural: there is no single theory that can be called 'critical criminological psychology' or 'critical criminology'. The critical stance encompasses a range of viewpoints and perspectives although there are ideas held in common between them. Broadly, critical perspectives assert that the mainstream, historically, has investigated crime and related topics in a very narrow way, focusing mainly on individual offenders and on crime as defined by the state (Friedrichs, 2009). Besides accepting legal definitions of crime in an uncritical way, mainstream criminology and criminological psychology have tended to focus only on a limited range of harmful acts. No reasonable person would deny the harm caused by street robbery or interpersonal violence. However, a critical perspective might ask why corporate fraud, unsafe working conditions, violation of environmental legislation and the incitement of conflict in other nation states attract relatively little public disapproval, condemnation from the authorities or investigation by academics even though they also result in economic and ecological harm and loss of life. A possible answer lies in the way the mass media, under the influence of powerful elites, direct public attention and concern toward only certain crimes, typically those committed by poor, uneducated and marginalised people (Box, 1983). Critical researchers, then, open up questions about power relations and social control and ask how institutions like the police, the courts, the government, the media and, indeed, academic research may play a role in producing and perpetuating inequality and injustice.

Although they use a wide variety of methodologies, there is a tendency for those working within the critical perspectives to question the claim that objective, scientific methodology should have a privileged status. Some believe that the purported objectivity of scientific methods is, in itself, an ideological position that serves the powerful. Consequently, many critical researchers favour qualitative, interpretive methodologies that allow them to engage with people's lived experience and subjective social reality. In relation to their theorising about crime, critical perspectives tend to emphasise the role of social processes and forces in producing criminality and victimhood. Along with this there comes a scepticism about essentialist explanations that locate the causes of behaviour inside the individual. Further, many of those working within critical perspectives reject the idea that academic research should be separated from activism. Rather than aiming merely to describe how the world is, they seek to bring about social change through their research activities. Friedrichs (2009) identifies a number of issues around which critical research into crime has tended to coalesce including:

- Understanding crime in relation to economic inequality under a capitalist system (e.g. why are poorer people over-represented in the criminal statistics?).
- Understanding violent and sexual crime in relation to gender as a cultural force that both drives offending and marginalises its victims (e.g. why is male violence against women so prevalent?).
- Understanding crimes perpetrated by the advantaged or privileged in society against those who are relatively powerless (e.g. why do people commit 'hate crimes' against ethnic and sexual minorities or people with disabilities?).
- Understanding the crimes of the powerful (e.g. why are the people responsible for corporate or ecological crime so rarely held accountable?).

Feminism, gender and crime

Over the second half of the 20th century feminism rose to prominence as the leading critical perspective on crime, criminology and criminological psychology. Definitions of feminism vary but they centre on advocacy for women's rights and gender equality. In relation to crime, as in other fields, the feminist project has been not just to understand the role of gender in crime and victimisation but also to press for practical changes that address injustice and support gender equality. Like other critical perspectives, feminism includes a plurality of viewpoints and its foci have changed over time in response to societal conditions and critiques that have come from both inside and outside the feminist movement.

An early feminist critique of mainstream criminology was that women were largely absent from it (e.g. Heidensohn, 1968; Smart, 1976). There are obvious sex differences in the rate of recorded crime but until relatively recently they went unremarked on in the academic literature. Until the 1980s almost all research on offenders used male samples and so practically nothing was known about women's offending. This androcentric bias meant that when women were discussed as offenders, explanations were generally based on questionable generalisations from male offenders or on stereotypes about the biological or psychological 'nature' of women. Feminist critics suggested that women in the criminal justice system were treated by the authorities as 'doubly deviant', first for committing a crime and second for transgressing against the stereotypes of women as passive and maternal. The experiences of women offenders were largely unresearched.

In relation to the victimisation of women, violence in the family tended to be ignored or not considered in the light of gender inequality. As researchers started to conduct studies of girls and women in the criminal justice system, new emphasis was given to victimisation, and particularly the way in which societal power relations around gender conspired to render 'invisible' crimes that most frequently affect women. For example, until 1991 there was no legal concept of rape within marriage in UK law, even though a 1989 survey of 1,007 women found that 14% of respondents reported having been forced to have sex by their husbands against their will (Painter, 1991). Similarly, until the 1970s it was rare for police to intervene in cases of domestic violence, which was widely regarded as a 'private matter' by law enforcement, a situation that has improved markedly in recent years due to feminist activism (Houston, 2014).

In recent years, attention has moved to the intersection between gender, race and class. This shift is rooted in a critique of some earlier feminist views that presented an essentialist view that assumed that the experiences and characteristics of women were universal. Contemporary analyses point to how people are affected by overlapping systems of oppression. The experiences of a white, middle class woman in relation to crime and justice may be very different from those of a black, lower class woman (Crenshaw, 1989), a fact to which the over-representation of indigenous and minority ethnicity women among the prison populations of many countries attests (Carrington & Death, 2014). Although the foci of feminist perspectives on crime have changed over time, there has been a constant emphasis on the relationship between gender and power and on how the social construction of gender operates to uphold men's power over women.

Woman offenders

A consistent feminist criticism of mainstream theories of crime is that they are actually theories of male criminal behaviour, based almost exclusively on research using male offenders against a backdrop of stereotypes about women. Apart from perpetuating gender stereotypes, this is bad science as the field collectively has failed to gather data about woman offenders (Naffine, in Carrington & Death, 2014, p.104). As a consequence there has been a neglect of how gender might influence men's and women's pathways into crime, the types of crime they commit, their selection of victims and their treatment by the authorities. For example, social learning theory (see Chapter 5) puts great emphasis on the peer group as a source of pro-crime attitudes, models and reinforcement for criminal acts. While this may be true for men, women's pathways into offending are often different. Women are more likely to be recruited into offending by an intimate partner with delinquent tendencies (Sharp, 2009). According to Sharp, part of the problem is that mainstream academic research into crime has a close relationship with the criminal justice system and tends to reflect its concerns. Since the criminal justice system is most concerned with crimes that immediately threaten public safety, and these crimes are usually committed by men, women's offending has comparatively been ignored.

Chesney-Lind and Pasko (2004) argue that the patriarchal nature of Western society means that any explanation of women's offending must take as its starting point the ways in which women are systematically disadvantaged. Their status as second-class citizens exposes them to early experiences of powerlessness and victimisation, which, in turn, provide the context for their later development of a delinquent or criminal career. Based on investigations with young female offenders in the US, Chesney-Lind and Pasko found that girls' first encounter with the criminal justice system tends to be for 'status offences' (acts that are only illegal when the person is underage), such as truanting, running away or engaging in sexual activity. Girls are sanctioned for such actions more heavily than boys because of the sexual double standard, whereby females are condemned as immoral for sexual behaviour that, in males, is tolerated or even encouraged. Acts such as running away and early sexual activity are often linked to abuse within the home or family so young women's offending is driven by their response to abuse. The moral condemnation it attracts, however, leads to labelling (see Chapter 5), which affects their self-concept and limits their opportunities to establish a legitimate status and identity. Drug and alcohol use are common in female offenders and contribute significantly to their imprisonment (Heidensohn & Silvestri, 2012), which further serves to lock female offenders into criminal trajectories. Female prisoners frequently have multiple vulnerabilities including drug and alcohol misuse, poor physical and mental health, the effects of earlier victimisation and a lack of education and employability skills. Female prisoners are also more likely than male to have dependent children; imprisonment frequently results in their removal, further increasing their vulnerability. Sharp (2009) argues, therefore, that because women's and men's pathways into offending are different, it is inappropriate to subject female offenders to a prison system designed to reform men.

Intimate partner violence

Another strand of feminist enquiry concerns how gender inequality affects the victimisation of women. It was noted above that early feminist critics highlighted the processes by which female victims have tended to be 'erased' by legal and policing arrangements that conspire to render them invisible. Much research has focused on heterosexual intimate partner violence (IPV) and violence in domestic settings, where feminists have generally argued that domestic violence is asymmetric (that is, men are more likely to be the perpetrators and women the victims). This claim has been disputed on the basis of data that suggest that women are violent towards their male partners at least as often as men are towards their female ones (e.g. Steinmetz, 1977). Dobash and Dobash (2015), however, point to a weakness of the 'objective' data that come from such surveys in that merely counting kicks, punches, slaps and so on strips violence of its meaning: it matters whether an act was carried out in order to threaten, intimidate, retaliate or in self-defence. When contextually sensitive measures of violence are used, the majority of perpetrators are men and the majority of victims of IPV are women. Using data from the US National Intimate Partner and Sexual Violence Survey (NISVS), Breiding et al. (2014) estimated that 8.8% of women are raped by an intimate partner during their lifetime; the corresponding figure for men being 0.5%. During their lifetime 15.8% of women and 9.5% of men experienced other forms of sexual violence. Severe physical violence was experienced by 22.3% of women and 14% of men. While these estimates do indicate that men are subject to violence in intimate relationships, the risk run by women is proportionally higher. Data from the 2013–2014 CSEW show that 46% of female murder victims were killed by a current or former intimate partner whereas the same was true of only 7% of male murder victims (ONS, 2017f).

Mainstream explanations of IPV tend to locate the causes of men's violence towards women inside the individual. For example, an evolutionary view might suggest that IPV in men reflects an evolved behavioural tendency. Unlike women, men cannot be sure that any offspring from their partnership actually carry their genes as the woman may have mated with another male. This introduces a risk that a man might invest his resources in rearing children who do not propagate his genes. In this view, sexual jealousy and the violence that goes with it serve to reduce the risk that a female partner will mate with someone else and, consequently, is an adaptive behaviour because it increases the probability of a man passing his genes on to his offspring (Goetz et al., 2008; see also Chapter 3).

Feminist analyses of IPV tend to reject the essentialism of the evolutionary account and point instead to its role in upholding the legitimacy of male violence against women. Feminists also tend to reject individualistic accounts of victimisation such as 'battered woman syndrome' (Walker, 1984), which construe the responses of victims of IPV as in some way defective or pathological. Rather, feminists have preferred to understand male violence as embedded in a multiplicity of social systems whose effect is to uphold men's dominance and privilege over women in intimate relationships. In this view, violence serves to intimidate and control women and isolate them from the support networks that otherwise might help them escape it. Women frequently remain in violent relationships because of the threat of further violence, economic disadvantage (which itself is related to gender inequality) and because of the prevailing 'moral order' that stresses a woman's obligations toward her family as part of her feminine identity.

Feminism has made a significant impact on how the police and the courts treat violence in domestic settings (Hoyle, 2007). In the 1970s the authorities typically did not take domestic violence seriously. The police were reluctant to intervene in IPV cases, preferring to refer them to social services when they took action at all. Under pressure from feminist researchers, policing moved towards arresting and charging perpetrators. Some police forces have removed 'taking no action' as an option for officers investigating IPV cases, leading to substantial increases in arrests for domestic violence. Legislators were also influenced by feminist research. For example, the Domestic Violence, Crime and Victims Act (2004) made common assault and breach of a non-molestation order arrestable offences, enabled the use of restraining orders on IPV perpetrators and extended legal protection to cohabiting couples on the same basis as married ones. However welcome these changes have been, there is now recognition that increased use of criminal sanctions may not protect victims of IPV adequately. The most vulnerable victims, those who are poor, of minority ethnicity, insecure immigration status and those with a criminal record, are still reluctant to report IPV to the authorities since by doing so they risk separation from their children, being arrested, deported and so on.

Chapter 10 discussed the use of psychological interventions in the rehabilitation of offenders. Besides offering insight into the needs of female offenders, feminist research has also addressed the issue of reforming perpetrators of IPV. According to Hoyle (2007), the majority of programmes aimed at addressing IPV are based on the Duluth Model, a framework for intervention based on the assumption that domestic violence is about power and control of women in the context of a patriarchal society. It is an educational approach that helps offenders recognise the relationship between their abusive actions and their need for power and control. The intention is to bring about attitude change in offenders so they become more favourable toward equality-based relationships. Although widely adopted, Duluth-based programmes have had a limited impact on IPV recidivism (Feder & Wilson, 2005). Hoyle (2007) suggests that the assumption that IPV is all about male power over women has meant that individual factors in IPV are sidelined when, in reality, a consideration of the risk factors that apply to individual perpetrators would make intervention more effective. Dutton and Corvo (2007) go further, questioning the core assumptions of the Duluth Model. They dispute the feminist claims that male IPV is not anger driven and that IPV is strongly related to patriarchal beliefs. They also question the view that power, control and violence are exclusively male issues, arguing that IPV is more symmetrical than Duluth proponents allow. Ehrensaft (2008) criticises the Duluth Model for its lack of a developmental perspective on violence and a reluctance to consider that female partners may contribute to a violent relationship out of a fear of victim blaming.

Feminism: general considerations

The limited success of attempts to reform IPV offenders notwithstanding, the impact of feminism on the study of crime and victimisation is unarguable. Feminism's activist stance has driven enormous advances in raising awareness of, and mobilising responses to, domestic violence. The foregrounding of feminist concerns has inspired research across the whole field of criminology and thereby addressed significant gaps in our understanding of offending and victimisation.

Perhaps inevitably, there has been backlash against feminism's influence on the study of crime and on society more generally. For example, since the 1990s there has been much discussion of a claimed rise in violence among young women. It was suggested in Chapter 2 that the narrowing of the gender gap in crime statistics actually reflects changes in the authorities' willingness to recognise and respond officially to violence by women. However, there has been no shortage of commentators ready to blame feminism for promoting female violence as a side effect of gender equality. Chesney-Lind and Pasko (2013) suggest that much of the media hype surrounding 'girl gangs' in the US is actually driven by concern about race. The gangs identified and condemned in the media are primarily black and Latina girls and women. Such gangs have been a constant feature in the US for many years but, prior to the 1990s, were largely ignored by the police, who were more concerned with policing girls' sexual behaviour.

Feminism has always been characterised by internal debate and so feminist ideas about crime and victimisation continue to change and develop. For example, there is increasing uneasiness about theories that position all crimes by women, including violent ones, as being a response to victimisation on the grounds that such explanations undermine women's agency and risk construing them as passive victims of circumstances (Carrington & Death, 2014). Such debates will no doubt continue to enliven a critical perspective that has gone, since the 1960s, from the marginal concern of a handful of fringe researchers to a mainstay of academic research into crime.

Critical perspectives on ethnicity, race and crime

Like feminism, critical perspectives on ethnicity, race and crime have challenged widely held assumptions about the nature and causes of offending, victimisation and the workings of the criminal justice system. In doing so, they have uncovered many ways in which mainstream criminological psychology and criminology have served to perpetuate racist and discriminatory ideas and practices.

A central question of critical perspectives on race and crime is why BEM groups are over-represented in the crime statistics. Chapter 2 identified two explanations. According to the differential involvement hypothesis, members of BEM groups commit more crime whereas the differential selection hypothesis suggests that they are more likely to end up in the crime statistics. If we accept differential selection then it becomes necessary to identify the ways in which BEMs are treated differently from white people in the criminal justice system. There are many possibilities. For example:

- Legislators may make laws that focus on the types of offence that are more likely to be committed by BEMs or which criminalise behaviour associated with minority groups.

- Police may scrutinise minorities more systematically than white people and are therefore more likely to observe illicit activity, leading to more arrests.

- The courts may be biased in their decisions about which criminal cases to pursue and the trial process may discriminate against minority groups either directly by returning biased verdicts (see Chapter 8) or indirectly by, for example, providing poor-quality legal representation to minority defendants.

The view that the criminal justice system is systematically biased against ethnic minorities has been developed in the US under the rubric of Critical Race Theory (see below).

If, by way of contrast, we accept the differential involvement view it is necessary to explain why BEM groups commit more crime. Broadly, there are two types of explanation. The social causation view is that minority groups are affected by their environment in ways that the white majority are not. Relevant factors could include poverty, environmental conditions, the experience of discrimination and so on. Under this view, crime is a consequence of structural inequalities in society. These factors tend to be foregrounded in critical perspectives on race, ethnicity and crime. The alternative is the 'intrinsic criminality' view, which suggests that there is something inherently criminal about members of minority ethnic groups. This notion has been present in criminological psychology since its early days. Those taking a critical perspective on the field link it with racism.

'Intrinsic criminality' and racism in criminological psychology

Chapter 2 described how members of ethnic minorities in the UK and US are over-represented in the crime statistics as both offenders and victims. The same pattern is discernible in Canada, Australia and New Zealand, where visible minorities including indigenous groups run a significantly higher risk of arrest and incarceration than white people (Gabbidon, 2010). The relationship between ethnicity and crime has been the subject of discussion since criminology was founded in the 19th century (see Chapter 1) and from its inception it has embodied racist understandings of people and society. For example, Lombroso suggested that the 'coloured races' of Europe were under-evolved and innately prone to savagery (Holmes, 2015). Such overt racism is relatively uncommon in the academic investigation of crime nowadays. The idea of a direct, biological link between a person's race and his risk of criminality was based on the understanding that each 'race' represented a distinct subgroup of the human species with many shared features. Investigation of the human genome has shown that, beyond the genes that affect skin coloration and physical stature, there are practically no genetic group differences between people classified as belonging to different 'races' (Cavalli-Sforza et al., 1994) and people classified as belonging to the same 'race' can be genetically very unalike (Bamshad & Olson, 2003). The majority of researchers, consequently, regard 'race' as a social construct rather than a biological one.

However, critical researchers have suggested that the theme of race as a biological influence on criminality has not disappeared from criminological psychology but rather has assumed different, subtler forms. Miller (1996) describes how individualistic, essentialist notions about the relationship between race, genetics, intelligence and criminality reappeared in the late 20th century in books such as *Crime and Human Nature* (Herrnstein & Wilson, 1985) and *The Bell Curve* (Herrnstein & Murray, 1996). Miller argues that such works, which are presented as academic research, are highly problematic in that they lend legitimacy to racist attitudes by attaching to them the credibility of science. The linking of crime to the 'hard science' of biology effectively closes down discussion of the social determinants of crime in minority groups. Not only does this confirm members of the public in racist attitudes they may hold but it also makes the public receptive to law and order policies that discriminate against minority groups (for example, mass incarceration; see Chapter 9). In Miller's analysis, the search for biological correlates of criminality should be treated with great suspicion as it inevitably ends up being used to support racist and discriminatory ideas, regardless of the intentions of the original researchers.

A more recent example is furnished by research into genetic influences on serotonin metabolism and their relationship with violence (see Chapter 3). Gibbons (2004) identified a variant of the MAOA gene linked with aggression, violence and risk taking, especially where the carrier had experienced abusive treatment as a child. Lea and Chambers (2007) observed that the MAOA variant occurred more frequently in some ethnic groups including Chinese, African and Polynesian samples. Gibbons used the term 'warrior gene' to denote the variant and this term was repeated both in academic research and the popular media. Gillett and Tamatea (2012) highlight a number of unfortunate consequences of this. The notion of a 'warrior gene' that is responsible for aggressive behaviour promotes an essentialist view of crime that is linked to 'race' via biology. First, this serves to legitimise punitive and reactionary law and order policies such as 'three strikes' laws and 'boot camps' that are used in a discriminatory way against members of marginalised groups such as the Maori in New Zealand. Second, it distracts attention from the social conditions that contribute to high rates of offending among indigenous groups in post-colonial societies, such as poverty and poor education. Third, it promotes a stereotype of Maori people that reduces them to a single idea – that they are aggressive people – while simultaneously denigrating the meaning of 'warrior' to Maori culture by linking it with impulsivity, recklessness and selfishness rather than discipline and the use of aggression in collective and goal-directed ways. Importantly, Gillett and Tamatea do not allege that Gibbons and others hold consciously racist or discriminatory attitudes or that they deliberately set out to uphold injustice through their research. Rather, they were oblivious to the consequences of their actions in the context of a society that systematically disadvantages members of minority groups.

Critical Race Theory

Critical Race Theory (CRT) is centred on the study of race, racism and power. It emerged in the US as a critical perspective on crime (among other things) in the

1970s. CRT draws on a variety of intellectual influences including Marxism, feminism and the US civil rights movement of the 1960s. Like feminism, CRT is transformative in that it explicitly aims to change society by eliminating racism from social institutions, including education and the criminal justice system (Ugwudike, 2015). Because it originated in the US, much of its critique is focused on US laws and institutions but its key ideas are gaining traction in the UK and elsewhere. According to Ross (2010), the grounding assumptions of CRT are (1) that the law is principally a pretext for the maintenance of white power over non-whites and (2) that this purpose is hidden by the purported rationality and objectivity of legal reasoning. CRT shares with (many aspects of) feminism the idea that 'reality' is socially constructed and bound up with the operation of power within society. Just as feminism argues that gender is central to understanding social processes, CRT argues that the functioning of a society like the US cannot be understood independently of the concept of race. It rejects the idea that racism is the result of the actions of a few individuals who hold racist attitudes. Rather, racism is perpetuated by all sorts of everyday actions by ordinary people who may actually be avowedly anti-racist in their views. Racism is produced by actions so pervasive that their significance is easily overlooked. Nonetheless, these everyday processes subordinate ethnic minorities in ways that confer an advantage on the privileged white majority. As we might expect, CRT rejects the notion of race as a biological phenomenon that underlies psychological and behavioural differences between people and groups. Instead, it holds that the inequalities that exist between different 'racial' groups result from social processes.

CRT's critique of racism is much broader than just crime and the justice system but many topics of interest to criminological psychologists and criminologists fall within its purview. For example, it argues that crime is defined in ways that reflect the concerns of the powerful. There are many acts that harm others but they are only criminalised by the law where it serves the interests of the dominant white majority. Consequently, financial malpractice that deprives people of their employment or savings goes unchallenged whereas activities like congregating in groups, graffiti or even the wearing of certain types of clothing are aggressively policed because they are things that black and Hispanic people do (Ross, 2010). When black communities were affected by the US crack cocaine epidemic in the 1980s and 1990s, this was treated as a law and order issue and resulted in the 'war on drugs' and mass incarceration (see Chapter 9) whereas the recent steep rise in the abuse of prescription opioids among white Americans is presented as a public health issue requiring medical intervention (Yankah, 2016). The differential criminalisation of white and non-white drug use is reflected in media coverage of drug use. A content analysis of representations of drug use in US newspapers between 2001 and 2011 showed that opioid addiction was depicted in markedly different ways depending on whether the people concerned were white or black/Hispanic (Netherland & Hansen, 2016). Stories about opioid use by white people tended to present addiction as surprising and unusual, as a tragic waste of life and in terms that construed addicts as blameless or sympathetic victims of circumstances. In contrast, drug use by non-whites was presented as typical; voluntary criminality was the central theme.

In CRT, media representations are important because they contribute to differential racialisation. This is a key concept in CRT that draws attention to the fact that different racial groups have different histories and this is reflected in their experiences of everyday reality. Consequently, the lived experience of a black, Hispanic and Jewish person will be qualitatively different. It also means that the same racial group may be treated differently at different times. This is often linked to economic factors. For example, an undocumented immigrant might be welcomed as a 'migrant worker' when she acts as a source of cheap labour but an 'illegal alien' if economic circumstances alter (Ross, 2010). Popular media representations (e.g. newspapers, cartoons, films etc.) of different racial groups then alter correspondingly. For example, black Americans have variously been depicted as simple and carefree at some times and as brutish and threatening at others, according to prevailing social and economic conditions (Delgado & Stefancic, 2012). These representations do not only reflect societal views; they also inform and sustain them. This has an impact on how minorities are treated both individually and by institutions such as the police and courts. For example, between the 1980s and the 2000s, media representations of Muslims in the British media changed from an older stereotype of 'Asian passivity' to one of aggressive militancy and unwillingness to integrate with British (i.e. white) society (Saeed, 2007). Such representations feed a suspicion of the 'otherness' of British Muslims and have made them a target for racist attacks by the public and surveillance and intervention by the authorities. The increased differential racialisation of Muslims may ironically fuel the perception of group injustice that may incline marginalised people to become radicalised (see Chapter 11).

CRT's critique of mainstream criminology and criminological psychology goes beyond adding race/ethnicity as another variable to analyse, inviting us instead to consider fundamental questions about what crime is and how it is produced as a social process. It also asks us to consider whether academic disciplines like criminological psychology and criminology might play a role in upholding and reproducing the racism that CRT claims is at the heart of society. Its critics have accused CRT of 'playing the race card', that is, blaming racism whenever a black person loses in the criminal justice system. Others have derided it as a paranoid mode of thinking that attributes racist intent to legal processes where there is none (Ross, 2010). The social constructionist stance of many critical race theorists, together with their preference for qualitative research methods that explore the subjective experiences of BME people have drawn criticism from those who regard it as unscientific and resting on an evidence base that is difficult to verify. It is also the case that, originating in the US, CRT tends to reflect the history and experiences of black Americans so some of its insights may not readily transfer elsewhere. However, CRT is becoming established in other countries in a variety of academic fields and it is to be expected that locally relevant variants will develop over the next few years.

Chapter summary

Critical perspectives on crime are those that question the positivist assumption that there is an objective reality to crime and criminality that can be established using the methods of science. Critical perspectives typically emphasise the socially constructed nature of crime and the role of social and economic power in defining social reality. They raise fundamental questions about what criminological psychologists should study and how. Many critical researchers have approached criminology from a feminist perspective, arguing that women have been ignored and stereotyped by the field. Feminist researchers have extended the study of crime to include women as offenders, arguing that the nature and motivation for their offending differs from that of men. Others have addressed the invisibility of women victims of IPV, where the activism of feminist researchers has brought about significant changes to police practices and the law. The over-representation of BME people in crime statistics has been a question for criminological research since its inception. Critical perspectives on crime, race and ethnicity have highlighted how biological and psychological research into the causes of crime has been used to uphold racist ideas. Critical Race Theory (CRT) has emerged since the 1970s as a multidisciplinary project to challenge societal and institutional racism. Among other things, it has analysed the centrality of race to how crime is defined and policed and the interplay between law and order policies, social attitudes and representations of race in the mass media. Both feminism and CRT have been critiqued on political grounds, for their social constructionist standpoint and their preference for qualitative research methodologies that acknowledge subjective experience. Feminism has weathered this backlash to establish itself as an essential viewpoint in the academic study of crime. It is, as yet, too early to conclude whether CRT will manage to do the same.

Further reading

Ugwudike, P. (2015). *An Introduction to Critical Criminology*. Bristol: Policy Press.
A comprehensive introduction to critical perspectives on crime and criminology exploring a very broad selection of viewpoints including both historical and contemporary thinking.

References

Ageton, S. S., & Elliott, D. S. (1974). The effects of legal processing on delinquent orientations. *Social Problems, 22*(1), 87–100.

Ahmed-Leitao, F., Spies, G., van den Heuvel, L., & Seedat, S. (2016). Hippocampal and amygdala volumes in adults with posttraumatic stress disorder secondary to childhood abuse or maltreatment: A systematic review. *Psychiatry Research, 256,* 33–43.

Ainsworth, P. B. (2000). *Psychology and Crime: Myths and Reality.* Harlow: Pearson Education.

Ainsworth, P. B. (2001). *Offender Profiling and Crime Analysis.* Cullompton: Willan Publishing.

Akers, R. (1973). *Deviant Behavior: A Social Learning Approach.* Belmont, CA: Wadsworth.

Akers, R. L. (1990). Rational choice, deterrence, and social learning theory in criminology: The path not taken. *Journal of Criminal Law and Criminology, 81*(3), 653–676.

Akers, R. L., Krohn, M. D., Lanza-Kaduce, L., & Radosevich, M. (1979). Social learning and deviant behavior: A specific test of a general theory. *American Sociological Review, 44*(4), 636–655.

Akers, R. L., (2009). *Social Structure and Social Learning: A General Theory of Crime and Deviance.* Livingston: NJ: Transaction Publishers.

Alison, L., Smith, M. D., Eastman, O., & Rainbow, L. (2003). Toulmin's philosophy of argument and its relevance to offender profiling. *Psychology, Crime & Law: PC & L, 9*(2), 173–183.

Allely, C. S. (2016). Prevalence and assessment of traumatic brain injury in prison inmates: A systematic PRISMA review. *Brain Injury, 30*(10), 1161–1180.

Allen, G., & Watson, C. (2017). *UK Prison Population Statistics (Briefing Paper Number SN/SG/04334).* London: House of Commons Library.

Allen, M. W., Bettinger, R. L., Codding, B. F., Jones, T. L., & Schwitalla, A. W. (2016). Resource scarcity drives lethal aggression among prehistoric hunter-gatherers in central California. *Proceedings of the National Academy of Sciences, 113*(43), 12120–12125.

Alleyne, E., Fernandes, I., & Pritchard, E. (2014). Denying humanness to victims: How gang members justify violent behavior. *Group Processes & Intergroup Relations, 17*(6), 750–762.

Alper, A., Buckhout, R., Chern, S., Harwood, R., & Slomovits, M. (1976). Eyewitness identification: Accuracy of individual vs. composite recollections of a crime. *Bulletin of the Psychonomic Society, 8*(2), 147–149.

Anda, R. F., Butchart, A., Felitti, V. J., & Brown, D. W. (2010). Building a framework for global surveillance of the public health implications of adverse childhood. experiences. *American Journal of Preventive Medicine, 39*(1), 93–98.

Anderson, C. A., Shibuya, A., Ihori, N., Swing, E. L., Bushman, B. J., Sakamoto, A., & Saleem, M. (2010). Violent video game effects on aggression, empathy, and prosocial behavior in eastern and western countries: A meta-analytic review. *Psychological Bulletin, 136*(2), 151–173.

Andrews, D. A., & Bonta, J. (2010). *The Psychology of Criminal Conduct*. London: Routledge.

Antonaccio, O., Botchkovar, E. V., & Hughes, L. A. (2017). Ecological determinants of situated choice in situational action theory: Does neighborhood matter? *Journal of Research in Crime and Delinquency, 54*(2), 208–243.

Aos, S., Phipps, P., Barnoski, R., and & Lieb., R. (2001). *The Comparative Costs and Benefits of Programs to Reduce Crime*. Olympia, WA: Washington State Institute for Public Policy.

Aos, S., Lieb, R., Miller, J. M. M., & Pennucci, A. (2004). *Benefits and Costs of Prevention and Early Intervention Programs for Youth*. Olympia, WA: Washington State Institute for Public Policy.

Aos, S., Miller, M., and Drake, E. (2006). *Evidence-Based Public Policy Options to Reduce Future Prison Construction, Criminal Justice Costs, and Crime Rates*. Olympia, WA: Washington State Institute for Public Policy.

Apel, R. (2013). Sanctions, perceptions, and crime: Implications for criminal deterrence. *Journal of Quantitative Criminology, 29*(1), 67–101.

Arbuthnot, J., Gordon, D. A., & Jurkovic, G. (1987). Personality. In H. C. Quay (Ed.) *Handbook of Juvenile Delinquency* (pp. 139–183). Chichester: Wiley.

Ashworth, A. (2010). *Sentencing and Criminal Justice*. Cambridge: Cambridge University Press.

Aspley Limited. (1993). *E-Fit*. Hatfield: Aspley Limited.

Auty, K. M., Farrington, D. P., & Coid, J. W. (2015). Intergenerational transmission of psychopathy and mediation via psychosocial risk factors. *British Journal of Psychiatry, 206*(1), 26–31.

Averdijk, M. (2011). Reciprocal effects of victimization and routine activities. *Journal of Quantitative Criminology, 27*(2), 125–149.

Baglivio, M. T., Wolff, K. T., Piquero, A. R., & Epps, N. (2015). The relationship between adverse childhood experiences (ACE) and juvenile offending trajectories in a juvenile offender sample. *Journal of Criminal Justice, 43*(3), 229–241.

Bakker, E. (2015). *Terrorism and Counterterrorism Studies: Comparing Theory and Practice*. Leiden: Leiden University Press.

Bakker, E., & De Bont, R. (2016). Belgian and Dutch jihadist foreign fighters (2012–2015): Characteristics, motivations, and roles in the war in Syria and Iraq. *Small Wars & Insurgencies, 27*(5), 837–857.

Baldus, D. C., Woodworth, G., Zuckerman, D., & Weiner, N. A. (1998). Racial discrimination and the death penalty in the post-Furman era: An empirical and legal overview with recent findings from Philadelphia. *Cornell Law Review, 83,* 1638.

Bamshad, M. J., & Olson, S. E. (2003). Does race exist? *Scientific American, 289*(6), 78–85.

Bandura, A. (1977). *Social Learning Theory.* Englewood Cliffs, NJ: Prentice-Hall.

Bandura, A. (1986). *Social Foundations of Thought and Action: A Social Cognitive Theory.* Englewood Cliffs, NJ: Prentice-Hall.

Bandura, A. (1990). Selective activation and disengagement of moral control. *Journal of Social Issues, 46*(1), 27–46.

Bandura, A., Ross, D., & Ross, S. A. (1963). Imitation of film-mediated aggressive models. *Journal of Abnormal and Social Psychology, 66*(1), 3–11.

Barnoski, R. (2004). *Outcome Evaluation of Washington State's Research-Based Programs for Juvenile Offenders.* Olympia, WA: Washington State Institute for Public Policy.

Bartlett, F. C. (1932). *Remembering: An Experimental and Social Study.* Cambridge: Cambridge University Press.

Bazemore, G. (2009). Restorative justice: Theory, practice, and evidence. In *21st Century Criminology: A Reference Handbook* (pp. 750–760). Thousand Oaks, CA: Sage.

Beaver, K. M., DeLisi, M., Wright, J. P., & Vaughn, M. G. (2009). Gene–environment interplay and delinquent involvement: Evidence of direct, indirect, and interactive effects. *Journal of Adolescent Research, 24*(2), 147–168.

Beaver, K. M., DeLisi, M., Vaughn, M. G., & Barnes, J. C. (2010). Monoamine oxidase: A genotype is associated with gang membership and weapon use. *Comprehensive Psychiatry, 51*(2), 130–134.

Beaver, K. M., Barnes, J. C., May, J. S., & Schwartz, J. A. (2011). Psychopathic personality traits, genetic risk, and gene–environment correlations. *Criminal Justice and Behavior, 38*(9), 896–912.

Becker, G. S. (1968). Crime and punishment: An economic approach. *Journal of Political Economy, 76*(2), 169–217.

Becker, H. S. (1963). *Outsiders: Studies in the Sociology of Deviance.* New York: Free Press.

Bellair, P. E. (1997). Social integration and community crime: Examining the importance of neighbor networks. *Criminology: An Interdisciplinary Journal, 35*(4), 677–704.

Belson, W. A. (1978). *Television Violence and the Adolescent Boy.* Ann Arbor, MI: Saxon House.

Bennett, T., Wright, R., & Wright, R. (1984). *Burglars on Burglary: Prevention and the Offender.* Aldershot: Gower.

Berkowitz, L. (1959). Anti-semitism and the displacement of aggression. *Journal of Abnormal and Social Psychology, 59,* 182–187.

Berkowitz, L. (1969). The frustration-aggression hypothesis revisited. In *Roots of Aggression: A Re-examination of the Frustration-Aggression Hypothesis.* New York: Atherton Press.

Bernburg, J. G., Krohn, M. D., & Rivera, C. J. (2006). Official labeling, criminal embeddedness, and subsequent delinquency. *Journal of Research in Crime and Delinquency, 43*(1), 67–88.

Besemer, S., Farrington, D. P., & Bijleveld, C. C. J. H. (2017). Labeling and intergenerational transmission of crime: The interaction between criminal justice intervention and a convicted parent. *PloS One, 12*(3), e0172419.

Blackburn, R. (1993). *The Psychology of Criminal Conduct: Theory, Research and Practice*. Chichester: Wiley.

Blair, J., Mitchell, D., & Blair, K. (2005). *The Psychopath: Emotion and the Brain*. Malden, MA: Blackwell.

Blank, H., & Launay, C. (2014). How to protect eyewitness memory against the misinformation effect: A meta-analysis of post-warning studies. *Journal of Applied Research in Memory and Cognition, 3*(2), 77–88.

Boduszek, D., & Hyland, P. (2011). The theoretical model of criminal social identity: Psycho-social perspective. *International Journal of Criminology and Sociological Theory, 4*(1), 604–615.

Boisjoli, R., Vitaro, F., Lacourse, E., Barker, E. D., & Tremblay, R. E. (2007). Impact and clinical significance of a preventive intervention for disruptive boys. *British Journal of Psychiatry, 191*, 415–419.

Bornstein, B. H., & Greene, E. (2011). Jury decision making: Implications for and from psychology. *Current Directions in Psychological Science, 20*(1), 63–67.

Bornstein, B. H., & Greene, E. (2017). *The Jury Under Fire: Myth, Controversy, and Reform*. Oxford: Oxford University Press.

Bornstein, B. H., Golding, J. M., Neuschatz, J., Kimbrough, C., Reed, K., Magyarics, C., & Luecht, K. (2017). Mock juror sampling issues in jury simulation research: A meta-analysis. *Law and Human Behavior, 41*(1), 13–28.

Borum, R. (2008). Terrorism. In B. L. Cutler (Ed.) *Encyclopedia of Psychology and Law*. Thousand Oaks, CA: Sage.

Bottomley, A. K., & Pease, K. (1986). *Crime and Punishment: Interpreting the Data*. Milton Keynes: Open University Press.

Bouffard, J. A., & Muftić, L. R. (2007). The effectiveness of community service sentences compared to traditional fines for low-level offenders. *Prison Journal, 87*(2), 171–194.

Bowlby, J. (1951). Maternal care and mental health. *Bulletin of the World Health Organization, 3*(3), 355–533.

Box, S. (1983). *Power, Crime and Mystification*. London: Tavistock.

Brantingham, P. J., & Brantingham, P. L. (1981). *Environmental Criminology*. Beverly Hills, CA: Sage.

Breiding, M. J., Smith, S. G., Basile, K. C., Walters, M. L., Chen, J., & Merrick, M. T. (2014). Prevalence and characteristics of sexual violence, stalking, and intimate partner violence victimization – National Intimate Partner and Sexual Violence Survey, United States, 2011. *Morbidity and Mortality Weekly Report. Surveillance Summaries, 63*(8), 1–18.

Bremner, J. D., & Vermetten, E. (2001). Stress and development: Behavioral and biological consequences. *Development and Psychopathology, 13*(3), 473–489.

Brewer, N., Keast, A., & Rishworth, A. (2002). Improving the confidence–accuracy relation in eyewitness identification: Evidence from correlation and calibration. *Journal of Experimental Psychology. Applied, 8*, 44–56.

Brigham, J. C., & Pfeifer, J. E. (1994). *Evaluating the Fairness of Lineups. Adult Eyewitness Testimony: Current Trends & Developments.* Melbourne: Cambridge University Press.

Brinded, P. M. J., Stevens, I., Mulder, R. T., Fairley, N., Malcolm, F., & Wells, J. E. (1999). The Christchurch prisons psychiatric epidemiology study: Methodology and prevalence rates for psychiatric disorders. *Criminal Behaviour and Mental Health, 9*(2), 131–143.

Britton, P. (1998). *The Jigsaw Man.* London: Corgi Books.

Brodsky, S. L., Griffin, M. P., & Cramer, R. J. (2010). The witness credibility scale: An outcome measure for expert witness research. *Behavioral Sciences & the Law, 28*(6), 892–907.

Brown, M., J. (1997). Psychology at the service of the police. In *Proceedings of the 15th ATP Conference* (pp. 21–27).

Brown, R., & Kulik, J. (1977). Flashbulb memories. *Cognition, 5*(1), 73–99.

Browne, K. D. (1995). Possible effects of video film on the behaviour of young offenders. In *Proceedings of the British Psychological Society* (Vol. 3, p. 114). Leicester: British Psychological Society.

Browne, K. D., & Hamilton-Giachritsis, C. (2005). The influence of violent media on children and adolescents: A public-health approach. *The Lancet, 365*(9460), 702–710.

Browne, K., & Pennell, A. (1998). *The Effects of Video Violence on Young Offenders. Home Office Research and Statistics Directorate: Research Findings No. 65.* London: HMSO.

Bruce, V. (1988). *Recognising Faces.* Hove: Lawrence Eerlbaum Associates.

Buckels, E. E., Trapnell, P. D., & Paulhus, D. L. (2014). Trolls just want to have fun. *Personality and Individual Differences, 67*(Supplement C), 97–102.

Buckholtz, J. W., & Meyer-Lindenberg, A. (2008). MAOA and the neurogenetic architecture of human aggression. *Trends in Neurosciences, 31*(3), 120–129.

Budd, T., Sharp, C., & Mayhew, P. (2005). *Offending in England and Wales: First Results from the 2003 Crime and Justice Survey.* London: Home Office.

Buonanno, P., & Raphael, S. (2013). Incarceration and incapacitation: Evidence from the 2006 Italian collective pardon. *American Economic Review, 103*(6), 2437–2465.

Caldwell, R. G. (1965). *Criminology,* 2nd ed. New York: Ronald Press.

Cale, E. M. (2006). A quantitative review of the relations between the 'Big 3' higher order personality dimensions and antisocial behavior. *Journal of Research in Personality, 40*(3), 250–284.

Calvert, S. L., Appelbaum, M., Dodge, K. A., Graham, S., Nagayama Hall, G. C., Hamby, S., et al. (2017). The American Psychological Association Task Force assessment of violent video games: Science in the service of public interest. *American Psychologist, 72*(2), 126–143.

Campbell, S., & Harrington, V. (1999). *Findings from the 1998/99 Youth Lifestyles Survey.* London: Home Office.

Canter, D. (1994). *Criminal Shadows: Inside the Mind of the Serial Killer.* London: HarperCollins.

Canter, D. (1995). Psychology of offender profiling. In R. Bull & D. Carson (Eds.) *Handbook of Psychology in Legal Contests* (pp. 343–335). Chichester: Wiley

Canter, D. (2005). Confusing operational predicaments and cognitive explorations: Comments on Rossmo and Snook et al. *Applied Cognitive Psychology, 19*(5), 663–668.

Canter, D. V., & Gregory, A. (1994). Identifying the residential location of rapists. *Forensic Science Society, 34*(3), 169–175.

Canter, D., & Heritage, R. (1990). A multivariate model of sexual offence behaviour: Developments in "offender profiling". *Journal of Forensic Psychiatry & Psychology, 1*(2), 185–212.

Canter, D. V., & Youngs, D. (2010). *Investigative Psychology: Offender Profiling and the Analysis of Criminal Action*. Chichester: Wiley.

Carré, J. M., Hyde, L. W., Neumann, C. S., Viding, E., & Hariri, A. R. (2013). The neural signatures of distinct psychopathic traits. *Social Neuroscience, 8*(2), 122–135.

Carrington, K., & Death, J. (2014). Feminist criminologies' contribution to understandings of sex, gender, and crime. In R. Gartner, & W. McCarthy (Eds.) *Oxford Handbook of Gender, Sex, and Crime* (pp. 99–122). Oxford: Oxford University Press.

Cases, O., Seif, I., Grimsby, J., Gaspar, P., Chen, K., Pournin, S., et al. (1995). Aggressive behavior and altered amounts of brain serotonin and norepinephrine in mice lacking MAOA. *Science, 268*(5218), 1763–1766.

Caspi, A., McClay, J., Moffitt, T. E., Mill, J., Martin, J., Craig, I. W., et al. (2002). Role of genotype in the cycle of violence in maltreated children. *Science, 297*(5582), 851–854.

Castellow, W. A., Wuensch, K. L., & Moore, C. H. (1990). Effects of physical attractiveness of the plaintiff and defendant in sexual harassment judgements. *Journal of Social Behavior and Personality, 5*(6), 547–562.

Cavalli-Sforza, L. L., Menozzi, P., & Piazza, A. (1994). *The History and Geography of Human Genes*. Princeton, NJ: Princeton University Press.

Cecil, K. M., Brubaker, C. J., Adler, C. M., Dietrich, K. N., Altaye, M., Egelhoff, J. C., et al. (2008). Decreased brain volume in adults with childhood lead exposure. *PLoS Medicine, 5*(5), e112.

Chen, C.-A., & Howitt, D. (2012). Self-serving aspects of social cognition among adult offenders. *Psychology, Crime & Law, 18*(7), 595–611.

Chesney-Lind, M., & Pasko, L. (2004). *Girls' Troubles and 'Female Delinquency'*. Thousand Oaks, CA: Sage.

Chesney-Lind, M., & Pasko, L. (2013). *The Female Offender: Girls, Women, and Crime*. Thousand Oaks, CA: Sage.

Christiansen, K. O. (1977). A preliminary study of criminality among twins. In S. A. Mednick, & K. O. Christiansen (Eds.) *Biosocial Bases of Criminal Behavior* (pp. 89–108). New York: Gardner.

Christianson, S. Å. (1992). Emotional stress and eyewitness memory: A critical review. *Psychological Bulletin, 112*(2), 284–309.

Christianson, S. Å., & Hübinette, B. (1993). Hands up! A study of witnesses' emotional reactions and memories associated with bank robberies. *Applied Cognitive Psychology, 7*(5), 365–379.

Cid, J. (2009). Is imprisonment criminogenic? A comparative study of recidivism rates between prison and suspended prison sanctions. *European Journal of Criminology, 6*(6), 459–480.

Clark, S. E. (2012). Costs and benefits of eyewitness identification reform: Psychological science and public policy. *Perspectives on Psychological Science: A Journal of the Association for Psychological Science, 7*(3), 238–259.

Clarke, C., & Milne, R. (2001). *A National Evaluation of the PEACE Investigative Interviewing Course*. London: Home Office.

Clarke, R. V. (1997). *Situational Crime Prevention: Successful Case Studies*, 2nd ed. Guilderland, NY: Harrow & Heston.

Clifford, B. R., & Hollin, C. R. (1981). Effects of the type of incident and the number of perpetrators on eyewitness memory. *Journal of Applied Psychology, 66*(3), 364–370.

Clifford, B. R., & Scott, J. (1978). Individual and situational factors in eyewitness testimony. *Journal of Applied Psychology, 63*(3), 352–359.

Cloninger, C. R., Christiansen, K. O., Reich, T., & Gottesman, I. I. (1978). Implications of sex differences in the prevalences of antisocial personality, alcoholism, and criminality for familial transmission. *Archives of General Psychiatry, 35*(8), 941–951.

Clough, J. (2015). *Principles of Cybercrime*. Cambridge: Cambridge University Press.

Cohen, A. K. (1955). *Delinquent Boys: The Culture of the Gang*. Glencoe, IL: Free Press.

Cohen, L. E., & Felson, M. (1979). Social change and crime rate trends: A routine activity approach. *American Sociological Review, 44*(4), 588–608.

Cohen, R. L., & Harnick, M. A. (1980). The susceptibility of child witnesses to suggestion: An empirical study. *Law and Human Behavior, 4*(3), 201.

Cooke, D. J., Michie, C., Hart, S. D., & Patrick, C. (2006). Facets of clinical psychopathy: Towards clearer measurement. In C. Patrick (Ed.) *Handbook of Psychopathic Personality Disorder* (pp. 91–106). New York: Guilford.

Cooley, C. M. (2006). The CSI effect: Its impact and potential concerns. *New England Law Review, 41*(3), 471–502.

Cooley, C. M., & Turvey, B. E. (2014). *Miscarriages of Justice: Actual Innocence, Forensic Evidence, and the Law*. Cambridge, MA: Academic Press.

Copson, G., Badcock, R., Boon, J., & Britton, P. (1997). Articulating a systematic approach to clinical crime profiling. *Criminal Behaviour and Mental Health: CBMH, 7*(1), 13–17.

Cornet, L. J. M., de Kogel, C. H., Nijman, H. L. I., Raine, A., & van der Laan, P. H. (2014). Neurobiological factors as predictors of cognitive-behavioral therapy outcome in individuals with antisocial behavior: A review of the literature. *International Journal of Offender Therapy and Comparative Criminology, 58*(11), 1279–1296.

Cornish, D. B., & Clarke, R. V. (1987). Understanding crime displacement: An application of rational choice theory. *Criminology: An Interdisciplinary Journal, 25*(4), 933–948.

Cornish, D. B., & Clarke, R. V. (2003). Opportunities, precipitators and criminal decisions: A reply to Wortley's critique of situational crime prevention. In M. J.

Smith, & D. B. Cornish (Eds.) *Theory for Practice in Situational Crime Prevention (Crime Prevention Studies, Vol. 16)*. Monsey, NY: Criminal Justice Press.

Coyne, S. M. (2007). Does media violence cause violent crime? *European Journal on Criminal Policy and Research, 13*(3–4), 205–211.

Crenshaw, K. (1989). Demarginalizing the intersection of race and sex: A black feminist critique of antidiscrimination doctrine, feminist theory and antiracist politics. *University of Chicago Legal Forum, 1*, 139–176.

Crowe, R. R. (1972). The adopted offspring of women criminal offenders: A study of their arrest records. *Archives of General Psychiatry, 27*(5), 600–603.

Crowe, T. D. (1991). *Crime Prevention through Environmental Design: Applications of Architectural Design and Space Management Concepts*. Boston, MA: Butterworth-Heinemann.

Cruse, D., & Leigh, B. C. (1987). 'Adam's Rib' revisited: Legal and non-legal influences on the processing of trial testimony. *Social Behaviour, 2*(4), 221–230.

Cullen, F. T., Jonson, C. L., & Nagin, D. S. (2011). Prisons do not reduce recidivism: The high cost of ignoring science. *Prison Journal, 91*(3 Supplement), 48S–65S.

Cutler, B. L., & Penrod, S. D. (1995). *Mistaken Identification: The Eyewitness, Psychology and the Law*. Cambridge: Cambridge University Press.

Daftary-Kapur, T., Dumas, R., & Penrod, S. D. (2010). Jury decision-making biases and methods to counter them. *Legal and Criminological Psychology, 15*(1), 133–154.

Dalgaard, O. S., & Kringlen, E. (1976). A Norwegian twin study of criminality. *British Journal of Criminology, 16*(3), 213–232.

Dalton, G., Gawrylowicz, J., Memon, A., Milne, R., Horry, R., & Wright, D. B. (2013). Public perceptions of identification procedures in the United Kingdom. *Policing: A Journal of Policy and Practice, 8*(1), 35–42.

Daly, G., & Pattenden, R. (2005). Racial bias and the English criminal jury trial. *Cambridge Law Journal, 64*(3), 678–710.

Damasio, A. R. (1996). The somatic marker hypothesis and the possible functions of the prefrontal cortex. *Philosophical Transactions of the Royal Society of London. Series B, Biological Sciences, 351*(1346), 1413–1420.

Davies, G. M. (1991). Research on children's testimony: Implications for interviewing practice. In C. R. Hollin, & K. Howells (Eds.) *Clinical Applications to Sex Offenders and their Victims* (pp. 93–115). Chichester: Wiley.

Davies, G. M., & Oldman, H. (1999). The impact of character attribution on composite production: A real world effect? *Current Psychology, 18*(1), 128–139.

Davies, G. M., & Valentine, T. (2007). Facial composites: Forensic utility and psychological research. *Handbook of Eyewitness Psychology, 2*, 59–83.

de Bruin, J. P., van Oyen, H. G., & Van de Poll, N. (1983). Behavioural changes following lesions of the orbital prefrontal cortex in male rats. *Behavioural Brain Research, 10*(2–3), 209–232.

DeAngelis, T. (2009). Understanding terrorism. *American Psychological Association, 40*(10), 60–64.

Deffenbacher, K. A. (1983). The influence of arousal on reliability of testimony. In S. M. A. Lloyd-Boystock, & B. R. Clifford (Eds.) *Evaluating Witness Evidence* (pp. 235–251). New York: Wiley.

Delgado, R., & Stefancic, J. (2012). *Critical Race Theory: An Introduction*. New York: New York University Press.

DeLisi, M. (2009). Psychopathy is the unified theory of crime. *Youth Violence and Juvenile Justice, 7*(3), 256–273.

Dettbarn, E. (2012). Effects of long-term incarceration: A statistical comparison of two expert assessments of two experts at the beginning and the end of incarceration. *International Journal of Law and Psychiatry, 35*(3), 236–239.

Devery, C. (2010). Criminal profiling and criminal investigation. *Journal of Contemporary Criminal Justice, 26*(4), 393–409.

Devine, D. J., Krouse, P. C., Cavanaugh, C. M., & Basora, J. C. (2016). Evidentiary, extraevidentiary, and deliberation process predictors of real jury verdicts. *Law and Human Behavior, 40*(6), 670–682.

Dhanani, S., Kumari, V., Puri, B. K., Treasaden, I., Young, S., & Sen, P. (2017). A systematic review of the heritability of specific psychopathic traits using Hare's two-factor model of psychopathy. *CNS Spectrums, 11*, 1–10.

Diamond, B., & Bachmann, M. (2015). Out of the beta phase: Obstacles, challenges, and promising paths in the study of cyber criminology. *International Journal of Cyber Criminology, 9*(1), 24–34.

Dion, K., Berscheid, E., & Walster, E. (1972). What is beautiful is good. *Journal of Personality and Social Psychology, 24*(3), 285–290.

Dobash, R. E., & Dobash, R. P. (2015). Domestic violence: Sociological perspectives. In J. D. Wright (Ed.) *International Encyclopedia of the Social & Behavioral Sciences*, 2nd ed. Oxford: Elsevier.

Dodd, D. H., & Bradshaw, J. M. (1980). Leading questions and memory: Pragmatic constraints. *Journal of Verbal Learning and Verbal Behavior, 19*(6), 695–704.

Dolnik, L., Case, T. I., & Williams, K. D. (2003). Stealing thunder as a courtroom tactic revisited: Processes and boundaries. *Law and Human Behavior, 27*(3), 267–287.

Donohue, J. J., III. (2009). Assessing the relative benefits of incarceration: Overall changes and the benefits on the margin. In S. Raphael, & M. A. Stoll (Eds.) *Do Prisons Make Us Safer?: The Benefits and Costs of the Prison Boom* (pp. 269–342). New York: Russell Sage Foundation.

Douglas, J., & Olshaker, M. (1996). *Mindhunter*. London: Heinemann.

Dowden, C., Bennell, C., & Bloomfield, S. (2007). Advances in offender profiling: A systematic review of the profiling literature published over the past three decades. *Journal of Police and Criminal Psychology, 22*(1), 44–56.

Drago, F., Galbiati, R., & Vertova, P. (2011). Prison conditions and recidivism. *American Law and Economics Review, 13*(1), 103–130.

Dror, I. E. (2009). On proper research and understanding of the interplay between bias and decision outcomes. *Forensic Science International, 191*(1), 17–18.

Dror, I. E. (2017). Human expert performance in forensic decision making: Seven different sources of bias. *Australian Journal of Forensic Sciences, 49*(5), 541–547.

Dror, I. E., Charlton, D., & Péron, A. E. (2006). Contextual information renders experts vulnerable to making erroneous identifications. *Forensic Science International, 156*(1), 74–78.

Dunaway, R. G., Cullen, F. T., Burton, V. S., & Evans, T. D. (2000). The myth of social class and crime revisited: An examination of class and adult criminality. *Criminology: An Interdisciplinary Journal, 38*(2), 589–632.

Dunning, D., & Perretta, S. (2002). Automaticity and eyewitness accuracy: A 10- to 12-second rule for distinguishing accurate from inaccurate positive identifications. *Journal of Applied Psychology, 87*(5), 951–962.

Dutton, D. G., & Corvo, K. (2007). The Duluth model: A data-impervious paradigm and a failed strategy. *Aggression and Violent Behavior, 12*(6), 658–667.

Eck, J. E. (2006). Preventing crime at places. In L. W. Sherman, D. P. Farrington, B. C. Welsh, & D. L. MacKenzie (Eds.) *Evidence-Based Crime Prevention*. New York: Routledge.

Ehrensaft, M. K. (2008). Intimate partner violence: Persistence of myths and implications for intervention. *Children and Youth Services Review, 30*(3), 276–286.

Eisner, M. (2003). Long-term historical trends in violent crime. *Crime and Justice, 30*, 83–142.

Eley, T. C., Lichtenstein, P., & Moffitt, T. E. (2003). A longitudinal behavioral genetic analysis of the etiology of aggressive and nonaggressive antisocial behavior. *Development and Psychopathology, 15*(2), 383–402.

Emler, N., & Reicher, S. D. (1995). *Adolescence and Delinquency: The Collective Management of Reputation*. Oxford: Blackwell.

Erickson, W. B., Lampinen, J. M., & Leding, J. K. (2014). The weapon focus effect in target-present and target-absent line-ups: The roles of threat, novelty, and timing. *Applied Cognitive Psychology, 28*(3), 349–359.

Estrada, F., Bäckman, O., & Nilsson, A. (2016). The darker side of equality? The declining gender gap in crime: Historical trends and an enhanced analysis of staggered birth cohorts. *British Journal of Criminology, 56*(6), 1272–1290.

EvoFIT Limited. (2001). *EvoFIT*. Preston: EvoFIT Limited.

Eysenck, H. J. (1964). *Crime and Personality*. Boston, MA: Houghton-Mifflin.

Ezkurdia, I., Juan, D., Rodriguez, J. M., Frankish, A., Diekhans, M., Harrow, J., et al. (2014). Multiple evidence strands suggest that there may be as few as 19,000 human protein-coding genes. *Human Molecular Genetics, 23*(22), 5866–5878.

Farrell, G. (2013). Five tests for a theory of the crime drop. *Crime Science, 2*(1), 1–8.

Farrell, G., & Pease, K. (2014). Repeat victimization. In G. Bruinsma, & D. Weisburd (Eds.) *Encyclopedia of Criminology and Criminal Justice* (pp. 4371–4381). New York: Springer.

Farrington, D. P. (1986). Age and crime. *Crime and Justice, 7*, 189–250.

Farrington, D. P. (1997). Early prediction of violent and non-violent youthful offending. *European Journal on Criminal Policy and Research, 5*(2), 51–66.

Farrington, D. P. (2000). Explaining and preventing crime: The globalization of knowledge. *Criminology, 38*, 1–24.

Farrington, D. P. (2007). Criminal profiling, principles and practice [Book review]. *International Journal of Offender Therapy and Comparative Criminology, 51*, 486–487.

Farrington, D. P., & Loeber, R. (1999). Transatlantic replicability of risk factors in the development of delinquency. In P. Cohen, C. Slomkowski, & L. N. Robins (Eds.) *Historical and Geographical Influences on Psychopathology* (pp. 299–329). Mahwah, NJ: Lawrence Erlbaum Associates.

Farrington, D. P., Biron, L., & LeBlanc, M. (1982). Personality and delinquency in London and Montreal. In J. Gunn, & D. P. Farrington (Eds.) *Abnormal Offenders, Delinquency and the Criminal Justice System*. Chichester: Wiley.

Farrington, D. P., Barnes, G. C., & Lambert, S. (1996). The concentration of offending in families. *Legal and Criminological Psychology, 1*(1), 47–63.

Fawcett, J. M., Russell, E. J., Peace, K. A., & Christie, J. (2013). Of guns and geese: A meta-analytic review of the 'weapon focus' literature. *Psychology, Crime & Law, 19*(1), 35–66.

Fazel, S., & Wolf, A. (2015). A systematic review of criminal recidivism rates worldwide: Current difficulties and recommendations for best practice. *PloS One, 10*(6), e0130390.

Feder, L., & Wilson, D. B. (2005). A meta-analytic review of court-mandated batterer intervention programs: Can courts affect abusers' behavior? *Journal of Experimental Criminology, 1*(2), 239–262.

Feldman, M. P. (1977). *Criminal Behaviour: A Psychological Analysis*. London: Wiley.

Feldman, M. P. (1993). *The Psychology of Crime*. Cambridge: Cambridge University Press.

Felitti, V. J., Anda, R. F., Nordenberg, D., Williamson, D. F., Spitz, A. M., Edwards, V., et al. (1998). Relationship of childhood abuse and household dysfunction to many of the leading causes of death in adults. The Adverse Childhood Experiences (ACE) Study. *American Journal of Preventive Medicine, 14*(4), 245–258.

Ferguson, C. J., & Kilburn, J. (2010). Much ado about nothing: The misestimation and overinterpretation of violent video game effects in eastern and western nations: Comment on Anderson et al. (2010). *Psychological Bulletin, 136*(2), 174–178.

Fergusson, D. M., Boden, J. M., Horwood, L. J., Miller, A. L., & Kennedy, M. A. (2011). MAOA, abuse exposure and antisocial behaviour: 30-year longitudinal study. *British Journal of Psychiatry, 198*(6), 457–463.

Finlay, W. M. L., & Lyons, E. (2002). Acquiescence in interviews with people who have mental retardation. *Mental Retardation, 40*(1), 14–29.

Finn, J. (2004). A survey of online harassment at a university campus. *Journal of Interpersonal Violence, 19*(4), 468–483.

Fisher, R. P., & Geiselman, R. E. (1992). *Memory Enhancing Techniques for Investigative Interviewing: The Cognitive Interview*. Springfield, IL: Charles C. Thomas.

Fisher, R. P., Geiselman, R. E., & Raymond, D. S. (1987a). Critical analysis of police interview techniques. *Journal of Police Science and Administration, 15*(3), 177–185.

Fisher, R. P., Geiselman, R. E., Raymond, D. S., Jurkevich, L. M., & Warhaftig, M. L. (1987b). Enhancing enhanced eyewitness memory: Refining the cognitive interview. *Journal of Police Science and Administration, 15*, 291–297.

Fonagy, P. (2003). The developmental roots of violence in the failure of mentalization. In F. Pfäfflin, & G. Adshead (Eds.) *A Matter of Security: The Application of Attachment Theory to Forensic Psychiatry and Psychotherapy.* (pp. 13–56). London: Jessica Kingsley.

Fontaine, R. G. (2012). Developmental social cognition and antisocial behavior. In R. G. Fontaine (Ed.) *The Mind of the Criminal* (pp. 31–66). Cambridge: Cambridge University Press.

Found, B. (2015). Deciphering the human condition: The rise of cognitive forensics. *Australian Journal of Forensic Sciences, 47*(4), 386–401.

Fox, B. (2017). It's nature and nurture: Integrating biology and genetics into the social learning theory of criminal behavior. *Journal of Criminal Justice, 49*, 22–31.

Fox, B. H., Perez, N., Cass, E., Baglivio, M. T., & Epps, N. (2015). Trauma changes everything: Examining the relationship between adverse childhood experiences and serious, violent and chronic juvenile offenders. *Child Abuse & Neglect, 46*, 163–173.

Frick, P. J., Cornell, A. H., Barry, C. T., Bodin, S. D., & Dane, H. E. (2003). Callous-unemotional traits and conduct problems in the prediction of conduct problem severity, aggression, and self-report of delinquency. *Journal of Abnormal Child Psychology, 31*(4), 457–470.

Friedrichs, D. O. (2009). Critical criminology. In J. M. Miller (Ed.) *21st Century Criminology: A Reference Handbook.* Thousand Oaks, CA: Sage.

Friendship, C., Mann, R. E., & Beech, A. R. (2003). Evaluation of a national prison-based treatment program for sexual offenders in England and Wales. *Journal of Interpersonal Violence, 18*, 744–759.

Frowd, C. D., Erickson, W. B., Lampinen, J. M., Skelton, F. C., Mcintyre, A. H., & Hancock, P. J. B. (2015). A decade of evolving composites: Regression- and meta-analysis. *Journal of Forensic Practice, 17*(4), 319–334.

Fuchs, S. A., Edinger, H. M., & Siegel, A. (1985). The organization of the hypothalamic pathways mediating affective defense behavior in the cat. *Brain Research, 330*(1), 77–92.

Gabbidon, S. L. (2010). *Race, Ethnicity, Crime, and Justice: An International Dilemma.* Thousand Oaks, CA: Sage.

Gaes, G. G., & Camp, S. D. (2009). Unintended consequences: Experimental evidence for the criminogenic effect of prison security level placement on post-release recidivism. *Journal of Experimental Criminology, 5*(2), 139–162.

Gale, J. A., & Coupe, T. (2005). The behavioural, emotional and psychological effects of street robbery on victims. *International Review of Victimology, 12*(1), 1–22.

Gallagher, C. A., Wilson, D. B., Hirschfield, P., Coggeshall, M. B., and MacKenzie, D. L. (1999). A quantitative review of the effects of sex offender treatment on sexual reoffending. *Corrections Management Quarterly, 3*, 19–29.

Gannon, T. A. (2009). Social cognition in violent and sexual offending: An overview. *Psychology, Crime & Law, 15*(2–3), 97–118.

Geiselman, R. E., Fisher, R. P., MacKinnon, D. P., & Holland, H. L. (1985). Eyewitness memory enhancement in the police interview: Cognitive retrieval mnemonics versus hypnosis. *Journal of Applied Psychology, 70*(2), 401–412.

Geiselman, R. E., Fisher, R. P., MacKinnon, D. P., & Holland, H. L. (1986). Enhancement of eyewitness memory with the cognitive interview. *American Journal of Psychology, 99*(3), 385–401.

Gendreau, P., Goggin, C., Cullen, F. T., & Andrews, D. A. (2000). The effects of community sanctions and incarceration on recidivism. *Forum on Corrections Research, 12*(2), 10–13.

Gibbons, A. (2004). Tracking the evolutionary history of a 'warrior' gene. *Science, 304*(5672), 818.

Gibbs, J. C., Potter, G. B., & Goldstein, A. P. (1995). *The EQUIP program.* Champaign, IL: Research Press.

Gibbs, L. E. (1974). The effects of juvenile legal procedures on juvenile offenders' self-attitudes. *Journal of Research in Crime and Delinquency, 11*(1), 51–55.

Gillett, G., & Tamatea, A. J. (2012). The warrior gene: Epigenetic considerations. *New Genetics and Society, 31*(1), 41–53.

Glenn, A. L., & Raine, A. (2014). Neurocriminology: Implications for the punishment, prediction and prevention of criminal behaviour. Nature Reviews. *Neuroscience, 15*(1), 54–63.

Goetz, A. T., Shackelford, T. K., Romero, G. A., Kaighobadi, F., & Miner, E. J. (2008). Punishment, proprietariness, and paternity: Men's violence against women from an evolutionary perspective. *Aggression and Violent Behavior, 13*(6), 481–489.

Goldman, L., Giles, H., & Hogg, M. A. (2014). Going to extremes: Social identity and communication processes associated with gang membership. *Group Processes & Intergroup Relations, 17*(6), 813–832.

Gómez, J. M., Verdú, M., González-Megías, A., & Méndez, M. (2016). The phylogenetic roots of human lethal violence. *Nature, 538*(7624), 233–237.

Gottschalk, M., & Ellis, L. (2010). Evolutionary and genetic explanations of violent crime. In C. Ferguson (Ed.) *Violent Crime: Clinical and Social Implications* (pp. 57–74). Thousand Oaks, CA: Sage.

Grabosky, P. N. (2001). Virtual criminality: Old wine in new bottles? *Social & Legal Studies, 10*(2), 243–249.

Grandjean, P., & Landrigan, P. J. (2014). Neurobehavioural effects of developmental toxicity. *Lancet Neurology, 13*(3), 330–338.

Griffith-Dickson, G., Dickson, A., & Robert, I. (2014). Counter-extremism and de-radicalisation in the UK: A contemporary overview. *Journal for Deradicalization, 1*, 26–37.

Griffiths, S. Y., & Jalava, J. V. (2017). A comprehensive neuroimaging review of PCL-R defined psychopathy. *Aggression and Violent Behavior, 36*, 60–75.

Grimland, M., Apter, A., & Kerkhof, A. (2006). The phenomenon of suicide bombing. *Crisis, 27*(3), 107–118.

Grossman, J. B., & Tierney, J. P. (1998). Does mentoring work?: An impact study of the Big Brothers Big Sisters Program. *Evaluation Review, 22*(3), 403–426.

Gudjonsson, G. H. (1996). *The Psychology of Interrogations, Confessions and Testimony.* Chichester: Wiley.

Gudjonsson, G. H. (2003). *The Psychology of Interrogations and Confessions: A Handbook.* Chichester: Wiley.

Gudjonsson, G. H., & Haward, L. R. C. (1998). *Forensic Psychology: A Guide to Practice.* London: Routledge.

Hales, J., Nevill, C., Pudney, S., & Tipping, S. (2009). Longitudinal analysis of the Offending, Crime and Justice Survey 2003–06. *London, Home Office: Online Research Report, 19.* Retrieved from https://lemosandcrane.co.uk/resources/ horr19c.pdf.

Hall, L. J., & Player, E. (2008). Will the introduction of an emotional context affect fingerprint analysis and decision-making? *Forensic Science International, 181*(1j–3), 36–39.

Haney, C. (2008). Death qualification of juries. In B. Cutler (Ed.) *Encyclopedia of Psychology and Law.* Thousand Oaks, CA: Sage.

Hans, V. P., & Vidmar, N. (1986). *Judging the Jury.* New York: Plenum.

Hanson, R. K., Gordon, A., Harris, A. J. R., Marques, J. K., and Murphy, W. (2002). First report of the collaborative outcome data project on the effectiveness of psychological treatment for sex offenders. *Sexual Abuse: A Journal of Research and Treatment, 14,* 169–194.

Hare, R. D., Clark, D., Grann, M., & Thornton, D. (2000). Psychopathy and the predictive validity of the PCL-R: An international perspective. *Behavioral Sciences & the Law, 18*(5), 623–645.

Harlow, C. W. (2003). *Education and Correctional Populations. (Special Report Bureau of Justice Statistics).* Washington, DC: US Department of Justice.

Harris, G. T., Rice, M. E., & Cormier, C. A. (1991). Psychopathy and violent recidivism. *Law and Human Behavior, 15*(6), 625–637.

Hastie, R., Penrod, S., & Pennington, N. (1983). *Inside the Jury.* Cambridge, MA: Harvard University Press.

Hattie, J. (2009). *Visible Learning: A Synthesis of Over 800 Meta-Analyses Relating to Achievement.* London: Routledge.

Hawkins, J. D., von Cleve, E., & Catalano, R. F. (1991). Reducing early childhood aggression: Results of a primary prevention program. *Journal of the American Academy of Child and Adolescent Psychiatry, 30,* 208–217.

Hawkins, J. D., Catalano, R. F., Kosterman, R., Abbott, R., & Hill, K. G. (1999). Preventing adolescent health risk behaviors by strengthening protection during childhood. *Archives of Pediatrics and Adolescent Medicine, 153,* 226–234.

Hay, C., & Forrest, W. (2009). The implications of family poverty for a pattern of persistent offending. In J. Savage (Ed.) *The Development of Persistent Criminality.* New York: Oxford University Press.

Hayden, R. M., & Anderson, J. K. (1979). On the evaluation of procedural systems in laboratory experiments: A critique of Thibaut and Walker. *Law and Human Behavior, 3*(1–2), 21–38.

Hazelwood, R. R. (1987). Analyzing the rape and profiling the offender. In R. R. Hazelwood, & A. W. Burgess (Eds.) *Practical Aspects of Rape Investigation: A Multidisciplinary Approach* (pp. 169–199). New York: Elsevier.

Hazelwood, R. R., & Douglas, J. E. (1980). The lust murderer. *FBI Law Enforcement Bulletin, 49*, 18–22.

Heidensohn, F. (1968). The deviance of women: A critique and an enquiry. *British Journal of Sociology, 19*, 160–175.

Heidensohn, F., & Silvestri, M. (2012). Gender and crime. In M. Maguire, R. Morgan, & R. Reiner (Eds.) *Oxford Handbook of Criminology*. Oxford: Oxford University Press.

Helfgott, J. B. (2015). Criminal behavior and the copycat effect: Literature review and theoretical framework for empirical investigation. *Aggression and Violent Behavior, 22*, 46–64.

Hennigan, K. M., Del Rosario, M. L., & Heath, L. (1982). Impact of the introduction of television on crime in the United States: Empirical findings and theoretical implications. *Journal of Personality, 42*(3), 461–477.

Her Majesty's Inspector of Constabularies (HMIC) (2014). Crime recording: Making the victim count. Retrieved November 6, 2017, from http://www.justiceinspec torates.gov.uk/hmicfrs/wp-content/uploads/crime-recording-making-the-victim-count.pdf.

Herrnstein, R. J., & Murray, C. (1996). *The Bell Curve: Intelligence and Class Structure in American Life*. New York: Simon & Schuster.

Herrnstein, R., & Wilson, J. Q. (1985). *Crime and Human Nature*. New York: Simon & Schuster.

Heydon, J. D. (1984). *Evidence: Cases and Materials*, 2nd ed. London: Butterworths.

Hindelang, M. J., Hirschi, T., & Weis, J. G. (1981). *Measuring Delinquency*. Beverly Hills, CA: Sage.

Hipp, J. R., & Wo, J. C. (2015). Collective efficacy and crime. In J. D. Wright (Ed.) *International Encyclopedia of Social and Behavioral Sciences*, 2nd ed. (pp. 169–173). Oxford: Elsevier.

Hirst, W., & Phelps, E. A. (2016). Flashbulb memories. *Current Directions in Psychological Science, 25*(1), 36–41.

Hjalmarsson, R., & Lindquist, M. J. (2013). The origins of intergenerational associations in crime: Lessons from Swedish adoption data. *Labour Economics, 20*, 68–81.

Hogg, M. A., Abrams, D., Otten, S., & Hinkle, S. (2004). The social identity perspective. *Small Group Research, 35*(3), 246–276.

Hollin, C. R. (1989). *Psychology and Crime: An Introduction to Criminological Psychology*. London: Routledge.

Hollin, C. R., & Clifford, B. R. (1983). Eyewitness testimony: The effects of discussion on recall accuracy and agreement. *Journal of Applied Social Psychology, 13*(3), 234–244.

Holmes, M. D. (2015). Crime, race and ethnicity. In J. D. Wright (Ed.) *International Encyclopedia of the Social & Behavioral Sciences*, 2nd ed. (pp. 182–188). Oxford: Elsevier.

Holt, T. J., Burruss, G. W., & Bossler, A. M. (2010). Social learning and cyber-deviance: Examining the importance of a full social learning model in the virtual world. *Journal of Crime and Justice, 33*(2), 31–61.

Home Office. (1994). *Criminal Statistics*. London: Home Office.

Hood, T. W., Siegfried, J., & Wieser, H. G. (1983). The role of stereotactic amygda-
lotomy in the treatment of temporal lobe epilepsy associated with behavioral
disorders. *Applied Neurophysiology*, 46(1–4), 19–25.

Horgan, J. (2009). *Walking Away from Terrorism: Accounts of Disengagement from Radi-
cal and Extremist Movements*. London: Routledge.

Horley, J. (2011). On the tyranny of professional labelling. *Psychotherapy and Politics
International*, 9(2), 127–133.

Horry, R., Memon, A., Wright, D. B., & Milne, R. (2012). Predictors of eyewitness
identification decisions from video lineups in England: A field study. *Law and
Human Behavior*, 36(4), 257–265.

Hough, M., & Mayhew, P. (1983). *The British Crime Survey: First Report* (Vol. 76). London: HMSO.

House of Commons. (2010). *Preventing Violent Extremism: Sixth Report of Session
2009–10, Report, Together with Formal Minutes, Oral and Written Evidence*. London:
The Stationery Office.

Houston, C. (2014). *How Feminist Theory Became (Criminal) Law: Tracing the Path to
Mandatory Criminal Intervention in Domestic Violence Cases*. Retrieved December 29,
2017, from https://papers.ssrn.com/sol3/papers.cfm?abstract_id=2896291.

Hovland, C. I., & Janis, I. L. (1959). *Communication and Persuasion: Psychological Studies of Opinion Change*. New Haven, CT: Yale University Press.

Howitt, D. (1998). *Crime, the Media, and the Law*. Chichester: Wiley.

Hoyle, C. (2007). Feminism, victimology and domestic violence. In S. Walklate (Ed.)
Handbook of Victims and Victimology (pp. 146–174). Portland, OR: Willan Publishing.

Hutchings, B., & Mednick, S. A. (1975). Registered criminality in the adoptive and
biological parents of registered male criminal adoptees. *Proceedings of the Annual
Meeting of the American Psychopathological Association*, 63, 105–116.

Inbau, F., Reid, J., Buckley, J., & Jayne, B. (2011). *Criminal Interrogation and Confessions*. Burlington, MA: Jones & Bartlett Publishers.

Irving, B., & McKenzie, I. K. (1989). *Police Interrogation: The Effects of the Police and
Criminal Evidence Act, 1984*. London: Police Federation.

Jackowski, A. P., De Araújo, C. M., De Lacerda, A. L. T., de Jesus Mari, J., & Kaufman,
J. (2009). Neurostructural imaging findings in children with post-traumatic stress
disorder: Brief review. *Psychiatry and Clinical Neurosciences*, 63(1), 1–8.

Jahoda, G. (1954). A note on Ashanti names and their relationship to personality.
British Journal of Psychology, 45(3), 192–195.

Jewkes, Y. (2011). Prisons. In M. Tondry (Ed.) *The Oxford Handbook of Crime and Criminal Justice* (pp. 872–896). Oxford: Oxford University Press.

Jolliffe, D., & Farrington, D. P. (2004). Empathy and offending: A systematic review
and meta-analysis. *Aggression and Violent Behavior*, 9(5), 441–476.

Jonas, K., Eagly, A. H., & Stroebe, W. (1995). Attitudes and persuasion. In M. Argyle, &
A. M. Colman (Eds.) *Social Psychology* (pp. 1–15). London: Longman.

Jones, T., MacLean, B., & Young, J. (1986). *The Islington Crime Survey: Crime, Victimization and Policing in Inner-City London*. Aldershot: Gower.

Kahan, D. M. (2015). Laws of cognition and the cognition of law. *Cognition*, 135,
56–60.

Kanz, K. M. (2015). Mediated and moderated effects of violent media consumption on youth violence. *European Journal of Criminology, 13*(2), 149–168.

Kapardis, A. (2002). *Psychology and Law: A Critical Introduction.* Cambridge: Cambridge University Press.

Kassin, S. M., & Gudjonsson, G. H. (2004). The psychology of confessions: A review of the literature and issues. *Psychological Science in the Public Interest: A Journal of the American Psychological Society, 5*(2), 33–67.

Kassin, S. M., & Neumann, K. (1997). On the power of confession evidence: An experimental test of the fundamental difference hypothesis. *Law and Human Behavior, 21*(5), 469–484.

Kassin, S. M., & Sukel, H. (1997). Coerced confessions and the jury: An experimental test of the 'harmless error' rule. *Law and Human Behavior, 21*(1), 27.

Kassin, S. M., & Wrightsman, L. S. (1985). Confession evidence. *The Psychology of Evidence and Trial Procedure,* 67–94.

Kassin, S. M., Drizin, S. A., Grisso, T., Gudjonsson, G. H., Leo, R. A., & Redlich, A. D. (2010). Police-induced confessions: risk factors and recommendations. *Law and Human Behavior, 34*(1), 3–38.

Kazdin, A. E., Kraemer, H. C., Kessler, R. C., Kupfer, D. J., & Offord, D. R. (1997). Contributions of risk-factor research to developmental psychopathology. *Clinical Psychology Review, 17,* 375–406.

Kelly, V. G., Merrill, G. S., Shumway, M., Alvidrez, J., & Boccellari, A. (2010). Outreach, engagement, and practical assistance: Essential aspects of PTSD care for urban victims of violent crime. *Trauma, Violence & Abuse, 11*(3), 144–156.

Kiesner, J., Poulin, F., & Nicotra, E. (2003). Peer relations across contexts: Individual-network homophily and network inclusion in and after school. *Child Development, 74*(5), 1328–1343.

Killias, M., Gilliéron, G., Villard, F., & Poglia, C. (2010). How damaging is imprisonment in the long-term? A controlled experiment comparing long-term effects of community service and short custodial sentences on re-offending and social integration. *Journal of Experimental Criminology, 6*(2), 115–130.

King, M. A., & Yuille, J. C. (1986). *The Child Witness.* Ottawa: Health and Welfare Canada, National Clearinghouse on Family Violence.

Kitson, A., Darnbrough, M., & Shields, E. (1978). Let's face it. *Police Research Bulletin, 30,* 7–13.

Kohlberg, L. (1976). Moral stages and moralization: The cognitive-development approach. In T. Lickona (Ed.) *Moral Development and Behavior* (pp. 31–53). New York: Holt, Rinehart & Winston.

Kovera, M. B. (2002). The effects of general pretrial publicity on juror decisions: An examination of moderators and mediating mechanisms. *Law and Human Behavior, 26*(1), 43–72.

Kovera, M. B., Penrod, S. D., Pappas, C., & Thill, D. L. (1997). Identification of computer-generated facial composites. *Journal of Applied Psychology, 82*(2), 235–246.

Kramer, T. H., Buckhout, R., & Eugenio, P. (1990). Weapon focus, arousal, and eyewitness memory: Attention must be paid. *Law and Human Behavior, 14*(2), 167–184.

Kruglanski, A. W., Crenshaw, M., Post, J. M., & Victoroff, J. (2007). What should this fight be called?: Metaphors of counterterrorism and their implications. *Psychological Science in the Public Interest: A Journal of the American Psychological Society, 8*(3), 97–133.

Kruglanski, A. W., Gelfand, M. J., Bélanger, J. J., Sheveland, A., Hetiarachchi, M., & Gunaratna, R. (2014). The psychology of radicalization and deradicalization: How significance quest impacts violent extremism. *Political Psychology, 35*, 69–93.

Kruk, M. R. (1991). Ethology and pharmacology of hypothalamic aggression in the rat. *Neuroscience and Biobehavioral Reviews, 15*(4), 527–538.

Kunst, M. J. J., Winkel, F. W., & Bogaerts, S. (2011). Posttraumatic anger, recalled peritraumatic emotions, and PTSD in victims of violent crime. *Journal of Interpersonal Violence, 26*(17), 3561–3579.

Kurki, L., & Morris, N. (2001). The purposes, practices, and problems of Supermax prisons. *Crime and Justice, 28*, 385–424.

Lalumière, M. L., Mishra, S., & Harris, G. T. (2008). In cold blood: The evolution of psychopathy. In J. D. Duntley, & T. K. Shackelford (Eds.) *Evolutionary Forensic Psychology: Darwinian Foundations of Crime and Law* (pp. 176–197). Oxford: Oxford University Press.

Langan, P. A., & Levin, D. J. (2002). Recidivism of prisoners released in 1994. *Federal Sentencing Reporter, 15*(1), 58–65.

Latimer, J., Dowden, C., & Muise, D. (2005). The effectiveness of restorative justice practices: A meta-analysis. *Prison Journal, 85*(2), 127–144.

Launay, C., & Py, J. (2015). Methods and aims of investigative interviewing of adult witnesses: An analysis of professional practices. *Pratiques Psychologiques, 21*(1), 55–70.

Lauritsen, J. L., Heimer, K., & Lynch, J. P. (2009). Trends in the gender gap in violent offending: New evidence from the National Crime Victimization Survey. *Criminology: An Interdisciplinary Journal, 47*(2), 361–399.

Lavergne, G. M. (1997). *A Sniper in the Tower: The Charles Whitman Murders.* Denton, TX: University of North Texas Press.

Lea, R., & Chambers, G. (2007). Monoamine oxidase, addiction, and the 'warrior' gene hypothesis. *New Zealand Medical Journal, 120*(1250), 5–10.

Leippe, M. R., & Eisenstadt, D. (2007). Eyewitness confidence and the confidence-accuracy relationship in memory for people. In R. C. L. Lindsay, D. F. Ross., J. D. Read, & M. P. Toglia (Eds.) *The Handbook of Eyewitness Psychology* (pp. 377–426). Mahwah, NJ: Lawrence Erlbaum Associates.

Leippe, M. R., Manion, A. P., & Romanczyk, A. (1992). Eyewitness persuasion: How and how well do fact finders judge the accuracy of adults' and children's memory reports? *Journal of Personality and Social Psychology, 63*(2), 181–197.

Lieberman, J. D., Carrell, C. A., Miethe, T. D., & Krauss, D. A. (2008). Gold versus platinum: Do jurors recognize the superiority and limitations of DNA evidence compared to other types of forensic evidence? *Psychology, Public Policy, and Law: An Official Law Review of the University of Arizona College of Law and the University of Miami School of Law, 14*(1), 27–62.

Liebling, A. (1992). *Suicides in Prison*. London: Routledge.

Liebling, A. (2007). Prison suicide and its prevention. *Handbook on Prisons*, 423–446.

Liebling, A., & Maruna, S. (2005). Introduction: The effects of imprisonment revisited. In *The Effects of Imprisonment* (pp. 1–32). London: Routledge.

Lieven, J., Pauwels, R., Weerman, F. M., Gerben, J., Bruinsma, N., & Bernasco, W. (2015). How much variance in offending, self-control and morality can be explained by neighbourhoods and schools? An exploratory cross-classified multi-level analysis. *European Journal on Criminal Policy and Research*, 21(4), 523–537.

Lin, J. H. (2013). Do video games exert stronger effects on aggression than film? The role of media interactivity and identification on the association of violent content and aggressive outcomes. *Computers in Human Behavior*, 29(3), 535–543.

Liu, J., Liu, X., Wang, W., McCauley, L., Pinto-Martin, J., Wang, Y., et al. (2014). Blood lead concentrations and children's behavioral and emotional problems: A cohort study. *JAMA Pediatrics*, 168(8), 737–745.

Livingston, M., Galster, G., Kearns, A., & Bannister, J. (2014). Criminal neighbourhoods: Does the density of prior offenders in an area encourage others to commit crime? *Environment & Planning A*, 46(10), 2469–2488.

Llewellyn, J. J., & Howse, R. (1998). *Restorative Justice: A Conceptual Framework; Prepared for the Law Commission of Canada*. Ottawa: Law Commission of Canada.

Lofstrom, M., & Raphael, S. (2016). Prison downsizing and public safety. *Criminology & Public Policy*, 15(2), 349–365.

Loftus, E. F., & Palmer, J. C. (1974). Reconstruction of automobile destruction: An example of the interaction between language and memory. *Journal of Verbal Learning and Verbal Behavior*, 13(5), 585–589.

Loftus, E. F., Miller, D. G., & Burns, H. J. (1978). Semantic integration of verbal information into a visual memory. *Journal of Experimental Psychology. Human Learning and Memory*, 4(1), 19–31.

Loftus, E. F., Loftus, G. R., & Messo, J. (1987). Some facts about 'weapon focus;. *Law and Human Behavior*, 11(1), 55–62.

Loftus, E. F., Greene, E. L., & Doyle, J. M. (1990). The psychology of eyewitness testimony. In D. C. Raskin (Ed.) *Psychological Methods in Criminal Investigations and Evidence* (pp. 3–46). New York: Springer.

Lopes, B., & Yu, H. (2017). Who do you troll and why: An investigation into the relationship between the dark triad personalities and online trolling behaviours towards popular and less popular Facebook profiles. *Computers in Human Behavior*, 77, 69–76.

Lösel, F., and Schmucker, M. (2005). The effectiveness of treatment for sexual offenders: A comprehensive meta-analysis. *Journal of Experimental Criminology*, 1, 117–146.

Loughran, T. A., Paternoster, R., Chalfin, A., & Wilson, T. (2016). Can rational choice theory be considered a general theory of crime? Evidence from individual-level panel data. *Criminology: An Interdisciplinary Journal*, 54(1), 86–112.

Lowell, A., Suarez-Jimenez, B., Helpman, L., Zhu, X., Durosky, A., Hilburn, A., et al. (2017). 9/11-related PTSD among highly exposed populations: A systematic review 15 years after the attack. *Psychological Medicine*, 1–17.

Ly, M., Motzkin, J. C., Philippi, C. L., Kirk, G. R., Newman, J. P., Kiehl, K. A., et al. (2012). Cortical thinning in psychopathy. *American Journal of Psychiatry*, *169*(7), 743–749.

Lygre, R. B., Eid, J., Larsson, G., & Ranstorp, M. (2011). Terrorism as a process: A critical review of Moghaddam's 'staircase to terrorism'. *Scandinavian Journal of Psychology*, *52*(6), 609–616.

Lynch, M., & Haney, C. (2009). Capital jury deliberation: Effects on death sentencing, comprehension, and discrimination. *Law and Human Behavior*, *33*(6), 481–496.

Lyons, H. A., & Harbinson, H. J. (1986). A comparison of political and non-political murderers in Northern Ireland, 1974–84. *Medicine, Science, and the Law*, *26*(3), 193–198.

Maass, A., & Köhnken, G. (1989). Eyewitness identification: Simulating the 'weapon effect'. *Law and Human Behavior*, *13*(4), 397–408.

MacCoun, R. J. (2005). Voice, control and belonging: The double-edged sword of procedural fairness. *Annual Review of Law and Social Science*, *1*, 171–201.

Mackay, D. A. (2012). Introduction to crime prevention. In D. A. Mackay, & K. Levan (Eds.) *Crime Prevention* (pp. 1–27). Burlington, MA: Jones and Bartlett Learning.

MacKenzie, D. L. (2006). *What Works in Corrections: Reducing the Criminal Activities of Offenders and Delinquents.* New York: Cambridge University Press.

Maguire, M., & McVie, S. (2017). Crime data and criminal statistics: A critical reflection. In A. Leibling, S. Maruna, & L. McAra (Eds.) *The Oxford Handbook of Criminology*, 6th ed. (Vol. 1, pp. 163–189). Oxford: Oxford University Press.

Mariano, M., Pino, M. C., Peretti, S., Valenti, M., & Mazza, M. (2017). Understanding criminal behavior: Empathic impairment in criminal offenders. *Social Neuroscience*, *12*(4), 379–385.

Mark, V. H., & Sweet, W. H. (1974). The role of limbic brain dysfunction in aggression. *Research Publications – Association for Research in Nervous and Mental Disease*, *52*, 186–200.

Marsh, K., & Fox, C. (2008). The benefit and cost of prison in the UK. The results of a model of lifetime re-offending. *Journal of Experimental Criminology*, *4*(4), 403–423.

Martinson, R. (1974). What works? Questions and answers about prison reform. *Public Interest*, *10*, 22–54.

Martire, K. A., Kemp, R. I., Watkins, I., Sayle, M. A., & Newell, B. R. (2013). The expression and interpretation of uncertain forensic science evidence: Verbal equivalence, evidence strength, and the weak evidence effect. *Law and Human Behavior*, *37*(3), 197–207.

Mason, D. A., & Frick, P. J. (1994). The heritability of antisocial behavior: A meta-analysis of twin and adoption studies. *Journal of Psychopathology and Behavioral Assessment*, *16*(4), 301–323.

Mastroe, C. (2016). Evaluating CVE: Understanding the recent changes to the United Kingdom's implementation of Prevent. *Perspectives on Terrorism*, *10*(2). Retrieved

November 15, 2017, from http://www.terrorismanalysts.com/pt/index.php/pot/ article/view/501/html.

Maxwell, G., & Morris, A. (2001). Putting restorative justice into practice for adult offenders. *Howard Journal of Criminal Justice, 40*(1), 55–69.

May, C. (1999). *Explaining Reconviction following a Community Sentence: The Role of Social Factors (Home Office Research Study No. 192)*. London: HMSO.

Mazzella, R., & Feingold, A. (1994). The effects of physical attractiveness, race, socioeconomic status, and gender of defendants and victims on judgments of mock jurors: A meta-analysis. *Journal of Applied Social Psychology, 24*, 1315–1338.

McAlaney, J., Thackray, H., & Taylor, J. (2016). The social psychology of cybersecurity. *The Psychologist, 29*(9), 686–689.

McAuliff, B. D., Ellis, L., & Phillips, M. (2011). 'May it please the court…' A social-cognitive primer on persuasion in legal contexts. In R. Wiener, & B. Bornstein (Eds.) *Handbook of Trial Consulting* (pp. 33–62). New York: Springer.

McCauley, C., & Moskalenko, S. (2017). Understanding political radicalization: The two-pyramids model. *American Psychologist, 72*(3), 205–216.

McCloskey, M., & Zaragoza, M. (1985). Misleading postevent information and memory for events: Arguments and evidence against memory impairment hypotheses. *Journal of Experimental Psychology, General, 114*(1), 1–16.

McCormick, C. T. (1972). *McCormick's Handbook of the Law of Evidence*. St. Paul, MI: West Publishing Company.

McDermott, R., Tingley, D., Cowden, J., Frazzetto, G., & Johnson, D. D. P. (2009). Monoamine oxidase A gene (MAOA) predicts behavioral aggression following provocation. *Proceedings of the National Academy of Sciences of the United States of America, 106*(7), 2118–2123.

McElhaney, K. B., Immele, A., Smith, F. D., & Allen, J. P. (2006). Attachment organization as a moderator of the link between friendship quality and adolescent delinquency. *Attachment & Human Development, 8*(1), 33–46.

McGloin, R., Farrar, K., & Krcmar, M. (2013). Video games, immersion, and cognitive aggression: Does the controller matter? *Media Psychology, 16*(1), 65–87.

McGrath, A. J. (2014). The subjective impact of contact with the criminal justice system. *Crime & Delinquency, 60*(6), 884–908.

McGuire, M. (2012). *Organised Crime in the Digital Age*. London: John Grieve Centre for Policing and Security.

McGurk, B. J., Carr, M. J., & McGurk, D. (1993). *Investigative Interviewing Courses for Police Officers: An Evaluation*. London: Home Office Police Department.

Mears, D. P., Cochran, J. C., & Cullen, F. T. (2015). Incarceration heterogeneity and its implications for assessing the effectiveness of imprisonment on recidivism. *Criminal Justice Policy Review, 26*(7), 691–712.

Meichenbaum, D. H., Bowers, K. S., & Ross, R. R. (1969). A behavioral analysis of teacher expectancy effect. *Journal of Personality and Social Psychology, 13*(4), 306–316.

Meissner, C. A., & Russano, M. B. (2003). The psychology of interrogations and false confessions: Research and recommendations. *Canadian Journal of Police & Security Services*, *1*, 53–64.

Meissner, C., Redlich, A., Michael, S., Evans, J., Camilletti, C., Bhatt, S., et al. (2014). Accusatorial and information-gathering interrogation methods and their effects on true and false confessions: A meta-analytic review. *Journal of Experimental Criminology*, *10*(4), 459–486.

Melander, L. A. (2010). College students' perceptions of intimate partner cyber harassment. *Cyberpsychology, Behavior and Social Networking*, *13*(3), 263–268.

Memon, A., Mastroberardino, S., & Fraser, J. (2008). Münsterberg's legacy: What does eyewitness research tell us about the reliability of eyewitness testimony? *Applied Cognitive Psychology*, *22*(6), 841–851.

Memon, A., Meissner, C. A., & Fraser, J. (2010). The cognitive interview: A meta-analytic review and study space analysis of the past 25 years. *Psychology, Public Policy, and Law: An Official Law Review of the University of Arizona College of Law and the University of Miami School of Law*, *16*(4), 340–372.

Mennis, J., & Harris, P. (2011). Contagion and repeat offending among urban juvenile delinquents. *Journal of Adolescence*, *34*(5), 951–963.

Mews, A., Di Bella, L., & Purver, M. (2017). *Impact Evaluation of the Prison-based Core Sex Offender Treatment Programme*. London: HMSO.

Meyer-Lindenberg, A., Buckholtz, J. W., Kolachana, B., Hariri, A. R., Pezawas, L., Blasi, G., et al. (2006). Neural mechanisms of genetic risk for impulsivity and violence in humans. *Proceedings of the National Academy of Sciences of the United States of America*, *103*(16), 6269–6274.

Miczek, K. A., Brykczynski, T., & Grossman, S. P. (1974). Differential effects of lesions in the amygdala, periamygdaloid cortex, and stria terminalis on aggressive behaviors in rats. *Journal of Comparative and Physiological Psychology*, *87*(4), 760–771.

Mielke, H. W., & Zahran, S. (2012). The urban rise and fall of air lead (Pb) and the latent surge and retreat of societal violence. *Environment International*, *43*, 48–55.

Milarsky, J. R., Kessler, R. C., Stipp, H., & Rubens, W. S. (1982). *Television and Aggression: A Panel Study*. New York: Academic Press.

Milgram, S. (1963). Behavioral study of obedience. *Journal of Abnormal Psychology*, *67*, 371–378.

Miller, J. G. (1996). *Search and Destroy: African-American Males in the Criminal Justice System*. Cambridge: Cambridge University Press.

Miller, L. S. (1984). Bias among forensic document examiners: A need for procedural change. *Journal of Police Science & Administration*, *12*(4), 407–411.

Miller, L. S. (1987). Procedural bias in forensic science examinations of human hair. *Law and Human Behavior*, *11*(2), 157–163.

Milne, B., & Bull, R. (1999). *Investigative Interviewing: Psychology and Practice*. Chichester: Wiley.

Ministry of Justice. (2011). *Evaluation of the Intensive Alternatives to Custody Pilots. Research Summary 3/11*. Retrieved February 2, 2018, from https://www.gov.uk/

government/uploads/system/uploads/attachment_data/file/217372/inten sive-alt-custody-research-summary.pdf.

Ministry of Justice. (2017a). *Proven Reoffending Statistics Quarterly Bulletin,* July 2014 to June 2015. London: HMSO.

Ministry of Justice. (2017b). *2010 to 2015 Government Policy: Reoffending and Rehabilitation.* London: HMSO.

Mitchell, I. J., & Beech, A. R. (2011). Towards a neurobiological model of offending. *Clinical Psychology Review, 31*(5), 872–882.

Mitchell, T. L., Haw, R. M., Pfeifer, J. E., & Meissner, C. A. (2005). Racial bias in mock juror decision-making: A meta-analytic review of defendant treatment. *Law and Human Behavior, 29*(6), 621–637.

Moffitt, T. E. (1993). Adolescence-limited and life-course-persistent antisocial behavior: A developmental taxonomy. *Psychological Review, 100*(4), 674–701.

Moffitt, T. E. (2005). The new look of behavioral genetics in developmental psychopathology: Gene–environment interplay in antisocial behaviors. *Psychological Bulletin, 131*(4), 533–554.

Moffitt, T. E., Caspi, A., Rutter, M., & Silva, P. A. (2001). *Sex Differences in Anti-social Behaviour: Conduct Disorder, Delinquency, and Violence in the Dunedin Longitudinal Study.* Cambridge: Cambridge University Press.

Moghaddam, F. M. (2005). The staircase to terrorism: A psychological exploration. *American Psychologist, 60*(2), 161–169.

Monahan, J., & Loftus, E. F. (1982). The psychology of law. *Annual Review of Psychology, 33*(1), 441–475.

Moore, N. T., May, D. C., & Wood, P. B. (2008). Offenders, judges, and officers rate the relative severity of alternative sanctions compared to prison. *Journal of Offender Rehabilitation, 46*(3–4), 49–70.

Moore, T. M., Scarpa, A., & Raine, A. (2002). A meta-analysis of serotonin metabolite 5-HIAA and antisocial behavior. *Aggressive Behavior, 28*(4), 299–316.

Morris, R. G., & Blackburn, A. G. (2009). Cracking the code: An empirical exploration of social learning theory and computer crime. *Journal of Crime and Justice, 32*(1), 1–34.

Moston, S. (1990). The ever-so gentle art of police interrogation. In *British Psychological Society Annual Conference, Swansea University* (Vol. 5, pp. 155–167). Leicester: British Psychological Society.

Nagin, D. S. (2013). Deterrence in the twenty-first century. *Crime and Justice, 42*(1), 199–263.

Nagin, D. S., Cullen, F. T., & Jonson, C. L. (2009). Imprisonment and reoffending. *Crime and Justice, 38*(1), 115–200.

Narag, R. E., Pizarro, J., & Gibbs, C. (2009). Lead exposure and its implications for criminological theory. *Criminal Justice and Behavior, 36*(9), 954–973.

Nash, R. A., Hanczakowski, M., & Mazzoni, G. (2015). Eyewitness testimony. In J. D. Wright (Ed.) *International Encyclopedia of the Social and Behavioral Sciences,* 2nd ed. (pp. 642–649). Oxford: Elsevier.

National College of Policing. (2016). *Investigative Interviewing*. Retrieved October 27, 2017, from https://www.app.college.police.uk/app-content/investigations/investigative-interviewing/.

National Consortium for the Study of Terrorism and Responses to Terrorism (START). (2017). *Global Terrorism Database*. Retrieved November 11, 2017, from https://www.start.umd.edu/gtd.

Nelson, J. R., Smith, D. J., & Dodd, J. (1990). The moral reasoning of juvenile delinquents: A meta-analysis. *Journal of Abnormal Child Psychology, 18*(3), 231–239.

Netherland, J., & Hansen, H. (2016). The war on drugs that wasn't: Wasted whiteness, 'dirty doctors', and race in media coverage of prescription opioid misuse. *Culture, Medicine and Psychiatry, 40,* 664–686.

Neumann, C. S., & Hare, R. D. (2008). Psychopathic traits in a large community sample: Links to violence, alcohol use, and intelligence. *Journal of Consulting and Clinical Psychology, 76*(5), 893–899.

Nevin, R. (2000). How lead exposure relates to temporal changes in IQ, violent crime, and unwed pregnancy. *Environmental Research, 83*(1), 1–22.

Nevin, R. (2007). Understanding international crime trends: The legacy of preschool lead exposure. *Environmental Research, 104*(3), 315–336.

Newman, O. (1972). *Defensible Space: Crime Prevention Through Urban Design*. New York: Macmillan.

Ngo, F., & Jaishankar, K. (2017). Commemorating a decade in existence of the International Journal of Cyber Criminology: A research agenda to advance the scholarship on cyber crime. *International Journal of Cyber Criminology, 11*(1). Retrieved November 16, 2017, from http://cybercrimejournal.com/FawnjaiSAvol11issue1IJCC2017.pdf.

Nietzel, M. T., & Dillehay, R. C. (1983). Psychologists as consultants for changes of venue: The use of public opinion surveys. *Law and Human Behavior, 7*(4), 309–335.

Norris, F. (2005). *Range, Magnitude, and Duration of the Effects of Disasters on Mental Health: Review Update 2005*. Dartmouth, MA: Dartmouth Medical School National Center for Posttraumatic Stress Disorder.

Novaco, R. W. (1975). *Anger Control: The Development and Evaluation of an Experimental Treatment*. Lexington, MA: Lexington Books.

O'Connor, C., Rees, G., & Joffe, H. (2012). Neuroscience in the public sphere. *Neuron, 74*(2), 220–226.

O'Donnell, J., Hawkins, J. D., Catalano, R. F., Abbott, R. D., & Day, L. E. (1995). Preventing school failure, drug use, and delinquency among low-income children: Long-term intervention in elementary schools. *American Journal of Orthopsychiatry, 65*(1), 87–100.

O'Leary, B. (2007). IRA: Irish Republican Army (Oglaigh na hEireann). *Terror, Insurgency and the State, 189*–228.

Odinot, G., Wolters, G., & van Koppen, P. J. (2009). Eyewitness memory of a supermarket robbery: A case study of accuracy and confidence after 3 months. *Law and Human Behavior, 33*(6), 506–514.

Ogilvie, C. A., Newman, E., Todd, L., & Peck, D. (2014). Attachment & violent offending: A meta-analysis. *Aggression and Violent Behavior, 19*(4), 322–339.

Oldfield, M. (1996). *The Kent Reconviction Survey.* Maidstone: Kent Probation Service.

ONS. (Office for National Statistics). (2016). *Focus on Property Crime: Year ending March 2016.* Retrieved November 11, 2017, from https://www.ons.gov.uk/people populationandcommunity/crimeandjustice/bulletins/focusonpropertycrime/yearendingmarch2016#levels-of-victimisation.

ONS. (2017a). *Race and the Criminal Justice System 2016.* Retrieved November 12, 2017, from https://www.gov.uk/government/statistics/race-and-the-criminal-justice-system-2016.

ONS. (2017b). *Crime in England and Wales: Year ending June 2017.* Retrieved November 11, 2017, from https://www.ons.gov.uk/peoplepopulationandcommunity/crimeandjustice/bulletins/crimeinenglandandwales/june2017#overview-of-crime.

ONS. (2017c). *Overview of Violent Crime and Sexual Offences.* Retrieved November 13, 2017, from https://www.ons.gov.uk/peoplepopulationandcommunity/crimeandjustice/compendium/focusonviolentcrimeandsexualoffences/year endingmarch2016/overviewofviolentcrimeandsexualoffences.

ONS. (2017d). *Domestic Abuse, Sexual Assault and Stalking.* Retrieved November 13, 2017, from https://www.ons.gov.uk/peoplepopulationandcommunity/crimeandjustice/compendium/focusonviolentcrimeandsexualoffences/yearendingmarch2016/domesticabusesexualassaultandstalking.

ONS. (2017e). *Public Perceptions of Crime in England and Wales: Year ending March 2016.* Retrieved November 19, 2017, from https://www.ons.gov.uk/peoplepopula tionandcommunity/crimeandjustice/articles/publicperceptionsofcrimein englandandwales/yearendingmarch2016.

ONS. (2017f). *Homicide.* Retrieved December 10, 2017, from https://www.ons.gov.uk/peoplepopulationandcommunity/crimeandjustice/compendium/focuson violentcrimeandsexualoffences/yearendingmarch2016/homicide#how-are-victims-and-suspects-related.

Osborn, S. G., & West, D. J. (1979). Conviction records of fathers and sons compared. *British Journal of Criminology, 19*(2), 120–133.

Ousey, G. C., & Lee, M. R. (2012). Community, inequality, and crime. In F. Cullen, & P. Wilcox (Eds.) *The Oxford Handbook of Criminological Theory* (pp. 352–373). Oxford: Oxford University Press.

Oxburgh, G., Ost, J., Morris, P., & Cherryman, J. (2014). The impact of question type and empathy on police interviews with suspects of homicide, filicide and child sexual abuse. *Psychiatry, Psychology and Law, 21*(6), 903–917.

Padawer-Singer, A., & Barton, A. H. (1975). The impact of pretrial publicity on jurors' verdicts. In R. J. Simon (Ed.) *The Jury System in America: A Critical Overview* (pp. 123–139). Beverly Hills, CA: Sage.

Painter, K. (1991). *Wife Rape in the United Kingdom.* A Paper Presented at the American Society of Criminology. Retrieved December, 13, 2017 from http://www.crim.cam.ac.uk/people/visitors/kate_painter/wiferape.pdf.

Painter, K. A., & Farrington, D.P. (1999). Street lighting and crime: Diffusion of benefits in the Stoke-on-Trent Project. In K. A. Painter, & N. Tilley (Eds.) *Surveillance of Public Space: CCTV, Street Lighting and Crime Prevention (Crime Prevention Studies, Vol. 10)*. Monsey, NY: Criminal Justice Press.

Painter, K. A., & Farrington, D.P. (2001). The financial benefits of improved street lighting, based on crime reduction. *Lighting Research and Technology, 33*, 3–12.

Palmer, E. J. (2003). An overview of the relationship between moral reasoning and offending. *Australian Psychologist, 38*(3), 165–174.

Palmer, E. J., & Hollin, C. R. (1996). Sociomoral reasoning, perceptions of own parenting and self-reported delinquency. *Personality and Individual Differences, 21*(2), 175–182.

Palmer, E. J., & Hollin, C. R. (1998). A comparison of patterns of moral development in young offenders and non-offenders. *Legal and Criminological Psychology, 3*(2), 225–235.

Paternoster, R., & Iovanni, L. (1989). The labeling perspective and delinquency: An elaboration of the theory and an assessment of the evidence. *Justice Quarterly: Academy of Criminal Justice Sciences, 6*(3), 359–394.

Pearse, J., & Gudjonsson, G. H. (1999). Measuring influential police interviewing tactics: A factor analytic approach. *Legal and Criminological Psychology, 4*(2), 221–238.

Pease, K. (1998). *Repeat Victimisation: Taking Stock (Crime Detection and Prevention Series Paper 90)*. London: Home Office.

Pennington, N., & Hastie, R. (1988). Explanation-based decision making: Effects of memory structure on judgment. *Journal of Experimental Psychology. Learning, Memory, and Cognition, 14*(3), 521–533.

Pennington, N., & Hastie, R. (1990). Practical implications of psychological research on juror and jury decision making. *Personality & Social Psychology Bulletin, 16*(1), 90–105.

Penrod, S. D., & Cutler, B. L. (1987). Assessing the competencies of juries. In I. B. Weiner & A. K. Hess (Eds.) *Handbook for Forensic Psychology* (pp. 293–318). Oxford: Wiley.

Petrosino, A. J., Guckenburg, S., & Turpin-Petrosino, C. (2013). *Formal System Processing of Juveniles: Effects on Delinquency. Crime Prevention Research Review No. 9*. Washington, DC: US Department of Justice, Office of Community Oriented Policing Services.

Pfeifer, J. E., & Ogloff, J. (1991). Ambiguity and guilt determinations: A modern racism perspective. *Journal of Applied Social Psychology, 21*(21), 1713–1725.

Pickel, K. L. (2008). Weapon focus. In B. Cutler (Ed.) *Encyclopedia of Psychology and Law* (Vol. 2) (pp. 862–864). Thousand Oaks, CA: Sage.

Pickel, K. L., Ross, S. J., & Truelove, R. S. (2006). Do weapons automatically capture attention? *Applied Cognitive Psychology, 20*(7), 871–893.

Piliavin, I., Gartner, R., Thornton, C., & Matsueda, R. L. (1986). Crime, deterrence, and rational choice. *American Sociological Review, 51*(1), 101–119.

Pinel, J. P., Treit, D., & Rovner, L. I. (1977). Temporal lobe aggression in rats. *Science, 197*(4308), 1088–1089.

Piquero, A. R., & Brame, R. W. (2008). Assessing the race–crime and ethnicity–crime relationship in a sample of serious adolescent delinquents. *Crime & Delinquency, 54*(3), 390–422.

Portnoy, J., & Farrington, D. P. (2015). Resting heart rate and antisocial behavior: An updated systematic review and meta-analysis. *Aggression and Violent Behavior, 22*, 33–45.

Ports, K. A., Ford, D. C., & Merrick, M. T. (2016). Adverse childhood experiences and sexual victimization in adulthood. *Child Abuse & Neglect, 51*, 313–322.

Powell, L. (2016). Counter-productive counter-terrorism. How is the dysfunctional discourse of Prevent failing to restrain radicalisation? *Journal for Deradicalization, 10*(8), 46–99.

Powers, S. I. (1988). Moral judgement development within the family. *Journal of Moral Education, 17*(3), 209–219.

Pratt, D., Piper, M., Appleby, L., Webb, R., & Shaw, J. (2006). Suicide in recently released prisoners: A population-based cohort study. *The Lancet, 368*(9530), 119–123.

Pratt, T. C., Cullen, F. T., Sellers, C. S., Thomas Winfree, L., Madensen, T. D., Daigle, L. E., et al. (2010). The empirical status of social learning theory: A meta-analysis. *Justice Quarterly, 27*(6), 765–802.

Ragatz, L. L., & Russell, B. (2010). Sex, sexual orientation, and sexism: What influence do these factors have on verdicts in a crime-of-passion case? *Journal of Social Psychology, 150*(4), 341–360.

Raine, A. (2008). From genes to brain to antisocial behavior. *Current Directions in Psychological Science, 17*(5), 323–328.

Raine, A. (2013). *The Anatomy of Violence: The Biological Roots of Crime*. London: Allen Lane.

Raine, A., & Portnoy, J. (2012). Biology of crime. In R. Loeber, & B. C. Walsh (Eds.) *The Future of Criminology* (pp. 30–39). New York: Oxford University Press.

Raine, A., & Yang, Y. (2006). Neural foundations to moral reasoning and antisocial behavior. *Social Cognitive and Affective Neuroscience, 1*(3), 203–213.

Raine, A., Buchsbaum, M., & Lacasse, L. (1997). Brain abnormalities in murderers indicated by positron emission tomography. *Biological Psychiatry, 42*(6), 495–508.

Raine, A., Mellingen, K., Liu, J., Venables, P., & Mednick, S. A. (2003). Effects of environmental enrichment at ages 3–5 years on schizotypal personality and antisocial behavior at ages 17 and 23 years. *American Journal of Psychiatry, 160*(9), 1627–1635.

Raine, A., Moffitt, T. E., Caspi, A., Loeber, R., Stouthamer-Loeber, M., & Lynam, D. (2005). Neurocognitive impairments in boys on the life-course persistent antisocial path. *Journal of Abnormal Psychology, 114*(1), 38–49.

Rasch, W. (1981). The effects of indeterminate detention: A study of men sentenced to life imprisonment. *International Journal of Law and Psychiatry, 4*(3–4), 417–431.

Rebellon, C. J., & Manasse, M. E. (2014). Rationalizing delinquency: A longitudinal test of the reciprocal relationship between delinquent attitudes and behavior. *Social Psychology Quarterly, 77*, 361–386.

Regoli, R. M., Hewitt, J. D., & DeLisi (2010). *Delinquency in Society*. Boston, MA: McGraw-Hill.

Renauer, B. C., Cunningham, W. S., Feyerherm, B., O'Connor, T., & Bellatty, P. (2006). Tipping the scales of justice: The effect of overincarceration on neighborhood violence. *Criminal Justice Policy Review*, 17(3), 362–379.

Resick, P. A. (1987). Psychological effects of victimization: Implications for the criminal justice system. *NPPA Journal*, 33(4), 468–478.

Rettig, S. (1966). Ethical risk taking in group and individual conditions. *Journal of Personality and Social Psychology*, 4(6), 648–654.

Reyes, J. W. (2007). Environmental policy as social policy?: The impact of childhood lead exposure on crime. *BE Journal of Economic Analysis & Policy*, 7(1), 1–70.

Richardson, D. R., Hammock, G. S., Smith, S. M., Gardner, W., & Signo, M. (1994). Empathy as a cognitive inhibitor of interpersonal aggression. *Aggressive Behavior*, 20(4), 275–289.

Rogers, M., Smoak, N. D., & Liu, J. (2006). Self-reported deviant computer behavior: A Big-5, moral choice, and manipulative exploitive behavior analysis. *Deviant Behavior*, 27(3), 245–268.

Rose, N. (2000). The biology of culpability: Pathological identity and crime control in a biological culture. *Theoretical Criminology*, 4(1), 5–34.

Rosenthal, R., & Jacobson, L. (1968). Pygmalion in the classroom. *Urban Review*, 3(1), 16–20.

Roshier, R. (1995). *A Comparative Study of Reconviction Rates in Cleveland*. Middlesboro, KT: Cleveland Probation Service.

Ross, H. L. (1973). Law, science, and accidents: The British Road Safety Act of 1967. *Journal of Legal Studies*, 2(1), 1–78.

Ross, L. E. (2010). A vision of race, crime, and justice through the lens of critical race theory. In E. McLaughlin, & T. Newburn (Eds.) *The SAGE Handbook of Criminological Theory*. Thousand Oaks, CA: Sage.

Ross, R. R., Fabiano, E. A., & Ewles, C. D. (1988). Reasoning and rehabilitation. *International Journal of Offender Therapy and Comparative Criminology*, 32, 29–35.

Ruback, R. B., & Thompson, M. P. (2001). *Social and Psychological Consequences of Violent Victimization*. Thousand Oaks, CA: Sage

Rutter, M. (1971). Parent–child separation: Psychological effects on the children. *Journal of Child Psychology and Psychiatry, and Allied Disciplines*, 12(4), 233–260.

Saeed, A. (2007). Media, racism and Islamophobia: The representation of Islam and Muslims in the media. *Sociology Compass*, 1(2), 443–462.

Sageman, M. (2004). *Understanding Terror Networks*. Philadelphia, PA: University of Pennsylvania Press.

Saks, M. J. (1977). *Jury Verdicts*. Lexington, MA: Heath.

Saks, M. J., & Koehler, J. J. (2005). The coming paradigm shift in forensic identification science. *Science*, 309(5736), 892–895.

Saks, M. J., & Marti, M. W. (1997). A meta-analysis of the effects of jury size. *Law and Human Behavior*, 21(5), 451–467.

Salerno, J. M., & Diamond, S. S. (2010). The promise of a cognitive perspective on jury deliberation. *Psychonomic Bulletin & Review*, 17(2), 174–179.

Salfati, C. G. (2000). The nature of expressiveness and instrumentality in homicide: Implications for offender profiling. *Homicide Studies, 4*(3), 265–293.

Sampson, R. J., Raudenbush, S. W., & Earls, F. (1997). Neighborhoods and violent crime: A multilevel study of collective efficacy. *Science, 277*(5328), 918–924.

Sanbonmatsu, L., Katz, L. F., Ludwig, J., Gennetian, L. A., Duncan, G. J., Kessler, R. C., & Lindau, S. T. (2011). *Moving to Opportunity for Fair Housing Demonstration Program: Final Impacts Evaluation.* Washington, DC: US Department of Housing & Urban Development.

Sauer, J. D., Drummond, A., & Nova, N. (2015). Violent video games: The effects of narrative context and reward structure on in-game and postgame aggression. *Journal of Experimental Psychology. Applied, 21*(3), 205–214.

Scheck, B., Dwyer, J., Neufeld, P. J., & Boatman, M. (2000). *Actual Innocence: Five Days to Execution, and Other Dispatches from the Wrongly Convicted.* New York: Doubleday.

Schlenger, W. E., Caddell, J. M., Ebert, L., Jordan, B. K., Rourke, K. M., Wilson, D., et al. (2002). Psychological reactions to terrorist attacks: Findings from the National Study of Americans' Reactions to September 11. *Journal of the American Medical Association, 288*(5), 581–588.

Schmid, A. (2004). Terrorism – the definitional problem. *Case Western Reserve Journal of International Law, 36*(2), 375–419.

Schofield, P. W., Butler, T. G., Hollis, S. J., Smith, N. E., Lee, S. J., & Kelso, W. M. (2006). Neuropsychiatric correlates of traumatic brain injury (TBI) among Australian prison entrants. *Brain Injury, 20*(13–14), 1409–1418.

Schofield, P. W., Malacova, E., Preen, D. B., & D'Este, C. (2015). Does traumatic brain injury lead to criminality? A whole-population retrospective cohort study using linked data. *PloS One, 10*(7): e0132558.

Scrimin, S., Moscardino, U., Capello, F., Altoè, G., Steinberg, A. M., & Pynoos, R. S. (2011). Trauma reminders and PTSD symptoms in children three years after a terrorist attack in Beslan. *Social Science & Medicine, 72*(5), 694–700.

Seigfried-Spellar, K. C., Villacís-Vukadinovi-, N., & Lynam, D. R. (2017). Computer criminal behavior is related to psychopathy and other antisocial behavior. *Journal of Criminal Justice, 51*, 67–73.

Sellin, T. (1938). Culture, conflict and crime. *American Journal of Sociology, 44*(1), 97–103.

Seltzer, R. (2006). Scientific jury selection: Does it work? *Journal of Applied Social Psychology, 36*(10), 2417–2435.

Seo, D., Patrick, C. J., & Kennealy, P. J. (2008). Role of serotonin and dopamine system interactions in the neurobiology of impulsive aggression and its comorbidity with other clinical disorders. *Aggression and Violent Behavior, 13*(5), 383–395.

Shapland, J., & Hall, M. (2007). What do we know about the effects of crime on victims? *International Review of Victimology, 14*(2), 175–217.

Sharp, S. F. (2009). Feminist criminology. In J. M. Miller (Ed.) *21st Century Criminology: A Reference Handbook* (pp. 245–252). Thousand Oaks, CA: Sage.

Shepherd, E. (2008). *Investigative Interviewing.* Oxford: Oxford University Press.

Sherman, L. W. (1990). Police crackdowns: Initial and residual deterrence. *Crime and Justice, 12*, 1–48.

Sherman, L. W., Strang, H., Mayo-Wilson, E., Woods, D. J., & Ariel, B. (2015). Are restorative justice conferences effective in reducing repeat offending? Findings from a Campbell Systematic Review. *Journal of Quantitative Criminology, 31*(1), 1–24.

Shulman, E. P., Cauffman, E., Piquero, A. R., & Fagan, J. (2011). Moral disengagement among serious juvenile offenders: A longitudinal study of the relations between morally disengaged attitudes and offending. *Developmental Psychology, 47*(6), 1619–1632.

Siegel, A., & Victoroff, J. (2009). Understanding human aggression: New insights from neuroscience. *International Journal of Law and Psychiatry, 32*(4), 209–215.

Sigurdsson, J. F., & Gudjonsson, G. H. (1996). The psychological characteristics of 'false confessors': A study among Icelandic prison inmates and juvenile offenders. *Personality and Individual Differences, 20*(3), 321–329.

Silke, A. (2008). Holy warriors. *European Journal of Criminology, 5*(1), 99–123.

Simons, D. J., & Chabris, C. F. (1999). Gorillas in our midst: Sustained inattentional blindness for dynamic events. *Perception, 28*(9), 1059–1074.

Slaughter, B., Fann, J. R., & Ehde, D. (2003). Traumatic brain injury in a county jail population: Prevalence, neuropsychological functioning and psychiatric disorders. *Brain Injury, 17*(9), 731–741.

Smart, C. (1976). *Women, Crime, and Criminology: A Feminist Critique*. London: Routledge & Kegan Paul.

Smith, P., Gendreau, P., & Goggin, C. (2002). *The Effects of Prison Sentences and Intermediate Sanctions on Recidivism: General Effects and Individual Differences*. Ottawa: Solicitor General Canada.

Snook, B., Eastwood, J., Gendreau, P., Goggin, C., & Cullen, R. M. (2007). Taking stock of criminal profiling. *Criminal Justice and Behavior, 34*(4), 437–453.

Snook, B., Cullen, R. M., Bennell, C., Taylor, P. J., & Gendreau, P. (2008). The criminal profiling illusion: What's behind the smoke and mirrors? *Criminal Justice and Behavior, 35*(10), 1257–1276.

Snook, B., Brooks, D., & Bull, R. (2015). A lesson on interrogations from detainees. *Criminal Justice and Behavior, 42*(12), 1243–1260.

Softley, P., & Great Britain Home Office. (1980). *Police Interrogation: An Observational Study in Four Police Stations*. London: HMSO.

Soukara, S., Bull, R., & Vrij, A. (2002). Police detectives' aims regarding their interviews with suspects: Any change at the turn of the millennium? *International Journal of Police Science & Management, 4*(2), 101–114.

Soukara, S., Bull, R., Vrij, A., Turner, M., & Cherryman, J. (2009). What really happens in police interviews of suspects? Tactics and confessions. *Psychology, Crime & Law: PC & L, 15*(6), 493–506.

Sparks, G. G., & Sparks, C. W. (2002). Effects of media violence. In J. Bryant, & D. Zillman (Eds.) *Media Effects: Advances in Theory and Research*, 2nd ed. (pp. 269–286). Mahwah, NJ: Lawrence Erlbaum Associates.

Spelman, W. (2000). The limited importance of prison expansion. In A. Blumstein, & J. Walman (Eds.) *The Crime Drop in America* (Vol. 97, pp. 123–125). New York: Cambridge University Press.

Steblay, N. K., Dysart, J. E., & Wells, G. L. (2011). Seventy-two tests of the sequential lineup superiority effect: A meta-analysis and policy discussion. *Psychology, Public Policy, and Law: An Official Law Review of the University of Arizona College of Law and the University of Miami School of Law, 17*(1), 99–139.

Steblay, N. M. (1997). Social influence in eye-witness recall: A meta-analytic review of lineup instruction effects. *Law and Human Behaviour, 21,* 283–298.

Steblay, N. M., Besirevic, J., Fulero, S., & Jimenez-Lorente, B. (1999). The effects of pretrial publicity on juror verdicts: A meta-analytic review. *Law and Human Behavior, 23*(2), 219–235.

Steffensmeier, D. J., Allan, E. A., Harer, M. D., & Streifel, C. (1989). Age and the distribution of crime. *American Journal of Sociology, 94*(4), 803–831.

Steinmetz, S. K. (1977). The battered husband syndrome. *Victimology, 2*(3–4), 499–509.

Stephenson, G. (1992). *The Psychology of Criminal Justice.* Oxford: Blackwell.

Stetler, D. A., Davis, C., Leavitt, K., Schriger, I., Benson, K., Bhakta, S., et al. (2014). Association of low-activity MAOA allelic variants with violent crime in incarcerated offenders. *Journal of Psychiatric Research, 58,* 69–75.

Stevenage, S. V., & Bennett, A. (2017). A biased opinion: Demonstration of cognitive bias on a fingerprint matching task through knowledge of DNA test results. *Forensic Science International, 276,* 93–106.

Stretesky, P. B., & Lynch, M. J. (2004). The relationship between lead and crime. *Journal of Health and Social Behavior, 45*(2), 214–229.

Sturidsson, K., Långström, N., Grann, M., Sjöstedt, G., Åsgård, U., & Aghede, E.-M. (2006). Using multidimensional scaling for the analysis of sexual offence behaviour: A replication and some cautionary notes. *Psychology, Crime & Law: PC & L, 12*(3), 221–230.

Sue, S., Smith, R. E., & Gilbert, R. (1974). Biasing effects of pretrial publicity on judicial decisions. *Journal of Criminal Justice, 2*(2), 163–171.

Summers, A., Hayward, R. D., & Miller, M. K. (2010). Death qualification as systematic exclusion of jurors with certain religious and other characteristics. *Journal of Applied Social Psychology, 40*(12), 3218–3234.

Surette, R. (2013). Cause or catalyst: The interaction of real world and media crime models. *American Journal of Criminal Justice, 38*(3), 392–409.

Sutherland, E. H. (1939). *Principles of Criminology.* Philadelphia, PA: Lippincott.

Sutherland, R., & Hayne, H. (2001). The effect of postevent information on adults' eyewitness reports. *Applied Cognitive Psychology, 15*(3), 249–263.

Sykes, G. (1958). *The Society of Captives: A Study of a Maximum Security Prison.* Princeton, NJ: Princeton University Press.

Symonds, M. (1980). The 'second injury' to victims. *Evaluation and Change, 7*(1), 36–38.

Szycik, G. R., Mohammadi, B., Hake, M., Kneer, J., Samii, A., Münte, T. F., et al. (2017). Excessive users of violent video games do not show emotional desensitization: An MRI study. *Brain Imaging and Behavior*, *11*(3), 736–743.

Tajfel, H., & Turner, J. C. (1979). An integrative theory of intergroup conflict. In W. G. Austin, & S. Worchel (Eds.) *The Social Psychology of Intergroup Relations* (pp. 33–47). Pacific Grove, CA: Brooks/Cole.

Tanaka, J. W., & Farah, M. J. (2003). The holistic representation of faces. In M. A. Peterson, & G. Rhodes (Eds.) *Perception of Faces, Objects, and Scenes: Analytic and Holistic Processes* (pp. 53–71). Oxford: Oxford University Press.

Taylor, K. T. (2001). *Forensic Art and Illustration*. Boca Raton, FL: CRC Press.

Taylor, T. J., Freng, A., Esbensen, F.-A., & Peterson, D. (2008). Youth gang membership and serious violent victimization: The importance of lifestyles and routine activities. *Journal of Interpersonal Violence*, *23*(10), 1441–1464.

Thibaut, J., & Walker, L. (1978). A theory of procedure. *California Law Review*, *66*(3), 541–566.

Thomson, D. M. (1995). Eyewitness testimony and identification tests. In N. Brewer, & C. T. Wilson (Eds.) *Psychology and Policing* (pp. 119–154). Hillsdale, NJ: Lawrence Erlbaum Associates.

Thornton, D. (1987). Moral development theory. In B. J. McGurk, & D. M. Thornton (Eds.) *Applying Psychology to Imprisonment: Theory and Practice* (pp. 129–150). London: HMSO.

Thornton, D., & Reid, R. L. (1982). Moral reasoning and type of criminal offence. *British Journal of Social Psychology*, *21*(3), 231–238.

Tilley, N. (1993). *Understanding Car Parks, Crime and CCTV: Evaluation Lessons from Safer Cities. Crime Prevention Unit Series Paper, No. 42*. London: HMSO.

Tittle, C. R. (1980). Labelling and crime: An empirical evaluation. In W. R. Gove (Ed.) *The Labelling of Deviance* (pp. 241–263). New York: Wiley.

Tittle, C. R., Villemez, W. J., & Smith, D. A. (1978). The myth of social class and criminality: An empirical assessment of the empirical evidence. *American Sociological Review*, *43*(5), 643–656.

Tong, L. S. J., & Farrington, D. P. (2006). How effective is the 'reasoning and rehabilitation' programme in reducing reoffending? A meta-analysis of evaluations in four countries. *Psychology, Crime and Law*, *12*, 3–24.

Tonry, M. (2014). Why crime rates are falling throughout the Western World. *Crime and Justice*, *43*(1), 1–63.

Tousignant, J. P., Hall, D., & Loftus, E. F. (1986). Discrepancy detection and vulnerability to misleading postevent information. *Memory & Cognition*, *14*(4), 329–338.

Tremblay, R. E., Vitaro, F., Bertrand, L., LeBlanc, M., Beauchesne, H., Boileau, H., et al. (1992). Parent and child training to prevent early onset of delinquency: The Montréal Longitudinal-Experimental study. In J. McCord, and R. E. Tremblay (Eds.) *Preventing Antisocial Behavior: Interventions from Birth Through Adolescence* (pp. 117–138). New York: Guilford.

Tremblay, R. E., Pagani-Kurtz, L., Masse, L. C., Vitaro, F. and Pihl, R. O. (1995). A bimodal preventive intervention for disruptive kindergarten boys: Its impact through mid-adolescence. *Journal of Consulting and Clinical Psychology, 63,* 560–568.

Tremblay, R. E., Mâsse, L. C., Pagani, L. and Vitaro, F. (1996). From childhood physical aggression to adolescent maladjustment: The Montreal Prevention Experiment. In R. D. Peters, and R. J. McMahon (Eds.) *Preventing Childhood Disorders, Substance Use, and Delinquency* (pp. 268–298). Thousand Oaks, CA: Sage.

Ugwudike, P. (2015). *An Introduction to Critical Criminology.* Bristol: Policy Press.

Vachon, D. D., Lynam, D. R., & Johnson, J. A. (2014). The (non)relation between empathy and aggression: Surprising results from a meta-analysis. *Psychological Bulletin, 140*(3), 751–773.

Van Vugt, E., Gibbs, J., Stams, G. J., Bijleveld, C., Hendriks, J., & van der Laan, P. (2011). Moral development and recidivism: A meta-analysis. *International Journal of Offender Therapy and Comparative Criminology, 55*(8), 1234–1250.

van Zomeren, M., Spears, R., & Leach, C. W. (2008). Exploring psychological mechanisms of collective action: Does relevance of group identity influence how people cope with collective disadvantage? *British Journal of Social Psychology, 47*(2), 353–372.

Vennard, J., & Hedderman, C. (1998). Effective interventions with offenders. In P. Goldblatt, & C. Lewis (Eds.) *Reducing Offending: An Assessment of Research Evidence on Ways of Dealing with Offending Behaviour (Home Office Research Study No. 187).* London: HMSO.

Verkampt, F., & Ginet, M. (2010). Variations of the cognitive interview: Which one is the most effective in enhancing children's testimonies? *Applied Cognitive Psychology, 24*(9), 1279–1296.

Verkampt, F., Ginet, M., & Colomb, C. (2014). The influence of social instructions on the effectiveness of a cognitive interview used with very young child witnesses. *European Review of Applied Psychology, 64*(6), 323–333.

Viding, E., Blair, R. J. R., Moffitt, T. E., & Plomin, R. (2005). Evidence for substantial genetic risk for psychopathy in 7-year-olds. *Journal of Child Psychology and Psychiatry, and Allied Disciplines, 46*(6), 592–597.

Viding, E. T., McCrory, E., & Seara-Cardoso, A. (2014). Psychopathy. *Current Biology, 24*(18), 871–874.

Villettaz, P., Killias, M., & Zoder, I. (2006). The effects of custodial vs non-custodial sentences on re-offending. *A Systematic Review of the State of Knowledge. Campbell Collaboration Crime and Justice Group, Lausanne.* Retrieved from https://www.campbellcollaboration.org/media/k2/attachments/Killias_Sentencing_review_corrected.pdf.

Villettaz, P., Gilliéron, G., & Killias, M. (2015). The effects on re-offending of custodial vs. non-custodial sanctions: An updated systematic review of the state of knowledge. *Campbell Systematic Reviews, 11*(1). Retrieved from http://search.proquest.com/ docview/1773904646/.

Volkow, N. D., & Tancredi, L. (1987). Neural substrates of violent behaviour: A preliminary study with positron emission tomography. *British Journal of Psychiatry: Journal of Mental Science, 151,* 668–673.

Wagenaar, W. A., & Groeneweg, J. (1990). The memory of concentration camp survivors. *Applied Cognitive Psychology, 4*(2), 77–87.

Wagenaar, A. C., Maldonado-Molina, M. M., Erickson, D. J., Ma, L., Tobler, A. L., & Komro, K. A. (2007). General deterrence effects of U.S. statutory DUI fine and jail penalties: Long-term follow-up in 32 states. *Accident; Analysis and Prevention, 39*(5), 982–994.

Walker, D. M. (1980). *The Oxford Companion to Law*. Oxford: Clarendon.

Walker, L. E. (1984). Battered women, psychology, and public policy. *American Psychologist, 39*(10), 1178–1182.

Walker, N., Farrington, D. P., & Tucker, G. (1981). Reconviction rates of adult males after different sentences. *British Journal of Criminology, 21*(4), 357–360.

Walster, E., & Festinger, L. (1962). The effectiveness of 'over-heard' persuasive communications. *Journal of Abnormal and Social Psychology, 65*, 395–402.

Walters, G. D. (2004). The trouble with psychopathy as a general theory of crime. *International Journal of Offender Therapy and Comparative Criminology, 48*(2), 133–148.

Walters, G. D. (2016). Proactive criminal thinking and deviant identity as mediators of the peer influence effect. *Youth Violence and Juvenile Justice, 15*(3), 281–298.

Ward, J. T., & Brown, C. N. (2015). Social learning theory and crime. In J. D. Wright (Ed.) *International Encyclopedia of the Social & Behavioral Sciences*, 2nd ed. (pp. 409–414). Oxford: Elsevier.

Ward, T., & Maruna, S. (2007). *Rehabilitation: Beyond the Risk Paradigm*. London: Routledge.

Weatherburn, D., & Moffatt, S. (2011). The specific deterrent effect of higher fines on drink-driving offenders. *British Journal of Criminology, 51*(5), 789–803.

Wells, G. L. (1984). The psychology of lineup identifications. *Journal of Applied Social Psychology, 14*(2), 89–103.

Wells, G. L., & Olson, E. A. (2003). Eyewitness testimony. *Annual Review of Psychology, 54*, 277–295.

Wells, G. L., & Quinlivan, D. S. (2009). Suggestive eyewitness identification procedures and the Supreme Court's reliability test in light of eyewitness science: 30 years later. *Law and Human Behavior, 33*(1), 1–24.

Wells, G. L., Steblay, N. K., & Dysart, J. E. (2012). Eyewitness identification reforms. *Perspectives on Psychological Science: A Journal of the Association for Psychological Science, 7*(3), 264–271.

Welsh, B. C., & Farrington, D. P. (2009). Public area CCTV and crime prevention: An updated systematic review and meta-analysis. *Justice Quarterly, 26*, 716–745.

Wermink, H., Blokland, A., Nieuwbeerta, P., Nagin, D., & Tollenaar, N. (2010). Comparing the effects of community service and short-term imprisonment on recidivism: A matched samples approach. *Journal of Experimental Criminology, 6*(3), 325–349.

West, D. J. (1982). *Delinquency, Its Roots, Careers, and Prospects*. Cambridge, MA: Harvard University Press.

West, D. J. (1988). Psychological contributions to criminology. *British Journal of Criminology, 28*(2), 77–92.

Westcott, H. L. (2006). *Child Witness Testimony: What Do We Know and Where Are We Going?* Oxford: Oxford University Press.

White, S. F., & Blair, J. R. (2015). Psychopathy. In J. D. Wright (Ed.) *International Encyclopedia of the Social & Behavioral Sciences*, 2nd ed. (pp. 451–456). Oxford: Elsevier.

Wick, S. E., Nagoshi, C., Basham, R., Jordan, C., Kim, Y. K., Nguyen, A. P., et al. (2017). Patterns of cyber harassment and perpetration among college students in the United States: A test of routine activities theory. *International Journal of Cyber Criminology, 11*(1). Retrieved November 20, 2017, from http://cybercrimejournal. com/Wicketallvol11issue1IJCC2017.pdf.

Wiener, R. L., Krauss, D. A., & Lieberman, J. D. (2011). Mock jury research: Where do we go from here? *Behavioral Sciences & the Law, 29*(3), 467–479.

Wiest, J. B., & Duffy, M. (2013). The impact of gender roles on verdicts and sentences in cases of filicide. *Criminal Justice Studies, 26*(3), 347–365.

Williams, H. (2012). *Repairing Shattered Lives: Brain Injury and its Implications for Criminal Justice.* Exeter: Exeter University Press.

Williams, K. M., McAndrew, A., Learn, T., Harms, P., & Paulhus, D. L. (2001). The dark triad returns: Entertainment preferences and antisocial behavior among narcissists, Machiavellians, and psychopaths. Retrieved November 20, 2017, from http:// www.psych.ubc.ca/~dpaulhus/research/DARK_TRIAD/PRESENTATIONS/ APA.01.DarkTriadreturns.pdf.

Williams, T. M. (1986). *The Impact of Television: A Natural Experiment in Three Communities.* Montreal: Academic Press.

Williams, W. H., Mewse, A. J., Tonks, J., Mills, S., Burgess, C. N. W., & Cordan, G. (2010a). Traumatic brain injury in a prison population: Prevalence and risk for re-offending. *Brain Injury, 24*(10), 1184–1188.

Williams, W. H, Cordan, G., Mewse, A. J., Tonks, J., & Burgess, C. N. W. (2010b). Self-reported traumatic brain injury in male young offenders: A risk factor for re-offending, poor mental health and violence? *Neuropsychological Rehabilitation, 20*(6), 801–812.

Wilson, W. J. (2012). *The Truly Disadvantaged: The Inner City, the Underclass, and Public Policy*, 2nd ed. Chicago, IL: University of Chicago Press.

Winter, K., Spengler, S., Bermpohl, F., Singer, T., & Kanske, P. (2017). Social cognition in aggressive offenders: Impaired empathy, but intact theory of mind. *Scientific Reports, 7*(1), 670.

Wolf, M. E., Ly, U., Hobart, M. A., & Kernic, M. A. (2003). Barriers to seeking police help for intimate partner violence. *Journal of Family Violence, 18*(2), 121–129.

Wood, P. B. (2009). Prison. In J. M. Miller (Ed.) *21st Century Criminology* (Vol. 2, pp. 730–740). Thousand Oaks, CA: Sage.

World Prison Brief. (2017). *World Prison Brief. United States of America.* Retrieved January 29, 2018 from http://www.prisonstudies.org/country/united-states-america.

Wozniak, K. H. (2016). The role of poverty in the differential etiology of violence. In J. Savage, & K. H. Wozniak (Eds.) *Thugs and Thieves* (pp. 191–205). New York: Oxford University Press.

Wright, R. T., & Decker, S. H. (1994). *Burglars on the Job: Streetlife and Residential Break-ins*. Lebanon, PA: UPNE.

Wuensch, K. L., Chia, R. C., Castellow, W. A., Chuang, C.-J., & Cheng, B.-S. (1993). Effects of physical attractiveness, sex, and type of crime on mock juror decisions. *Journal of Cross-Cultural Psychology, 24*(4), 414–427.

Yankah, E. N. (2016). When addiction has a white face. *New York Times*, 9th February 2016. Retrieved December 28, 2016 from https://www.nytimes.com/2016/02/09/opinion/when-addiction-has-a-white-face.html.

Yar, M. (2005). The novelty of 'cybercrime': An assessment in light of routine activity theory. *European Journal of Criminology, 2*(4), 407–427.

Yates, P. J., Williams, W. H., Harris, A., Round, A., & Jenkins, R. (2006). An epidemiological study of head injuries in a UK population attending an emergency department. *Journal of Neurology, Neurosurgery, and Psychiatry, 77*(5), 699–701.

Yovel, J., & Mertz, E. (2004). The role of social science in legal decisions. In A. Sarat (Ed.) *The Blackwell Companion to Law and Society* (pp. 410–431). Oxford: Blackwell Publishing Ltd.

Yuille, J. C., & Cutshall, J. L. (1986). A case study of eyewitness memory of a crime. *Journal of Applied Psychology, 71*(2), 291–301.

Zaalberg, A., Nijman, H., Bulten, E., Stroosma, L., & Van Der Staak, C. (2010). Effects of nutritional supplements on aggression, rule-breaking, and psychopathology among young adult prisoners. *Aggressive Behavior, 36*(2), 117–126.

Zamble, E. (1992). Behavior and adaptation in long-term prison inmates: Descriptive longitudinal results. *Criminal Justice and Behavior, 19*(4), 409–425.

Zamble, E., & Porporino, F. J. (1988). *Coping, Behavior, and Adaptation in Prison Inmates*. New York: Springer.

Index

References to tables are shown in **bold**.